Understanding
Active
Directory
Services™

Daniel Blum

PUBLISHED BY
Microsoft Press
A Division of Microsoft Corporation
One Microsoft Way
Redmond, Washington 98052-6399

Library of Congress Cataloging-in-Publication Data
Blum, Daniel.
        Understanding Active Directory Services / Daniel Blum.
            p. cm.
        ISBN 1-57231-721-3
        1. Directory services (Computer network technology)   I. Title.
    TK5105.595.B58   1999
    005.7'1369--dc21   99-23386
                                                                    CIP

Printed and bound in the United States of America.

1 2 3 4 5 6 7 8 9   QMQM   4 3 2 1 0 9

Distributed in Canada by Penguin Books Canada Limited.

A CIP catalogue record for this book is available from the British Library.

Microsoft Press books are available through booksellers and distributors worldwide. For further information about international editions, contact your local Microsoft Corporation office or contact Microsoft Press International directly at fax (425) 936-7329. Visit our Web site at mspress.microsoft.com.

Acquisitions Editor: David Clark
Project Editor: Lynn Finnel

This book is dedicated to my family and my coworkers,
who had to put up with me during the writing process.
It is also dedicated to people who helped me by reviewing material
or providing information, such as Andreas Luther, Michele Rubenstein,
Peter Brundrett, Peter Houston, Shaun Hayes, Mark Brown,
and Margaret Johnson, as well as to the
hard-working Microsoft Press editorial staff.

Contents

Chapter Nine

Security Overview: Kerberos, Certificates, and Access Control 229

Chapter Ten

Migrating to Active Directory Services 265

Chapter One

Introducing Active Directory Services

Deploying distributed software objects, distributed computer file systems, single logon and public key security, and centralized administration are some of the most important information technology (IT) objectives of our time. But, ironically, these grand objectives will succeed or fail largely on the strength of an electronic network *directory*, a humble network component that many vendors and most enterprises have neglected for years. This is a book about Microsoft Windows 2000 Active Directory directory services, a general-purpose directory product that will do much to move directories into their rightful place at the center of customer network, security, and applications environments.

Directories are essential to distributed computing.

Directory Basics

A network directory (or just directory) is a file or database where users or applications can get reference information about objects on the network. There are special-purpose directories that serve only one purpose or application, and there are general-purpose directories that fulfill many functions. This chapter sets the stage for the rest of the book by defining special- and general-purpose directories and showing how they are different. It reviews the checkered past of directories, identifies opportunities for improvement and consolidation of directories today, and explains why enterprise-class directories are crucial to developing and managing

This chapter describes basic directory concepts and indicates where Active Directory services fits in.

directory-enabled applications and directory-enabled networking. This chapter also describes, in detail, where Active Directory technology fits, spells out why this technology is important, and draws a chapter-by-chapter map for the reader.

Special-Purpose Directories

A directory is any list (or lists) of items with a minimum set of attributes.

Most customers have deployed dozens, perhaps hundreds, of directories as components of applications and networks used in various divisions, departments, and workgroups of an enterprise. Any list of items (people, printers, servers) with even a minimum set of attributes (name, location, address, model number) can be a directory. Every network application has some type of directory as well as rules about who can access it and the rights that they have when they do so.

Special-purpose directories are embedded in products.

Special-purpose directories, as the name implies, apply to only one physical device, such as a file server, or one application, such as an e-mail system like Microsoft Exchange Server. These special-purpose directories are often embedded within the product, serving as an address book or administration tool.

General-Purpose Directories

Interest in general-purpose directories has grown.

Lately, as enterprises become aware of the hidden costs of managing multiple directories, interest has grown in directories that can serve more than one application—in other words, general-purpose directories like Novell's Novell Directory Services (NDS) or Netscape's Directory Server.

General-purpose directories can support many applications and network services.

As discussed in my company's report on directory-enabled computing,[1] general-purpose, functional directory services are an important element of the distributed computing infrastructure. Together with messaging services, security services, and component software frameworks, directory services will play a fundamental role in

---

1. Most recently in *Directory-Enabled Computing: The Directory's Expanding Role*, by Larry Gauthier and Jamie Lewis, The Burton Group, September 1998. *http://www.tbg.com*.

creating a new way of using networks. Special-purpose directories of the past, however, cannot enable such dramatic changes.

General-purpose directories that enable diverse applications, security, and network infrastructure components to be cost-effectively deployed and managed at an organization-wide level are central to defining the next generation of networked services and applications. Applications and components from multiple vendors will use such directories again and again. These directories provide enterprise-wide visibility, management, and security over network users, resources, and objects. In a large enterprise, they do not live on a single server, and they usually involve the collaboration of multiple products.

General-purpose directories improve network manageability.

In most cases, general-purpose directory products must interoperate not only with numerous applications and clients, but also with directory products from other vendors. This means that general-purpose directory products must be flexible and standards-based. General-purpose directories are more than a single product; they are really an integrated directory environment involving multiple products. In this chapter, we will note that general-purpose directories can assume three or more roles: at the network operating system (NOS) level, as an enterprise-wide directory, and as part of an electronic commerce–level directory operation. We will also show where and why Active Directory technology fits into the picture. First, however, we will begin with a short history of directories and a business case, or an economic justification, for general-purpose directories.

General-purpose directories must be standards-based.

Directory History: A Checkered Past

In a directory strategy document, Microsoft once described directories as tools for organizing, managing, or locating objects on a network. Network objects are things that users (and applications) need to know about to do their jobs—items such as users, printers, documents, e-mail addresses, databases, distributed components, and other resources. In their simplest form, directory services act like telephone book white pages; typing in a person's name, for example, returns an address and telephone number.

Directories have always been essential for locating information on a network.

Directory services can also act like the yellow pages, for example, providing a list of all the printers in a building. The need for directories has always been universal among customers, administrators, and the applications they use. To meet this need, people built special-purpose directories; and now the problem is that there are just too many of them!

DNS was developed to make resource location on the Internet more manageable and scalable.

At the dawn of networked computing in the 1960s and 1970s, network objects and their locators were hard-wired into the programs themselves, or were stored in parameter files on a host or workstation. At one time, for example, users maintained a file called *hosts* that held the names and addresses of all the machines on the Internet. When a machine changed its address, users updated the file and the applications continued to run. Users copied the *hosts* file everywhere to keep themselves synchronized. Eventually, however, the *hosts* file became too large and the changes too frequent. The Internet moved to a more dynamic, server-based directory called the Domain Name System (DNS), which, if given a hostname that includes the host's domain (such as *www.rapport.com*), returns the IP address of the host. DNS was the first—and the most successful—standardized directory.

DNS was not enough, and many other network-based directories soon evolved.

However, decades were to pass before the Internet and DNS hit critical mass in the industry. Over time, the industry also developed directories for Novell NetWare, Microsoft LAN Manager, Banyan VINES, DECnet, IBM's SNA , and many other proprietary networks. None of these systems used DNS, because DNS and the Internet were still fairly obscure. But vendors did follow the DNS approach of building server-based directories.

DNS lacked fine-grained information about people and other objects, which led to development of other, less successful, directory standardization efforts.

Although DNS and other early network directories were relatively advanced, they only contained information about host computers, domains, and addresses. In a rich network computing environment, users also need to store information about people, organizations, services, resources, applications, and so on. Recognizing this, in the mid-1980s, international standards groups tried to create a rich, object-oriented directory standard called X.500. As we will see, it took years for a successor to X.500, the Lightweight Directory Access Protocol (LDAP), to take off.

In the meantime, not finding rich information repositories in their friendly neighborhood directory, thousands of application developers and users set about building special-purpose directories, such as e-mail directories, human resources directories, telephone directories, and just about any other kind of special-purpose directory imaginable. Even worse, other vendors continued to rely on workstation-based directories, such as the Windows registry or its equivalent. In the typical enterprise, customers face dozens of directory islands, similar to the dilemma shown in Figure 1-1.

Lacking directory standards, general-purpose directories did not evolve, and directories proliferated.

Figure 1-1 *Too many directories!*

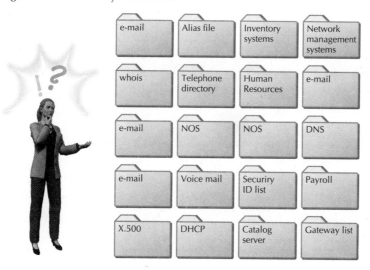

Costs of the Status Quo

We can sum up the implications of directory proliferation in one four-letter word: cost. Unfortunately, directory costs are hidden, and companies usually ignore them. Directories are almost always bundled with their parent application. E-mail systems, network operating systems (NOS), and human resources (HR) systems cannot run without directories, so developers usually do not charge extra for them. But that does not mean directories are free.

Directory islands create huge hidden costs.

The costs are hidden in
duplicate support
requirements and lost
productivity.

Some hidden directory costs stem from supporting duplicate systems that contain the same information. These hidden costs are mainly people costs, and they include training, setup, configuration, and administration. For example, entries for each user on the enterprise network might be found in the e-mail database (Daniel.Blum), the NOS directory (dblum), the human resources database (Daniel J. Blum), and all the others in Figure 1-1's motley crew. Each time a change must be made to a user entry on hiring, termination, organizational restructuring, site move, network upgrade, or some other action, some or all of the directories must be updated.

Low-quality directory
information content de-
grades user productivity.

Invalid or out-of-date directory information creates additional hidden costs. Users cannot locate each other in the directory, and then cannot communicate. Messages are lost, leading to misunderstandings. New employees cannot access systems they need to use. Users must log on to multiple systems with many passwords that are therefore poorly managed. Customers incur security risks when employees leave the company and logon IDs are not removed.

Significant opportunity
costs are hidden in the
current state of
directories.

Then there are the opportunity costs. When the enterprise or business unit needs a new application, chances are that application needs a directory to manage users, routing, security, groups, and other information. However, the manual effort necessary to support the application's directory interferes with deploying the application. With so much work to be done and so little time to do it in, opportunities are lost because resources or budget are not available to deploy the application. And when an application *is* deployed, the lack of a directory infrastructure might limit its management, security, and overall integration into the enterprise network.

A Business Case for General-Purpose Directories

Once an integrated di-
rectory infrastructure
replaces directory is-
lands, enterprises will
reap increased value and
large cost savings.

What if enterprises could consolidate directory islands into an integrated general-purpose directory infrastructure that allows a single point of administration for most applications? This ideal directory environment would reduce the costs of training, setup, configuration, and administration. It would be easier to directory-enable new applications. Information would be more up-to-date. With every new application leveraging the directory infrastructure, cost savings would increase. These ideas form the core of the economic justification, or the business case, for general-purpose directory services. Figure 1-2 illustrates the concept of many applications and services sharing a general-purpose directory infrastructure.

Figure 1-2 *General-purpose directory infrastructure for many applications.*

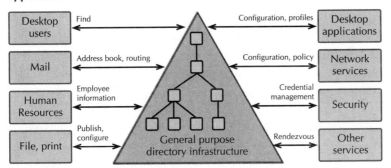

A manageable general-purpose directory infrastructure offers enterprises the opportunity to reduce workstation or PC maintenance costs, currently estimated at thousands of dollars per year per PC. Directories can centrally store desktop profile and configuration items that might otherwise need to be held in workstation-based files, scripts, or registries. When information is in the workstation, making changes requires hands-on touch management of each workstation, but when information is moved to the network directory, changes need be made only once. Early directory-enabled tools, such as Novell's Z.E.N.works and Netscape Mission Control Desktop, have proven this concept, which Microsoft has adopted in its Zero Administration Initiative for Windows (ZAW).

General-purpose directory infrastructures will reduce PC cost of ownership.

Desktop users will be able to find information in the directory through easy-to-use white-pages views, yellow-pages views, or even a simple desktop shortcut. E-mail systems will obtain address book and routing information from the directory system. Credentials for security systems will be much easier to manage

General-purpose directories can support many applications and make security systems more manageable.

once consolidated in a general-purpose directory, as will locator information for shared file and print systems. Users will be able to find objects on the network easily, services will be able to publish and configure information enterprise-wide, and it will be possible to extend security privileges flexibly to extranets or trading partner communities.

Directories also enable enterprises to extend their intranets into virtual private networks (VPNs), or extranets, for secure database access, messaging, collaboration, and other services with mobile employees, trading partners, customers, and suppliers. Because of their ability to provide an LDAP-accessible repository for user contact information, authentication data, and authorization profiles, directories are critical for business-to-business, business-to-consumer, and other forms of electronic commerce.

Finally, general-purpose directories integrated into the networking infrastructure will offer enterprises new opportunities for intelligent networking. For example, through the LDAP and the Directory-Enabled Networks (DEN) consortium initiative, router vendors are working with directory vendors to develop schematics for managing security, policy, and other configuration information needed by routers. Once this work is complete, routers will be much more intelligent about allocating network resources, services, and privileges on a per-user basis. For example, a policy server could query the directory to see if a user has authorization to allocate bandwidth for video conferencing, or whether a particular external trading partner has permission to pass through a firewall. With such mechanisms in place, directories do more than reduce costs; they also add enormous value.

Building General-Purpose Directories

Throughout 1998 and 1999, my company has received a deluge of consulting opportunities to help large Global 1000 companies design and deploy integrated directory services. In the fierce competition for corporate funding, directory projects often survive. The chief information officer (CIO) of one large Midwestern company we worked with pared a list of more than 50 projects down to 6, but left the enterprise directory project intact, saying: "This might be the most important IT project in our company today." Increasingly, customers recognize that directories are important, and developers understand that they must address customer directory needs. Specialized-directory systems that do not interoperate with others are on their way out, and general-purpose directory infrastructures are on their way in.

From Theory to Reality

But it is a long way from theorizing about general-purpose directories to building them. General-purpose directories must be comprehensive enough to address publishing and managing people information, organizational information, and resource information. Until recently, neither a single centralized enterprise directory nor a single network operating system (NOS) directory could—on its own—provide the entire general-purpose directory solution. So-called enterprise directories have tended to be centralized repositories of people information, largely divorced from the network resources that must be linked to people through permissions and access controls. Early NOS directories from Microsoft and Novell had closer ties to resources, but did not contain enough information about people or enterprise applications. Today, both Novell and Microsoft (with NDS and Active Directory services, respectively) are trying to provide a single, logically centralized enterprise directory solution. Much of the Novell NetWare 5 and Windows 2000 development effort has gone into placing global locator or configuration information in the directory and managing it there.

> It is difficult for a single physical directory to provide an entire general-purpose directory solution.

For years, users and some vendors assumed that the International Telecommunication Union's (ITU) X.500 directory would become a ubiquitous enterprise, indeed a global, directory. But, plagued by complexity and lukewarm support from major vendors, X.500 did not reach the mark. In 1996, however, momentum began to grow behind the Lightweight Directory Access Protocol (LDAP) as

> X.500 and LDAP standards were early efforts to create general-purpose directories.

a relatively simple protocol that provides directory clients with the ability to access directory servers by way of a single, standards-based approach. Major vendors, such as Netscape, Microsoft, IBM/Lotus, and Novell, have since implemented LDAP V3.

LDAP provides interoperability between directory clients and servers, but does little for integration of existing directories into general-purpose directories.

Although LDAP provides a clean front end to multivendor directory services, most back end (server) directories remain proprietary. Working groups of the Internet Engineering Task Force (IETF) are currently addressing advanced LDAP functionality, including replication, access control, schema definitions, and knowledge references—but these efforts are moving slowly. The result is that, although LDAP enables clients and servers to access general-purpose directories, it does not do much to promote interoperability or integration between existing directories on the server side. The LDAP protocol is necessary, but not sufficient, to create general-purpose directories.

Integration tools, called meta-directory services, are necessary to consolidate and manage information in general-purpose directories.

Difficulties in using LDAP to actually integrate disparate directories have given rise to a class of integration tools, called *meta-directory services,* whose function is to create centralized repositories, called *enterprise directories.* Technically, meta-directory services create a *join,* or a unified view, of the different directories in an organization, and make that unified view accessible via LDAP and Web-based access protocols.[2] Meta-directory services also manage the relationships between existing directories, allowing data to flow between them in a flexible, but controllable fashion. Thus, some degree of meta-directory functionality is a necessary condition for creating a general-purpose directory.

Architecture of General-Purpose Directories

General-purpose directory infrastructures need an LDAP, meta-directory, and repository or database technology mix.

From the earlier discussion, we can see that general-purpose directories must comprise an appropriate technology mix, including LDAP on the front end, meta-directory services on the back end, and repositories or databases presenting different views of directory information calibrated to different classes of uses. Figure 1-3

---

2. See *The Meta-directory FAQ* at *http://www.tbg.com/tbghome/metafaq.htm.*

diagrams an architecture for general-purpose directories. The model shows three layers: an applications layer, a repository layer, and an integration layer, and further divides applications and repositories into three classes: an e-commerce directory view, a NOS directory view, and an enterprise directory view. The NOS directory view is physically realized in a distributed manner, whereas the enterprise and e-commerce directory views are more centralized. The e-commerce directory views are accessible to various extranet or electronic commerce applications and external users. Meta-directory services manage relationships between people, accounts, resources, and other objects that appear in one or more of the integrated directory views. In addition, they manage the relationships among the various general-purpose repositories, or views, and any remaining special-purpose directories.

Figure 1-3 *Different sides of a general-purpose directory solution.*

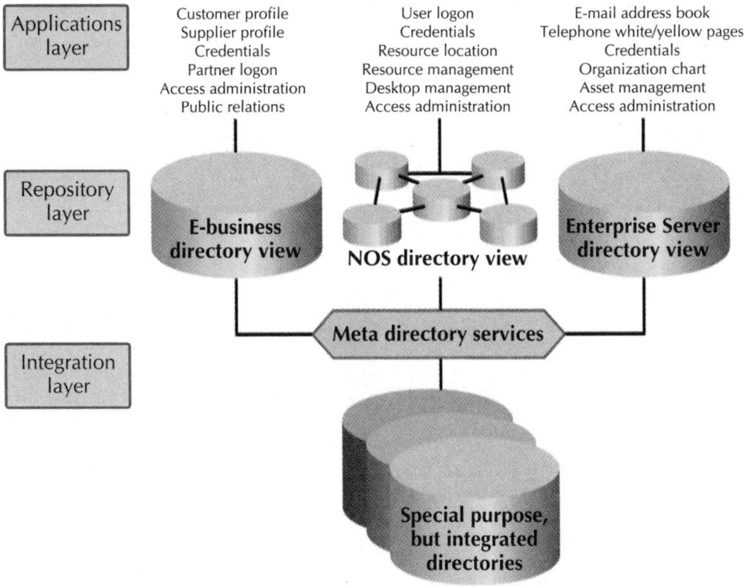

We have seen that no single physical directory repository can yet provide the full general-purpose directory and that a general-purpose directory must encompass meta-directory services, enterprise views, NOS views, and e-commerce views. It has been

It has been difficult to find a single product that can provide the whole general-purpose directory technology mix.

difficult or impossible to find a single product to meet all general-purpose directory needs. Historically, enterprise directories have been relatively centralized and information rich, whereas NOS directories have been highly distributed and information poor. Enterprise directories have primarily dealt with people information, whereas NOS directories have dealt with both people and resource information, but in a fairly limited manner. NOS directories are calibrated for frequent access and to be integral to the management of the network, and thus they are quite distributed. Enterprise and e-commerce directories are calibrated to provide rich information views (such as a phone book) to enterprise or e-commerce applications, and deploying them usually takes place in a more centralized manner.

Enterprise directories and NOS directory products are converging to provide more pieces of the general-purpose directory solution.

Recently, however, there has been a significant convergence of enterprise and NOS directories. Both Microsoft Active Directory services and Novell's Novell Directory Services (NDS) are changing the paradigm; sooner or later each will be able to operate as both an enterprise directory and a NOS directory, and each will soon incorporate meta-directory capabilities. The broadening of NOS directory product lines promises significant benefits for customers who will have fewer, more integrated directories to maintain, an increasingly single point of administration, and greater immediacy of directory updates.

Where Active Directory Services Fits

Active Directory services begins as a NOS directory but can take on additional roles.

The multi-faceted architecture shown in Figure 1-3 is necessary to achieve general-purpose directories in a large enterprise. However, this architecture begs the question of whether a single product can provide all views. As we will see, however, Active Directory services is first and foremost a NOS directory, but it has many attributes of an enterprise directory; customers can even tailor it to operate as an e-commerce directory. On its first release, Active Directory technology lacked meta-directory services, but that will change. Microsoft did acquire ZOOMIT, a meta-directory pioneer, and intends to incorporate ZOOMIT technology into Active Directory technology by the second half of 2000. Over time, Microsoft will seek to expand the role of Active Directory technology into all the areas we have described as elements of a general-purpose directory architecture.

Microsoft clearly believes that general-purpose directories are important. At the Microsoft Professional Developer's Conference in October 1998, CEO Bill Gates characterized Microsoft's top priority for the Windows 2000 operating system and the Windows Distributed interNet Applications Architecture (DNA) as "simplicity." The next slide in Gates' presentation began with the words "Active Directory." Together with Microsoft IntelliMirror and the latest Component Object Model (COM+)—and other Microsoft technologies now rolling out—Active Directory technology forms part of the next-generation Windows infrastructure.

Because of Microsoft's position in the operating system environment, Active Directory services clearly will have a major effect. Customers have been awaiting it eagerly and, although the product is arriving on the market later than expected, it should experience wide deployment over the next two to four years. Holding as it does users, accounts, resources, groups, security policies, and other objects, Active Directory technology will be a defining element in the Windows 2000 world. Like a traffic cop, it will have a say in all logon and many policy decisions.

Customers and developers, whether they are Microsoft advocates, iconoclasts, or competitors, should understand that although Active Directory technology is not the only general-purpose directory solution, it clearly will become one of the most important. Active Directory technology, on its own, might or might not become the best general-purpose directory, but because Microsoft has integrated it so tightly with Windows clients and servers, it will be part of most enterprise customer environments. As we said earlier, a general-purpose directory environment could consist of a few integrated directory systems, and Active Directory services will usually be one of them.

> Providing a general-purpose directory through Active Directory technology is a high priority for Microsoft.

> Active Directory technology will have a major effect on the Windows operating system and on the industry.

> Customers and developers must factor Active Directory technology into their plans.

Active Directory Services Features

Active Directory services enables general-purpose directory functionality.

Active Directory technology enables general-purpose directory functionality at the NOS level or sometimes at the enterprise level, through the following features:

- Serves as the base NOS directory, enabling users to log on and obtain Windows 2000 file and print services
- Provides a secure single logon to multiple applications hosted on Windows 2000 servers
- Designed for high availability with multimaster replication capabilities and partitioning of the database across multiple domains
- Publishes a Global Catalog view of subset information from multiple domain directories, including universal groups that can be referenced in access controls for multiple domains
- Unifies support for DNS and LDAP as well as other standard directory protocols and name formats; unifies public key infrastructure (PKI) and Kerberos support. In many cases, these standards enable Active Directory services to serve multivendor client and server products in a heterogeneous network, working with what is already available.
- Provides directory services for electronic messaging users of Microsoft Exchange Server and Microsoft Outlook
- Offers easy graphical administration with the possibility to delegate administrative responsibility for managing user and resource information through a hierarchical domain and organizational unit structure
- Exposes Active Directory Service Interfaces (ADSI) and object extensibility for the system programmer and the scripting language developer
- Enables remote control and configuration of desktop behavior through a Group Policy Editor (GPE) tool that can set defaults for domains, organizational units, or sites

- Enables the automated, self-healing, cost-reduction features of Windows Installer
- Enables distributed deployment of COM or COM+ software executable objects that customers can invoke remotely with minimal configuration on the desktop
- Provides backward compatibility with previous versions of the Microsoft Windows NT operating system

About This Book

I have written *Understanding Microsoft Active Directory Services* because I think Active Directory technology is an extremely important new development. We saw a major change with the transition from the static *hosts* file on the ARPANET (the network from which the Internet evolved), to DNS with its greatly expanded scalability. I believe that an equally seminal change is taking place with Active Directory technology in the Windows environment. Multiple applications and software components that currently register user or network component naming, addressing, and configuration parameters in the Windows registry will be able to configure these parameters centrally in Active Directory services instead. Centrally administered policy-based management and policy-based networking will replace expensive and inflexible hands-on management at the workstation level. Moreover, albeit with some caveats, Active Directory services' support for industry standards, such as DNS and LDAP, will make the benefits of general-purpose directories available to third-party developers in both Windows and non-Windows infrastructures.

A Word About Timing

I have written and researched this book using the release candidate versions of Active Directory directory services. Working with Microsoft Press, I have made every effort to ensure that the content is up-to-date with the final release of Windows 2000, as well as to anticipate the kinds of issues and planning concerns that customers and developers must prepare for. Thanks to many

This book is appearing early in the life cycle of Active Directory technology.

months of Active Directory technology testing, research, analysis, and consultation with the Microsoft Product Group and Active Directory technology users, I believe that this book is not only highly accurate but also demonstrates a high degree of foresight. However, because of time constraints, there will be some things I did not anticipate, and for these I can only apologize in advance.

Who Should Read This Book

This book is for readers in the IT and developer communities who need to understand the whole Active Directory technology from a conceptual architecture, development, and deployment perspective. Its target audience is senior management and senior technical staff, including CEOs, CIOs, CFOs, directors, technical managers, program managers, project managers, chief engineers, senior programmers, network planners or architects, senior administrators, and many others. The material serves this diverse audience through its tight, easy-to-follow organization, and its consistent whole-product focus on what is important and why customers should care.

Upper management readers from IT or developer organizations can surf the high points of the book for a basic understanding of Active Directory services and to learn about issues in managing Windows. Senior technical readers can pick up the high points and more. Readers can use this book as a quick conceptual reference, or drill down for details of immediate concern. Other aspiring types can gain from the book as well. True, it is a high-level conceptual view of the whole Active Directory product and, as such, we provide only a few administrator screen shots and a few lines of code. But by obtaining an overview of the whole product, readers will learn to "talk the talk" necessary for career advancement in customer or developer organizations that reward those who can see the big picture.

Chapter-by-Chapter Roadmap

The book proceeds from the general to the specific to provide customers with a basis for understanding Microsoft Active Directory services. In Chapter 2, we take a broad-brush view of industry standards for directories, and in Chapter 3, we look at the position of Active Directory services in the Microsoft product line. Chapter 4 presents an overview of Active Directory technology. Chapter 5 covers the end user's and administrator's perspectives, and Chapter 6 covers the developer's perspective. Chapters 7, 8, and 9 provide more technical details on topics such as namespaces, domains, schema, replication, sites, Kerberos, PKI, and access control, but keep the spotlight on what is important, and what are the best practices for customers and developers. Chapter 10 concludes the book with a discussion of how to migrate to Active Directory services, and the changes to look for in the future.

Chapter 2: Active Directory Services and Industry Standards

Directory standards, such as the DNS and LDAP, enable multivendor applications to locate resources on a network. Chapter 2 covers DNS (the Internet name-to-address resolution service) in detail and also covers the LDAP client/server directory access protocol and application programming interface (API). The chapter describes the similarities and differences between LDAP and its X.500 predecessor (which Microsoft does not implement). By reading this chapter, customers and developers will learn the essential details of the LDAP and DNS protocols that underlie Active Directory services. Understanding LDAP and DNS will help the reader to comprehend not only Active Directory services itself, but also how it fits into a larger directory environment.

Chapter 3: Active Directory Services in the Microsoft Product Line

Active Directory technology both leverages and enables the rest of the Windows 2000 infrastructure and various Microsoft products. In short, Active Directory services plays a key role in the Microsoft product line architecture. Chapter 3 reviews Microsoft's networking past, present, and future from LAN Manager to Microsoft Exchange Server to Windows 2000, with a particular focus on the directory functionality that each stage offers. It provides a high-level overview of Microsoft Distributed interNet Application (DNA) strategy. The chapter then overviews Windows 2000's distributed systems, with particular emphasis on the security architecture, distributed file system (Dfs), and Distributed Component Object Model (DCOM). The chapter discusses the unifying and integrating role of Active Directory technology in Microsoft BackOffice Server, Exchange Server, Transaction Server, and other applications. End users and developers should read this chapter for a better understanding of Microsoft's overall product line and Windows distributed system functionality, as well as to learn about the integration opportunities that Active Directory technology offers.

Chapter 4: Active Directory Services Architecture

Chapter 4 overviews Active Directory architecture as a whole, describing its essential architecture elements, including the information model and both client and server functionality. It discusses the overall role of Active Directory services in a Windows 2000 network for enabling logon, access control, navigation, and many other capabilities. On the client side, the chapter looks at the behavior of various Windows clients in a Windows 2000 network, the Active Directory Service Interfaces (ADSI) API, and the use of directory/provider interfaces to LDAP, Windows NT 4.0, and Novell NetWare servers. On the server side, the chapter reviews Active Directory database architecture, multimaster replication, and integration with Windows NT security services. Finally, it highlights planning considerations, such as migrating from earlier versions of Windows NT. As a microcosm of the rest of the book, this chapter helps the customer, the administrator, the planner, and the developer to put all the pieces of the Active Directory services puzzle into perspective.

Chapter 5: First Contact with Active Directory Services

Chapter 5 captures the look and feel of Active Directory technology by taking readers on a guided tour of the Active Directory client (or end user) functionality, server administration, and other features. It provides important guidance for readers who are taking a hands-on approach to learning Active Directory technology, perhaps from a home office or an isolated laboratory in their corporate network. On the client side, the chapter covers the My Network Places features and search functionality. On the administration side, the chapter discusses the processes of installing, upgrading, and configuring Active Directory services, as well as the Active Directory Users and Computers and Active Directory Domains and Trusts management snap-in tools.

Chapter 6: ADSI Programming and the Developer

Active Directory Service Interfaces (ADSI) provides API-enabling applications and administrative utilities to easily manipulate Windows 2000 directory information. This chapter is for developers at customer organizations and software companies. It provides guidance for developers of applications that need to access information in Active Directory services, applications that need to define and store information in Active Directory services, applications that need to manage Active Directory services, or all of these. The chapter discusses the Component Object Model (COM) architecture of ADSI itself, and common directory programming tasks, such as binding, querying, searching, publishing a service, managing security, and updating the schema. The chapter also provides practical advice on the do's and don'ts of developing to Active Directory technology to increase the performance and manageability of Active Directory applications.

Chapter 7: Planning Namespaces, Domains, and Schema

Defining Active Directory domain and schema models is a key step in deploying Active Directory services. Chapter 7 defines Active Directory namespace concepts and the manner in which they relate to the LDAP/X.500 and DNS global namespaces. The chapter introduces planning considerations and guidelines for creating domain forests, domain trees, and single domains. It identifies other domain planning considerations, such as designing for stability or choosing between geographic or organizational naming structures within an enterprise. Next, it introduces the types of containers (including domains, configuration, and organizational units) that Active Directory services uses, and describes Active Directory schema and naming conventions for users, groups, computers, and other objects. It explains LDAP/X.500 information model concepts, such as object classes, object class inheritance, and attributes. This chapter overviews both the out-of-the-box Active Directory schema and the pros and cons of extending the schema, as well as describing available schema management tools. It contains examples of Active Directory namespaces, domains and schema extensions, and numerous recommendations to customers and developers.

Chapter 8: Understanding Replication and Sites

Active Directory replication enables information to be partitioned across a forest of domains, yet remain highly available to all domain controllers and other computers in the forest. Chapter 8 discusses the importance of replication in general, as well as various techniques for replicating information within both single-vendor and multivendor environments. The chapter describes the Active Directory multi-master replication technology and how it affects customers and developers. It describes how replication of information occurs both within a domain and between domains in a domain forest. It covers optimizing Microsoft's intersite and intrasite replication and administration interfaces, and proposes some planning guidelines.

Chapter 9: Security Overview: Kerberos, Certificates, and Access Control

Serving as the enabling directory for Windows 2000 single sign-on and as the public key infrastructure (PKI) repository, Active Directory services sits at the center of Microsoft's distributed security architecture. Chapter 9 helps readers to master the basics of Kerberos Key Distribution Centers (KDCs) and the ability of Kerberos to authenticate clients to services and enable services to impersonate the client while delegating access to other services. The chapter covers the built-in Windows NT and Windows 2000 role-based access control and authorization model. In addition, it helps readers to master PKI concepts, such as digital signatures, certificates, certification authorities, certificate enrollment, and certificate trusts, both from the generic industry perspective and from the perspective of Microsoft Certificate Services, which are integrated with Active Directory services and Microsoft Group Policy. Finally, Chapter 9 looks at the granular Active Directory access control model, including concepts such as access control inheritance and administration, and concludes with a discussion of best practices in the area of Windows security from the customer's and the developer's perspectives.

Chapter 10: Migrating to Active Directory Services

This chapter discusses migrating to Active Directory services and looks at the future of Active Directory services and directories in general. Windows 2000 customers will need to determine the timing of their deployment, plan and execute a migration program, and then stabilize and optimize their environments. Planning considerations for small to mid-size enterprises will differ from those of large, complex enterprises. Thus, the timing and style of Active Directory services deployment will vary. New problems, solutions, and best practices for deploying Active Directory services will emerge, and the overall competitive landscape for directory products will change significantly. Meta-directory services will be important in ensuring coexistence and interoperability between multiple Active Directory forests and between Active Directory services and multivendor products. Finally, Active Directory itself will evolve, and so will the directory industry as a whole. As general-purpose directories like Active Directory proliferate, they will increasingly become the platform not only for managing applications and networking environments, but also for a myriad of directory-enabled applications or application frameworks that we are only just beginning to envision.

Summary

As Microsoft's new embedded Windows 2000 directory system, Active Directory directory services offers users an opportunity to deploy major parts of a general-purpose directory solution that will bring significant business benefits. All Microsoft client and server functionality will begin to converge on Active Directory technology as the common repository for publishing, locating, and navigating information about objects of interest on the network. As we will see, multiple Microsoft initiatives, including the new Component Object Model (COM+), Zero Administration Initiative for Windows (ZAW), and Windows 2000 distributed systems, have their basis in Active Directory technology. In addition, because Active Directory directory services is a comprehensive, standards-based offering from a vendor that has demonstrated the persistence and clout to establish its technologies as de facto industry standards, many third-party developers will follow Microsoft's lead and begin coding their applications to use it.

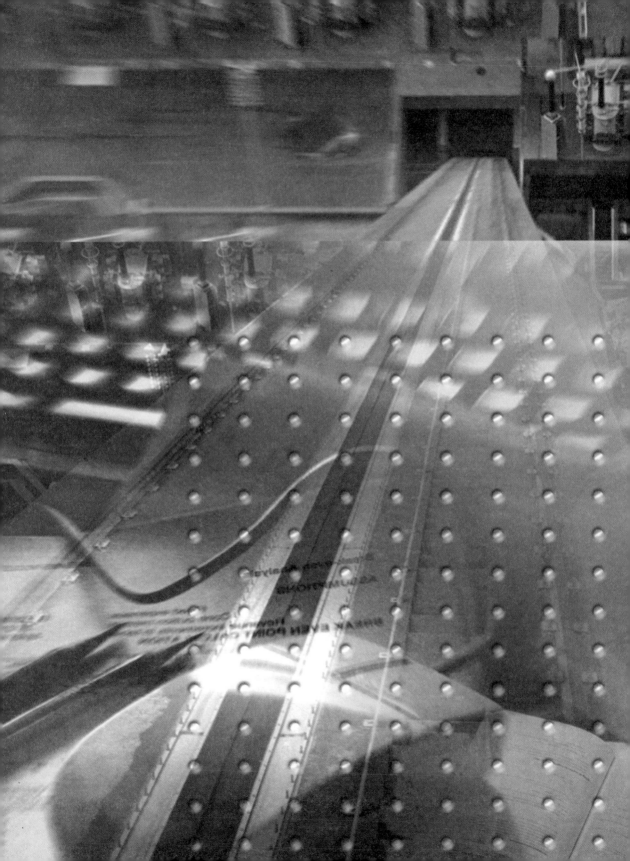

Chapter Two

Active Directory Services and Industry Standards

Efforts to standardize directories have been underway for the last 15 to 20 years. These efforts have come from two major standards organizations: the International Telecommunication Union (ITU) and the International Organization for Standardization (ISO), working jointly, and the Internet Engineering Task Force (IETF). In addition, standards impetus has often come from vendor efforts to extend the standards individually or through consortia. Over time, however, standards leadership has decisively shifted to the IETF.

The ITU, ISO, and IETF have developed directory standards.

These organizations have developed three standards: Domain Name System (DNS), X.500, and Lightweight Directory Access Protocol (LDAP). Microsoft Active Directory directory services implements LDAP and DNS while providing extensions in many areas, including integrated security and replication. It is important for customers and developers to understand the multivendor standards that Active Directory services supports and Microsoft's extensions and value adds—and the divergence or convergence of the two. An awareness of the strengths and limitations of the standards makes it possible for customers to develop strategies or best practices for leveraging standards and the products that implement them. In the future, we will see both Active Directory technology and industry standards evolve and move forward, generally on parallel or converging tracks.

Active Directory customers and developers need to understand DNS, X.500, and LDAP standards.

Directory Standards Survey

Active Directory technology has its basis in the standards developed by the ITU/ISO and the IETF. Closely integrated with its standards-based directory support, Active Directory services and Microsoft Windows 2000 also support Kerberos and public key infrastructure (PKI) industry security standards. Because all security systems require lists of users, credentials, policies, and access controls, it makes sense to integrate security standards, such as Kerberos, with directories. This chapter discusses LDAP and DNS; a detailed coverage of Kerberos and PKI is deferred to Chapter 9, "Security Overview: Kerberos, Certificates, and Access Control."

Why Standards? The Customer Perspective

Customers require both directory and security standards to integrate multivendor networking and applications environments. Progress in standards will influence both the evolution of Active Directory technology and the ability of users and suppliers to develop integrated enterprise directories. The key directory standards that exist today help customers achieve interoperability and higher efficiency on intranets by enabling a plethora of applications from both Microsoft and other vendors to leverage enterprise information about people and resources. These applications produce anything from organization charts to policy-based, intelligent networking. Standards also help customers to lower costs by reducing the number of interfaces, administered directories, replication infrastructures, and authentication/access control models that require support.

Standards also benefit electronic commerce: users can publish their public credentials (or certificates) and e-mail addresses in directories and use this information to exchange secure e-mail with trading partners. Directory-enabled secure e-mail is an increasingly important capability, as companies begin to send everything from purchase orders and contract authorizations to electronic payments over the Internet. In an LDAP-enabled directory, configuring groups provides access control criteria to determine, for example, whether an authenticated extranet user may run a particular application on a particular Web site or view a sensitive document. Virtual private networks (VPNs), which must authenticate devices belonging to remote employees and business partners, can be verified against an LDAP-enabled directory.

The Makers and Shakers of Directory Standards

The International Telecommunication Union (ITU) represents the Postal Telephone and Telegraph (PTT) and other telephone network operators. With a Web site at *www.itu.int,* the ITU is an international organization within which governments and the private sector coordinate global telecom networks and services. ITU originally developed the OSI and X.400 standards for networking and messaging.

The International Organization for Standardization (ISO) is a worldwide federation of the national standards bodies from more than 130 countries. ISO represents manufacturers and users of a broad range of technologies. It maintains a Web site at *www.iso.ch.* ISO collaborated with ITU on X.400 and X.500 standardization.

The Internet Engineering Task Force (IETF) is the standards-making body of the Internet. Affiliated with the Internet Society, the IETF maintains a Web site at *www.ietf.org.* The IETF has published a wealth of protocols, requirements documents, operational recommendations, and other informational documents as Request for Comments (RFCs). Some of these RFCs are designated as standards-track RFCs; others are not. The IETF also publishes Internet Draft documents that may or may not become RFCs. The IETF has developed many informational and standards-track RFC and Internet Draft documents for DNS, X.500, and LDAP.

Why Standards? The Developer Perspective

Standards allow developers to expand their market and to reduce their costs of development.

Developers benefit from standards such as LDAP and DNS because they simplify the customer's directory environments. Rather than build a product with custom directory functionality that is expensive to code and costly to administer, developers can attach their product to whatever LDAP directory the customer has installed. This speeds application deployment and thereby increases sales.

Developers who use LDAP can get their applications to run on multiple platforms.

Standards also make it possible for developers to maximize their market share using products that work with whatever technology a customer has installed. No longer must a directory-enabled application be pigeon-holed as Windows NT-only or Novell NetWare-only; now applications can be LDAP-enabled, and while there might be nuances that differ between installations, cross-platform portability gets much easier. It is less costly for developers to write code against a generic LDAP directory than against multiple proprietary ones.

DNS, X.500, and LDAP

To provide users and developers with the benefits of directory standards, the IETF developed DNS, ITU/ISO developed X.500, and IETF developed LDAP.

The IETF developed the Domain Name System (DNS) to provide simple, user-friendly name-to-IP-address resolution. The ITU and ISO developed X.500 to support the rich information requirements of electronic mail and other applications. Initially, the IETF developed LDAP as a simplified subset of X.500, but since then it has extended LDAP independently of X.500. Let us take a closer look at how these systems work and their relevance to Active Directory services.

DNS is an Internet-wide, name-to-address mapping service.

Domain Name System (DNS)   DNS has just enough capabilities to be successful at distributed global name-to-address resolution. It has been successful in creating an Internet-wide, name-to-address mapping service. Thanks to DNS, users almost never need to enter IP addresses directly; every browser, e-mail program, or other Internet client has DNS name-to-address resolution built in.

DNS has its basis in a hierarchical, global namespace with central registration of top-level domain names (such as *rapport.com)* and distributed management of subdomains (such as *sales.florida. rapport.com*). It is the division of labor between the centralized Internet infrastructure and decentralized Internet domains that makes DNS so scalable. Customers in any country can register their namespace without conflicting with others, and they then can manage that namespace however they see fit. Any changes within a domain need only be made once—the rest of the Internet adapts automatically.

DNS defines enough protocols to support its limited mission (name-to-address resolution), but not so many as to make the standard too complex for widespread implementation. Because DNS created just enough infrastructure and mechanics to enable a global directory within a limited scope, it has proliferated— supporting an Internet of hundreds, then thousands, then millions of host computers.

Today, as customers seek to drive down intranet cost of ownership, DNS is undergoing several kinds of enhancement while still retaining its original limited scope. These enhancements, as well as the details of the DNS protocol, are described later in this chapter. Some of this information is important to know when planning for Windows 2000, because Active Directory technology can either provide DNS service or work with your existing DNS—either way, it is necessary to support some of the newer dynamic DNS standards, as we will explain shortly.

The X.500 standards   X.500 was first developed by the ITU and ISO in 1988 as part of the Open Systems Interconnection (OSI) effort. The 1988 X.500 standard specified a multivendor distributed directory standard incorporating a hierarchical, object-oriented information model, a client-to-directory access protocol (DAP), a directory-to-directory system protocol (DSP), and an Authentication Framework (called X.509) based on public key cryptography.

Pilot X.500 directory systems soon sprang up on the Internet but failed to spread beyond the academic and commercial research communities.

Many vendors did not support X.500, despite enhancements made to it in 1993.

A 1993 revision of X.500 added functionality to support directory replication, directory access control, and schema publication and discovery. A number of vendors gradually implemented these features and then produced a handful of full-fledged X.500 products. Notable abstentions from the list of X.500 supporters were Microsoft, Netscape, Novell, and many other vendors. Critics cited concerns with the complexity of X.500, the difficulty of making X.500 implementations coexist with users' installed base of directory products, incompatibility with DNS naming, and the absence of a global X.500 name registration infrastructure as reasons not to invest in the technology. Despite the efforts of a dedicated X.500 community, by 1996 it had become clear to most analysts in the industry that X.500 was not destined to become the dominant global directory system.

LDAP initially provided a client-to-directory access protocol based on X.500.

The Lightweight Directory Access Protocol (LDAP)   The X.500 spaceship is simply too big and too complex to fly, but Internet engineers and visionaries have never given up on the idea of developing rich directory services to support multiple applications and information needs. The IETF's LDAP effort pragmatically leverages the X.500 specification as its first-stage rocket in a second run at developing rich directory services.

LDAP uses data structures that are simpler than those of X.500's original DAP.

The first generation of LDAP technology (early 1990s) was just a client-to-directory access protocol using simpler data structures than X.500's DAP. These simpler data structures reduced the working set memory requirements in clients and also made the LDAP specification easier to implement. Initially, the RFC 1777 LDAP V2 protocol piggybacked on the X.500 Directory System Agent (DSA) infrastructure; there was no thought of building out a stand-alone LDAP infrastructure.

Before long, however, growing disillusionment with X.500's slow adoption spawned multiple academic community efforts to develop LDAP servers that could exist independently of X.500, and a working group in the IETF considered ways to expand LDAP functionality. The turning point came in 1996, when Netscape and more than 40 vendors simultaneously announced their intention to build LDAP products. Among these vendors were Microsoft, Novell, and every X.500 player of note—in short, everyone who's anyone. By 1997, the IETF rolled out a new LDAP V3 specification. LDAP V2, LDAP V3, and the features of X.500 that they leverage are described below.

Major vendors began building native LDAP functionality onto servers as early as 1996, and LDAP was significantly enhanced by the IETF in 1997.

Going forward, both LDAP and DNS will be needed As LDAP gathered momentum, some doubters asked: "DNS is successful; why do we need two directory standards?" The fact is that to evolve the simple data structures at the core of DNS into the more elaborate structures desired for a rich directory information system would require major changes. Yet DNS is too deeply ingrained into too many legacy systems for significant changes to occur easily. The object-oriented information model used by LDAP and X.500 is more suited to rich directory requirements than the simplistic data structures at the core of the DNS. On the other hand, while future LDAP specifications could theoretically replace DNS, they will not because of DNS's massive installed base.

For historical reasons, LDAP and DNS will co-exist as dual standards for directory systems.

The evolution of two directory systems—one DNS-based and the other LDAP-based—is now inevitable. Figure 2-1 diagrams the types of information that will be stored in LDAP and DNS, respectively. Think of DNS as a basic, entry-level naming service that will continue to provide name-to-address resolution services, and think of LDAP as a general-purpose directory access protocol for containing user information, application information, and resource information.

Figure 2-1 *There will be two directory standards: LDAP and DNS.*

LDAP: User or application information	**DNS: Domain or host addressing information**
• Authentication and access control information • Profiles • Names, addresses, organizations • Other information	• Host addresses • Domain information • Mail routes • Service location

All standards have their limitations, and they are always changing.

Standards have their limitations   For all their benefits, standards tend to be complex and there are limits to the interoperability they provide. For example, LDAP lacks replication and access control capabilities, and the information stored in different vendors' directories varies. There is no guarantee that an LDAP application will work perfectly with any LDAP-enabled directory without some extra effort on the part of developers. Customers need a better understanding of what they can reasonably expect when developers simply implement the "standard." Developers need to understand when it is, or is not, appropriate to use LDAP, anticipate how the standard will change over time, and put in the right "hooks" for extensions. LDAP is still evolving in some respects. This chapter helps customers and developers track, anticipate, and plan for the LDAP of the future.

While important, standards support is not a panacea.

There are certain problems that LDAP/X.500 does not yet solve. These problems include: support for many legacy application-specific directories; cross-platform LDAP data definitions (schema) and replication; caching directory information in an offline PC or laptop; and tracking volatile, rapidly changing information such as currently logged-in IP addresses. Microsoft backing of DNS and LDAP standards will improve customers' prospects for interoperability and add considerable momentum to industry efforts to evolve the standards. But there will still be challenges for customers, and challenges or opportunities for developers. For example, directory information copied from an Active Directory directory to another LDAP directory will lose any associated access controls.

Also, a product designed to configure and create data definitions in a non-Microsoft LDAP directory cannot automatically do the same in an Active Directory directory. The IETF is working to add more interoperability features, such as replication and access control, to LDAP, but there is no clear time frame for when IETF will standardize such features, or whether Microsoft will support them.

Directory Architecture: Understanding the Big Picture

Before moving on to our overview of the DNS and LDAP standards, it will be helpful to establish a generic architecture model for distributed directories, as diagrammed in Figure 2-2, and to define some terminology used in this book. The model provides a valuable conceptual tool for understanding and evaluating any directory system, including one based on Active Directory technology. Chapter 4, "Active Directory Services Architecture," will review Active Directory technology in terms of this model.

A full-directory architecture includes client, server, naming, application programming interface (API), access protocol, replication, and many other components.

Figure 2-2 *Generic directory architecture.*

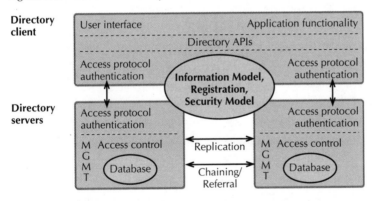

Few standards or products cover all of the whole-directory architecture. X.500 and LDAP, for example, do not specify databases or user interfaces, and Active Directory technology does not support chaining of requests from one server to another.

Individual products or standards may implement some, most, or even all of a full-directory architecture.

Directory Architecture Components

- **Client:** A client acts on behalf of a person or an application to provide simple text string searches, or elaborate graphical user interface (GUI) browsing logic. Some clients are used only for lookup, while others are also used for administration and configuration. User interfaces are not standardized in LDAP, DNS, or other specifications, but implementations such as Active Directory services do provide a client interface.

- **Application programming interface (API):** Clients may be split or layered into a user interface program and a protocol provider and then accessed through an API, such as the LDAP 'C' API, the Java Naming and Directory Interface (JNDI), or Active Directory Service Interfaces (ADSI).

- **Access protocol:** A directory client accesses a directory server via a protocol, such as LDAP. It is essential to standardize protocols so that multivendor products can communicate.

- **Server:** The directory server, often called a Directory System Agent (DSA), answers requests from directory clients through supported access protocols. The server contains the directory database, access controls, and other content.

- **Information model:** All directory products and standards must have their basis in a well-specified information model or schema. Directories generally follow the X.500 information model with hierarchical naming structures, which contain entries. Entries consist of attributes, which contain values.

- **Database:** A database is a file composed of directory information, indexes, and other records, each containing fields together with a set of operations for searching, sorting, recombining, and other functions. Reliability and performance is of the essence. Transacted storage models help protect against data loss through corruption.

- **Chaining protocol:** A chaining protocol enables two servers, or DSAs, implementing the same standard or product specification to respond cooperatively to user queries.

- **Replication protocol:** A replication protocol allows two or more DSAs implementing the same standard or product specification to synchronize all or part of their information content so that when content changes are made to one DSA, these changes are automatically sent to the other DSA.

- **Security and access control:** Directory security includes the ability to authenticate users and log them on to the directory, and then to impose access controls on their use of the directory. Directories also enable applications and network security by storing passwords, keys, Kerberos credentials, or X.509 certificates in a secure manner.

- **Directory management:** It is necessary to configure, tune, and manage a distributed directory over time. Management of directory content is usually performed through an administration client, which might or might not be Web-based. It is important for a directory product to come with a full suite of utilities.

Mastering the Domain Name System (DNS)

Fully defined in the IETF Request for Comment documents, RFCs 1034, 1035, and 1123, among others, DNS provides a distributed, global naming service based on a hierarchical information structure. Each node of a DNS database tree is called a *domain*. Domains can contain both hosts and other domains, called *subdomains*. Domain names form a hierarchy and are created along functional, national, geographic, or organizational boundaries. For example, the registered country codes (uk, us, de) are root domains. There are also functional root domains, such as com (commercial), edu (educational), mil (military), org (organizational), and net (public network).

Within organizations, subdomains tend to be created along administrative support boundaries. For example, if within the company *rapport*, the development and sales departments support their own networks, chances are the domain would be subdivided by department. The development department's domain would be *dev.rapport.com* and the sales department's domain would be *sales.rapport.com*. Each level of the DNS is or can be an area of autonomous administration. Hosts on the Internet have both domain name addresses (such as *bigserver.rapport.com*) and IP addresses (such as 207.46.130.149). The DNS client, or *resolver*, automatically translates the name address to the numerical IP address.

DNS Zones

DNS information is physically stored in a database called a *zone*. A zone is some portion of the DNS namespace whose database records exist and are managed in a particular zone file. It is possible to configure a single DNS server to manage one or multiple zone files. Each zone begins at a specific domain node—referred to as the zone's *root domain*. As you will see in Figure 2-3, zone files or databases do not necessarily contain the complete tree of subdomains under the zone's root node; the development department's "dev" is broken off into its own zone database.

DNS defines a hierarchical information structure to represent domains that are autonomously administered by users.

The ubiquitous DNS client is called a resolver.

DNS information content is held in DNS databases called zones, which can contain one or more subdomains held on a DNS server.

Figure 2-3 *DNS subdomains and zones.*

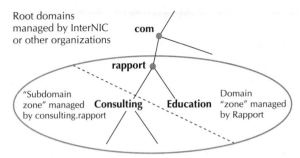

DNS servers (also known as name servers) control zones. The three kinds of name servers are primary, secondary, and master. A *primary name server* gets the data for its zones from local files and is the authoritative server (handles all changes) for the zone. A *secondary name server* receives data, via the DNS protocol, from another name server. A zone can have multiple secondary servers and should have at least one for purposes of redundancy and data backup. While DNS uses a single master replication model, a secondary name server can in turn replicate a zone to another secondary name server in order to avoid overloading the primary name server. Finally, a secondary name server must have a designated name server from which to receive the updated DNS information. This name server is referred to as the *master name server.* A master name server can be a primary or even a secondary name server for a particular zone.

Zones are controlled by a primary name server and replicated to one or more secondary name servers.

There are other nuances with name servers. Because DNS servers must contact other servers for remote information, and such contact could require interaction other than through the Internet, it is possible to designate certain servers as *forwarders.* Behind the firewall, DNS servers can be designated as *slaves* that must go through a forwarder. Some DNS servers are also called *caching servers,* meaning they do not have authority for any zone, but only cache information.

DNS servers can also act as forwarders or caching servers.

The DNS protocol
defines both recursive
and iterative queries.

Figure 2-4 displays an example of a behind-the-firewall name server (slave) that is issuing recursive queries to a name server, which is acting as a forwarder. The forwarder then issues multiple iterative queries on behalf of the requesting server to track down the requested domain information. Once a server has obtained the information, it normally caches it for however long the Time To Live parameter in the DNS address record (the *A* record) allows.

Figure 2-4 *DNS service in operation.*

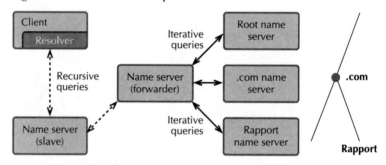

Other DNS Capabilities

The DNS supports in-
verse queries using the
in-addr.arpa domain.

Inverse queries are queries that look up an IP address in the DNS to retrieve the name of the resident host or domain name. An important use for these queries is to verify calling addresses. The DNS uses a special domain called *in-addr.arpa* to support inverse queries. An entry must be set up for every host where *in-addr.arpa* is the root and IP addresses are treated as artificial nodes or subdomains in this part of the DNS tree. Once an address is found in the DNS inverse tree, its entry contains a pointer (PTR) record to the appropriate host name. For example, to retrieve the host name for 192.57.40.1, the resolver asks for the name *1.40.57.192.in-addr.arpa.*

The DNS supports
electronic mail routing
using mail exchange
(MX) records.

Another service provided by DNS is routing support for electronic messaging relay. DNS mail exchange (MX) records, such as the ones in Figure 2-5, control message relay on the Internet.

In the example, the host *sales.rapport.com,* is served by a mail hub called *hub.rapport.com* and by a service provider called *svc.net.* Note that MX records appear for both the hub and the *svc.net.* Associated with each MX record is a number representing the cost or distance. These records are searched in ascending order. In this case, the MX records are set up so that message transfer agents (MTAs) will attempt to route directly to the destination first. If that fails, they will try the hub, then the *svc.net.* Note that when an MTA is in the MX list and is trying to route a message to a destination, it discards all records with a higher cost than its own. If there are multiple records of equal cost, the MTA tries them at random.

Figure 2-5   *DNS electronic mail routing information.*

```
hub.rapport.com     A    195.273.150.1
sales.rapport.com   A    195.273.150.3
         MX  0 sales.rapport.com
         MX 10 hub.rapport.com
         MX 20 svc.net
svc.net          A    128.340.200.1
```

DNS Extensions

A number of changes have been made to the DNS over the past few years to improve DNS replication, consistency, and manageability. Incremental zone transfer copes with ever-larger zone files by improving the granularity of DNS replication so that only the changed subset of a zone needs to be transferred. Change notification reduces the time during which at least one secondary name server has data that is inconsistent with the primary server; it uses a notify mechanism to facilitate fast convergence of servers, greatly improving the consistency of data in the zones.

Incremental zone transfer, change notification, dynamic update, and service location have been added to the DNS.

Secure, dynamic updates are another important extension area for DNS. As users have begun to deploy Dynamic Host Configuration Protocol (DHCP) servers to support automatic IP address assignments to both desktop and mobile (laptop) workstations, the frequency of DNS updates has increased. To support integrated DNS and DHCP, it is necessary to update small portions of a large zone incrementally and to propagate the updates dynamically in a secure manner. RFCs 2136 and 2137 specify Dynamic DNS capabilities.

Dynamic DNS capabilities allow a DNS program to be updated automatically when a Dynamic Host Configuration Protocol (DHCP) assigns IP addresses to a host on the network.

Active Directory services supports Dynamic DNS in its integrated DNS offering, and it is highly recommended that any third-party DNS systems used in a Windows 2000 network provide Dynamic DNS.

The DNS Service Resource Record (SRV RR) allows a client to find a service (such as FTP or LDAP) on the network, knowing only the name of a domain the service is in.

DNS has also been extended to provide better facilities for enabling clients to find hosts that offer particular services, such as DNS servers themselves (NS records), mail exchangers (MX records), and LDAP servers. Using the Service Resource Record (SRV RR), a client can find an LDAP service or some other service for a domain (*rapport.com*) even if the host name where the service is based is unknown. Microsoft implements SRV RR (RFC 2052) in Active Directory services to allow clients to find domain controllers. To illustrate the integration of DHCP, DNS, and LDAP that these newer DNS standards make possible, Figure 2-6 shows the process by which a Windows 2000 client—newly plugged into a network—gets an IP address, finds a DNS server, and finally locates a domain controller where it connects.

Figure 2-6   *DHCP, Dynamic DNS, and LDAP working together.*

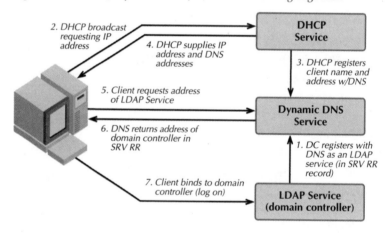

DNS Implementations

Most DNS implementations today are based on a program called BIND, but newer implementations are emerging.

The Berkeley Internet Name Domain program, better known as BIND, was developed at Berkeley in 1984 for the 4.3 BSD UNIX operating system and has shipped with myriad vendor implementations for many years. DNS servers based on BIND read in a BIND-specific text file called the BIND boot file. DNS servers do not need to comply with this file format to be DNS RFC compliant.

More recent implementations of DNS, such as Active Directory services, enable new capabilities, such as GUIs, multimaster zone replication, and Dynamic DNS support. Active Directory technology can also read in BIND file format, for those users who wish to migrate their DNS into Windows 2000, or it can coexist with other Dynamic DNS products.

Recent DNS implementations are more sophisticated.

Mastering the Lightweight Directory Access Protocol (LDAP)

Active Directory services implements LDAP as its native directory service protocol for accessing and managing information about people, resources, policies, access controls, and other objects on the network. The following discussion provides the essential information you need to understand how LDAP works, conceptualize the complicated X.500 information that underlies LDAP, and learn what management and security features to expect or build into LDAP products.

Active Directory services implements LDAP.

LDAP emerged as the de facto industry standard for client/server protocol access to rich directory information held in a variety of multivendor server repositories. LDAP's basic operation is diagramed in Figure 2-7.

Figure 2-7 *LDAP basic operation.*

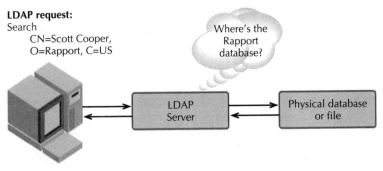

LDAP request:
Search
    CN=Scott Cooper,
    O=Rapport, C=US

Where's the Rapport database?

LDAP Server

Physical database or file

LDAP result:
Common Name: Scott Cooper
RFC 822 address: scottc+@rapport.com
Telephone: (614) 555-1586

LDAP V2 (RFC 1777) was originally intended only as a client complement to X.500, but the Internet community's aspirations for LDAP soon expanded to encompass the standardization of server functionality as well. An intermediate step in this direction has been the IETF approval of a series of LDAP V3 RFCs, 2251 through 2256, with Proposed Standard status. Further work on LDAP replication and access control was ongoing at the IETF in 1999 as this book went to press.

LDAP V2 provides a client/server directory access model, which is being enhanced with LDAP V3 and a variety of other initiatives.

LDAP Information Model

The LDAP protocol has its basis in an information framework model defined in the X.501 recommendation. The X.500 model assumes there are one or more servers called *Directory System Agents* (DSAs) that jointly provide access to a directory information tree (DIT). It also defines a *schema*, or set of logical data definitions, for directory content.

LDAP uses a hierarchical information model initially defined in X.500.

LDAP's Hierarchical Naming Model

Each DSA is responsible for a portion of the namespace; for example, in Figure 2-8, separate DSAs control the Rapport and Microsoft organization/domains. In general, DSAs are responsible for one or more naming contexts, or collections of entries that begin at an entry in the tree and include all its subordinates and their subordinates, down to the entries that are mastered by different DSAs. The overall *directory information tree*, or DIT, is made up of hierarchically related entries, each with one and only one parent, or container entry. Figure 2-8 shows the basic information model.

Each DSA is responsible for a portion of the X.500 namespace.

You probably noticed in Figure 2-8 that a box denotes each entry in the tree. Above the line in each box is the entry's name; below the line are the entry's contents. In the LDAP information model, names are hierarchical distinguished names (DNs). A *distinguished name* consists of its *relative distinguished name* (or RDN) plus the RDNs of all its container (or parent) entries. Thus, the RDN for Aaron Con is *CN=Aaron Con* and the full DN is *CN=Aaron Con, OU=Logistics, DC=Microsoft, DC=com*.

All entries in the DIT have distinguished names (DNs) and relative distinguished names (RDNs).

Figure 2-8 *LDAP hierarchical data model.*

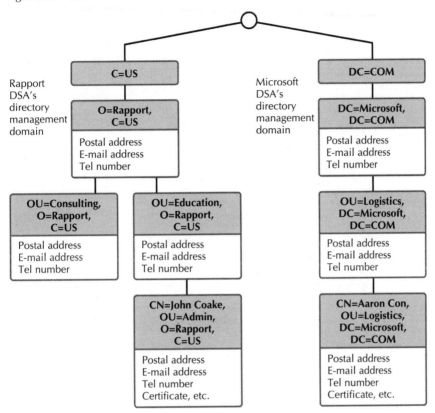

Hybrid Domain Component Naming in LDAP

There are various naming choices for representing the upper levels of the directory hierarchy. The examples in Figure 2-8 show the X.500 approach on the left for the Rapport organization, and a hybrid DNS/LDAP approach on the right for Microsoft organization. With the hybrid namespace, the *CN=Aaron Con* and *OU=Logistics* entries look like vintage LDAP/X.500, but the domain components *DC=Microsoft* and *DC=COM* part have their origin in the DNS world.

Microsoft could just as well have used a pure X.500 naming plan and called itself *O=Microsoft, C=US*. The problem with the X.500 plan is that, while DNS has an established global registration infrastructure to define domains like *Microsoft.com*, X.500 has no

Microsoft and other vendors use a hybrid naming structure that marries the DNS hierarchy with the LDAP hierarchy.

Hybrid DNS/LDAP naming leverages the DNS registration infrastructure.

Attribute Descriptions

LDAP defines a number of attribute descriptions, some of which appear in this chapter as abbreviations for the example names. Common attribute descriptions are:

CN: common name

OU: organizational unit

DC: domain component

O: organization

C: country

UID: unique ID

effective way to register a multinational enterprise that is not under one country, and even within countries the registration infrastructure is often quite expensive or obscure. In the United States, for example, it costs $2,500 just to register *O=Rapport* with the American National Standards Institute (ANSI). To reduce customer registration costs, and also to unify the DNS and LDAP infrastructures as much as possible, Microsoft uses the hybrid name form to combine the LDAP organizational units with DNS domain components.

Entry Content

An entry belongs to an object class that defines the attributes the entry contains.

Now that we have established the entry naming, what about the entry contents? Entries actually contain attributes holding information like telephone numbers and e-mail addresses. The object class—or type—of entry establishes which attributes an entry contains. Thus, every LDAP entry belongs to an object class and consists of a collection of attributes. *Object classes* define the schema for entries; they specify which attributes in an entry are mandatory, which are optional, and which are used for naming.

Moving down to the content of the entry, then, each attribute has a type element and value elements. The *type element* is identified by a short descriptive name and an object identifier (OID). The *type* governs whether there can be a single value or more than one value in an attribute. It also governs the syntax to which the values must conform, and the kinds of matching that can be performed on values during a lookup. One or more of the values (such as *CN=Aaron Con*) that are part of the entry's RDN are called *distinguished values*. Figure 2-9 shows an example of the attribute content for a User entry.

Attributes have both a type and a value.

Figure 2-9 *Contents of a directory entry.*

cn: Sam Clemens
sn: Clemens
uid: sclemens
telephonenumber: +1 999 999 9999
postal address: 123 Ivy Lane, Mountain View, CA 20010

Object Classes

One of the potentially attractive features of using object-oriented techniques for defining LDAP information types is that it is possible to reuse the definitions. Once one object class is defined, it is possible to derive a specialized version of the same class as a *subclass* of the original, which is then itself known as the *superclass* of the specialized subordinate class. Object classes are not limited to one superclass; multiple inheritance is permissible in the standard as long as the structure rules and other characteristics of the superclasses are not in conflict.

Object class definitions can be reused, or inherited, in a flexible manner.

Use of subclasses allows for economy in specification and also makes it possible, when processing the subclass, to reuse much of the software designed and built to support the superclass type. A subclass specialization inherits all of the characteristics, or attributes, of its superclass. For example, Organizational Person is a subclass of Person, which specifies additional optional attributes. In addition to various attributes over and above what the superclass Person may contain, Organizational Person may contain a job title. The bottom line is that the entries typically belong to more than one object class and contain a conglomeration of type definitions.

Object subclasses inherit attributes from their superclasses.

Various international standards, RFCs, and industry specifications define object class and attribute types that one can use with LDAP. One such specification is the *Lightweight Internet Person Schema* (LIPS), upon which a number of vendors agreed in late 1996 at the Network Applications Consortium. Other, less complete specifications have been proposed in various IETF RFCs. In general, users and developers can extend the LDAP schema, defining their own object classes and attributes to store in the directory. In Chapter 7, "Planning Namespaces, Domains, and Schema," we will discuss how this should be done with Active Directory services.

> Users and developers can leverage LDAP's object-oriented information framework to create new object classes and attributes where required.

Schema Publication

Servers use some attributes, termed *operational attributes*, to configure the directory system itself. Operational attributes are retrievable from the root of a DSA's naming context (called rootDSE) and provide information about the server's supported naming contexts, supported schema, alternate (backup) server, supported protocol extensions, supported controls, and supported authentication features. Other operational attributes that may be part of any entry include creatorsName, createTimestamp, modifiersName, and modifyTimestamp.

> LDAP servers support operational attributes, which are used for administration and system operation.

The *subschemaSubentry* identifies the distinguished name in a subschema entry that contains the schema definitions of a naming context. Directory servers use subschema entries for publishing and discovering the object classes and attribute types supported. A single subschema entry contains all schema definitions used by entries in that particular part of the directory tree.

> An LDAP server's object class and attribute schema are published in the directory and can be discovered by clients.

LDAP Protocol: Requests and Referrals

The LDAP client communicates with an LDAP server via protocol data units (PDUs) called *LDAPMessages*. An LDAPMessage can envelop multiple LDAP operations and is usually mapped over TCP/IP transport, although RFC 1798 makes it possible for short LDAPMessages to be mapped over the connectionless User Datagram Protocol (UDP) as well. Typically, an LDAP interaction

> LDAP operations are enveloped by LDAPMessages.

begins with a Bind request and response to authenticate the client and server, and then continues with additional operations, such as Searches. Figure 2-10 shows an LDAP protocol scenario.

Figure 2-10 *LDAP operational scenario.*

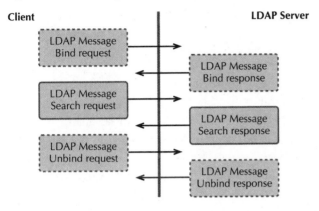

LDAP Directory Request Types

- **Compare:** retrieves or checks the attributes of a single object
- **Search:** accesses a single object, or collections of objects, retrieving some or all of the attributes from each
- **Abandon:** cancels other ongoing operations
- **Add:** adds an entry beneath a named superior in the DIT
- **Delete:** removes a named object from the DIT
- **Modify:** modifies the attributes of a named object in the DIT
- **Modify DN:** renames an entry by modifying its RDN
- **Unbind:** terminates a protocol session
- **Extend:** (added in LDAP V3) enables extensions to the LDAP protocol

An LDAPMessage uses a simple *string syntax* wherever possible.

Each LDAPMessage contains a *MessageID*, which makes it possible for the client and the server to correlate the request/response halves of multiple, asynchronously processed requests. An LDAPMessage itself is made up of various syntactic building blocks, but in keeping with the lightweight spirit of LDAP, an effort is made to use a simple textual representation for attribute type and value information, although complex types, such as security certificates, are sent in binary format.

LDAP supports Referrals, which advise the client to contact another server.

A server that does not hold the information requested by a client may return a Referral to the client in LDAPResults. This *Referral* provides a reference, in the form of a Uniform Resource Locator (URL), to another server (or set of servers), which is accessible from LDAP or other protocols. Referrals can be returned in response to any operation request (except Unbind and Abandon, which do not have responses). For example, Active Directory domain controllers use referrals to point clients at information in an external domain.

LDAP Protocol Setup: The Bind Operation

LDAP servers "listen" on a TCP port; LDAP clients invoke operations.

LDAP clients normally invoke connections on an LDAP server upon request by the user or application. The location of the LDAP server can be statically configured in a file on the client, or it is obtainable from the DNS. LDAP servers "listen" for incoming TCP/IP calls on TCP port 389. Once a connection comes in, the server will allocate resources to that connection and enable LDAP operations over it.

The Unbind operation disconnects LDAP sessions.

An LDAP connections normally remain open until the client closes it using the Unbind operation. However, inactivity timeouts or other server-based problems could lead the server to disconnect. If this happens with LDAP V2, the client gets no notice, but with LDAP V3, the server might notify the client prior to disconnect using the LDAP V3 Extend operation. Unbind on the client side can occur when an operation is complete, when the user exits LDAP-related screens, or when there has been a period of inactivity on the connection, depending on the client logic. For reasons of efficiency, it is advisable for clients to close connections on completing their work or, when using LDAP heavily, to process multiple requests over the same open connection.

The Bind operation exchanges authentication information between the client and server. Bind requests are required in LDAP V2, but not in LDAP V3. In LDAP V3, the client need not send a Bind request in the first protocol data unit (PDU) of a connection. However, the LDAP V3 server will treat any operation sent without a prior Bind request as unauthenticated, and will provide only minimal information access to the unauthenticated (and therefore anonymous) client.

The Bind operation is used for authentication.

Simple Authentication and Security Layer (SASL)   In the Bind request, the client specifies its version, the user name it is binding as, and its simple or (for LDAP V3 only) strong credentials. *Simple credentials* basically contain a password and should not be used over open networks where they might be sniffed or intercepted. *Strong credentials* use the Simple Authentication and Security Layer (SASL) protocol (RFC 2222) to negotiate a form of strong authentication, such as HTTP Digest, Kerberos, or the Transport Layer Security (TLS).

The Bind request's Simple Authentication and Security Layer (SASL) supports Secure Sockets Layer (SSL), Kerberos, HTTP Digest, and other security methods.

LDAP Search and Other Queries

Using the Search operation, a client can request that a server perform a search on its behalf. A rich set of search parameters makes Search a very flexible tool. Typical uses of Search are to match a single entry and read attributes from it, enumerate the names of all entries below a particular entry, or filter an entire subtree of entries.

LDAP supports lookup through the Search operation, which allows for a variety of query strategies.

A Search request begins with the distinguished name of an entry, called a *base object*. Next, a Scope parameter tells the server to search in one of three ways: 1) only the base object, 2) the base object and its direct subordinates, or 3) the base object and all its descendants in the subtree below. Note that when the Scope identifies a multiple entry search, the search might affect multiple

Search requests work down from a base object, possibly exploring multiple naming contexts.

LDAP servers holding naming contexts in the subtree to be searched. In this case, an LDAP V3 server will return a number of LDAP referrals to servers lower down in the tree.

A Filter parameter defines flexible matching criteria for in-scope entries, an Attributes parameter tells the server which attributes to return to the user, and the derefAliases parameter controls whether or not aliases (if present) are followed during different stages of the search. The Filter parameter allows for everything from a simple equality match of a single item, match if an attribute type is present, wild card or phonetic match of a string item, and ordinal (greater than, less than, greater than or equal to, and so on) matching of numeric items. Multiple item filters are also possible, enabling the user to specify "this item *and* that item" as well as *or* and *not* conjunctions. Figure 2-11 diagrams a typical LDAP Search operation.

Figure 2-11   *LDAP search.*

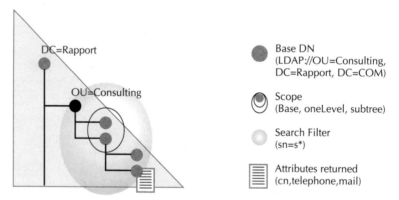

Base DN
(LDAP://OU=Consulting, DC=Rapport, DC=COM)

Scope
(Base, oneLevel, subtree)

Search Filter
(sn=s*)

Attributes returned
(cn,telephone,mail)

Search request extensions   Recent IETF LDAP extensions, such as the server-side paging of search results, server-side sorting of search results, and virtual list views, can make possible user-friendly browsing of large numbers of directory entries. Paging lets a client request that the search results be returned in blocks of *n* entries, where *n* could carve chunks of 100 entries out of a result set of thousands. *Virtual list views* is a term for yet another Internet Draft affecting searching that will make today's commonly implemented paged search obsolete. Virtual list views allow the client to use the LDAP protocol to scroll through the server-side result sets. Active Directory services supports server-side paging and sorting, but not virtual list views as yet.

Active Directory services also provides various LDAP extensions that are not yet LDAP standards, such as binary attribute value searching and searching through ranges of an attribute (such as group members) with a very large multivalue set. These features, available through ADSI, will not work with other vendors' directories.

Some ADSI extensions to LDAP are proprietary and do not work with other products.

Compare operation   The Directory Compare operation allows a user or application to request that a server check for the presence of an attribute value within a directory object. Instead of reading the entry's contents, as would normally be done with a Search operation, the client sends the server an assertion of what it believes the target value to be. The server then returns a *compareTrue* or *compareFalse* answer.

Compare provides another option for lookup that conserves client resources.

An example where the Compare operation proves useful is in password verification, or any circumstance where a value maintained in the directory is not readable. Another use for Compare is to check for a value's presence in an attribute that contains so many values that downloading and checking them in the client would be inefficient. This happens with group member lists and other large lists maintained as values within an attribute.

Use the Compare operation to check passwords or list memberships.

LDAP Uniform Resource Locators (URLs)
RFC 2255 defines an LDAP URL format used within the LDAP protocol to encode search references or other kinds of referrals. An example of using the LDAP URL for referral is: *ldap:// ldap.rapport.com/OU=Consulting,DC=rapport,DC=com*. This tells the client to look for the name starting with *OU=consulting* in the host *ldap.rapport.com.* The LDAP URL also provides the syntax for invoking searches with specified filters, and lists of attributes to return.

Customers can use the LDAP URL directly, as well as within the LDAP protocol.

LDAP Update Operations

LDAP provides the Add request to add a new entry under an existing parent entry, the Delete request to delete an existing entry, the Modify request to add, remove, or replace attribute values, and the Modify DN request to rename an existing entry. The DSA receiving the Update request will not follow aliases if they are present in the name of the entry (or parent) to be updated, but will return a referral if the referenced entry is held by another DSA. Adding or deleting information from an entry will enforce any object class restrictions defined for that entry type.

LDAP Update operations can also be submitted as a batch using the *LDAP Data Interchange Format* (LDIF). LDIF is typically used for bulk import and export directory information between LDAP-based directory servers, or to describe a set of changes that are to be applied to a directory. LDIF is useful in full-directory synchronization operations or incremental synchronization operations between dissimilar directory products.

LDAP Update limitations Readers should also be aware that, for the most part, the LDAP protocol is designed to support single-entry updates, not multiple-entry updates. For example, the Add operation provides protocol only to add a leaf entry, not a container. The Delete and Modify DN operations also do not provide protocol to alter a container with contents crossing multiple DSAs. Thus, while Active Directory services and other products will allow administrators to "prune" and "graft" container entries, customers must not expect to be able to perform arbitrary movements of entries and subtrees between servers, especially when different vendors provide the servers.

LDAP Application Programming Interfaces (APIs)

To use LDAP's directory lookup and update operations against an LDAP server, an application (such as an e-mail client) must have software that supports the LDAP protocol as defined in the RFCs. It is possible to embed protocol support directly within the application or to contain it within a separate program library that is

LDAP provides Add, Delete, and Modify Update operations.

LDIF allows LDAP updates to be supplied to a server in batch mode.

LDAP tree Update functions do not work across multivendor directory environments.

APIs that can be used to access LDAP include the IETF standard 'C' API, Microsoft ADSI, and Java-based APIs.

accessible through a set of API calls. Such an API is specified in RFC 1823, the LDAP 'C' language API. The IETF, however, is in the process of extending this API to accommodate the latest changes in LDAP V3.

Active Directory services includes a published ADSI API set that embeds the RFC 1823 'C' and also provides higher-level interfaces to LDAP through languages such as Visual Basic and Java. The various levels and layers of ADSI itself are fully described in Chapter 6, "ADSI Programming and the Developer." Other LDAP APIs have been published in the Java community, such as the Java Naming and Directory Interface (JNDI).

ADSI enables multiple programming languages to use LDAP.

The Future of LDAP and DNS

As of 1999, DNS is a stable protocol undergoing incremental enhancement, while LDAP continues to evolve. While LDAP interoperability between multivendor clients and servers is largely assured, the industry remains no closer to having standards-based interoperability between different brands of directory servers, such as Active Directory services and Novell's Novell Directory Services (NDS). This is because LDAP was designed as a client-to-directory protocol and work has just begun to recast it as a directory-to-directory protocol—a much more difficult problem. Legacy directory servers, LDAP directory servers, and X.500 DSAs will continue to proliferate and to be only partially compatible.

DNS is a stable protocol, but LDAP is still emerging.

Going forward, the most important IETF directory standards requirements for LDAP are access control, replication, and schema interoperability. Crafting these standards could take some time. Replication, in particular, could take a few more years to straighten out, as could access control. In the meantime, each vendor has its own implementation of access control. However, since Active Directory services and other products use proprietary access control, any such configuration will be lost if data is copied from one vendor's directory to another.

The IETF is developing LDAP enhancements for multivendor replication, access control, directory and schema definitions.

Another important area where work must be done is in harmonizing the information model so as to reduce duplicate schema elements between directories. Users and developers should minimize their use of custom schemas and monitor the standards processes. Where straightforward standards-based approaches fail to harmonize schemas and namespaces, meta-directory integration tools will be necessary for managing diverse LDAP and non-LDAP directories.

Efforts such as the Distributed Management Task Force (DMTF) Directory-Enabled Networks (DEN) schema definitions for routers are extremely important, both for schema standardization and for positioning LDAP and dynamic DNS/DHCP to move down the communications stack, enabling intelligent networks with quality of service, IPSec, VPN capabilities, and other enhancements. A new world of converged voice/data networks is emerging, with directories at the center of the infrastructure.

Summary

DNS, LDAP, and X.500 provide standards for directory services that are vital in enabling customers to integrate applications and operating environments, and in enabling developers to leverage a broad market for their wares.

X.500 defined a rich set of directory standards, covering most of the full-directory architecture elements, including client, server, access protocol, authentication and access control, chaining, replication, management, APIs, and others. Although major vendors have not deployed X.500 widely, many of X.500's original concepts—particularly the hierarchical, object-oriented information model—are reflected in LDAP.

Sidenotes (left margin):

Information schemas must become more standard between multivendor directories.

The Directory-Enabled Networks (DEN) standards will make possible intelligent, personalized networks with improved service support.

In summary, DNS, LDAP, and X.500 are the directory standards.

LDAP emerged as a simplified subset of X.500.

LDAP is evolving from a client-access protocol, originally designed as an interface to X.500, into a protocol capable of providing a more complete set of directory standards. Moreover, it is becoming operationally integrated with the well-established DNS protocol. For all LDAP's growing pains, the release of Active Directory services itself will do much to assure that LDAP's rapid adoption continues.

Active Directory services integrates LDAP with DNS and is driving more widespread adoption of the standard.

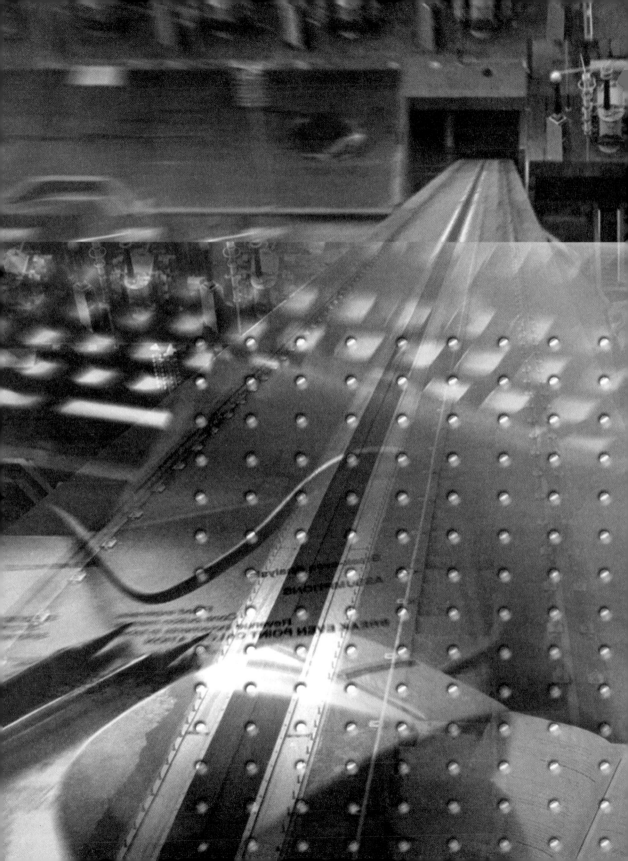

Chapter Three

Active Directory Services in the Microsoft Product Line

Microsoft's vision as a software company is to put information at people's fingertips through a new generation of software solutions that take advantage of distributed computing and the Internet. Microsoft provides computer operating systems and software tools, personal computing applications, business applications, and Internet services. Because Microsoft Active Directory technology is the most critical component of Microsoft's DNA roadmap, we begin this chapter with an overview of past, present, and future Microsoft networking products, highlighting the directory systems of each.

The Microsoft Distributed interNet Applications Architecture (DNA) is Microsoft's distributed computing and Internet roadmap.

A Microsoft Directory Retrospective

In the 1980s, Microsoft's MS-DOS emerged as the dominant personal computing operating system. In 1985, Microsoft released the first versions of Microsoft Windows, which gradually replaced MS-DOS after Windows 3.0 became available in 1990. The early versions of Windows were written for a 16-bit CPU processor platform.

In the 1980s, Microsoft marketed MS-DOS, 16-bit Windows, and LAN Manager.

LAN Manager in the 1980s

Microsoft also made a foray into network-based computing, taking on the local area network (LAN) file and print market through Microsoft LAN Manager, first released in 1989. Like other early network operating system products, LAN Manager created an entire proprietary networking infrastructure; Microsoft developed the network basic input/output (NetBIOS) APIs to redirect clients to use the LAN Manager server, the NetBIOS Enhanced User Interface (NetBEUI) protocol between clients and servers, the server message block (SMB) file-sharing protocol, and the Windows NT LAN Manager (NTLM) security protocol. As we review Microsoft Windows NT Server and Active Directory functionality throughout this book, it will become apparent that the earlier LAN Manager protocols are still supported.

Early directory capabilities were primitive.

These early product client operating systems and networking products contained nothing special in the way of directories. At the time of LAN Manager, having only a rudimentary directory system was not a competitive disadvantage; directories in the first versions of Novell's NetWare were also primitive. Of the major LAN vendors at that time, only Banyan pushed the directory concept with StreetTalk, which incorporated a hierarchical information model and distributed protocols that made it possible to access and administer networks of many servers in a more flexible manner. The X.500 standards, first issued in 1988, specified a hierarchical and object-oriented directory system that was far ahead of its time.

Distributed Windows Computing Initiatives in 1992

In 1992, Microsoft articulated its vision of 32-bit Windows-based personal computing.

In 1992, Microsoft set out a framework for the future of Windows, which included the 32-bit programming model and the new Microsoft Component Object Model (COM). Around the same time, Microsoft began to articulate the vision of a distributed, object-oriented file system (code-named Cairo) and started to develop a scalable electronic messaging product that later became Microsoft Exchange Server.

In the mid-1990s, Microsoft delivered Windows 95 and Windows NT. With COM, these operating systems are still at the center of Microsoft's continuing innovation. Delivering other initiatives, such as Cairo and Exchange Server, proved to be more difficult. Although Exchange Server was released in early 1996, the fully functional distributed system is only now arriving with Microsoft Windows 2000.

Despite delays in realizing parts of the vision, sales of Microsoft Windows NT Workstation and Exchange Server operating systems flourished in the mid-1990s. Microsoft Windows NT 4.0 Server provided a general-purpose application server, graphical management, and compatibility with many MS-DOS and Windows 3.*x* applications. Windows NT 4.0 also provided early TCP/IP support, as well as file and print capabilities. As many developers began moving applications to the Windows NT platform, Windows NT 4.0 began making inroads against Novell in the network operating system (NOS) market, and against UNIX servers in the enterprise market.

The Windows NT Server and Domain-Bound Directories

Microsoft's Windows NT 3.*x* and 4.0 servers are grouped into domains, or groups of machines and users whose account and access privileges are managed by the same administrator or support group and controlled by selected machines called domain controllers (DCs). Because midsize to large enterprises often require multiple domains, users often need access to resources in a remote domain. However, in Windows NT's flat domain-bound namespace, cross-domain access is neither transparent nor automatic with Windows NT 3.*x* and Windows NT 4.0; it requires significant manual intervention, both to define interdomain trust relationships and to configure information about the users or groups of users who have cross-domain privileges.

The directory functionality of Windows NT 3.*x* and Windows NT 4.0 will be revisited in Chapter 4, "Active Directory Services Architecture." For now, it is enough to note that the directory functionality in these systems is limited and has hampered Microsoft's enterprise-distributed computing initiatives.

Directory limitations also limited DCOM and Dfs.

The Distributed Component Object Model (DCOM) and Windows NT 4.0 distributed file system (Dfs) were early installments on Microsoft's promised distributed, object-oriented file and applications environment. DCOM makes it possible for a program to execute code in an object residing anywhere on the network, and Dfs creates a logical file or directory system and naming structure that spans servers. Without a powerful directory, however, Dfs was still not fully transparent to users and administrators, and COM applications still generally ran on a single machine. There was no namespace to locate and provide network objects and resources in a scalable manner across a large enterprise.

Microsoft Meets the Internet

In the mid-1990s, surging Internet adoption triggered a midcourse correction in many of Microsoft's strategies.

In 1995, as Microsoft struggled with Exchange Server, DCOM, and early parts of the Dfs, Internet and Web browser technology proliferated in both the business intranet and consumer Internet markets. Microsoft saw opportunity in the massive groundswell of demand for standards-based Internet products, but also came to an unexpected realization: the Java-based browser as a cross-platform "universal client" could pose a serious threat to Microsoft's dominance of the desktop market.

Microsoft's Internet strategy began with Internet Explorer and Internet Information Server.

The Internet opportunity and the browser threat led to a midcourse correction in Microsoft's Windows and Windows NT development strategy. Not only did Microsoft launch Microsoft Internet Explorer, Microsoft Internet Information Server (IIS), and Microsoft Network Internet/Web offerings, but also refocused the Exchange Server, Windows NT 5.0,[1] and DCOM initiatives to support or use Internet standards such as Lightweight Directory Access Protocol (LDAP), Domain Name System (DNS), and others. In short, Microsoft's DNA roadmap was drawn.

---

1. Windows NT 5.0 was later rebranded Windows 2000.

Microsoft Windows DNA: The Big Picture

In 1997, Microsoft announced the Windows DNA strategy. The Windows DNA application architecture embraces and integrates both the Web and client/server models of application development. It extends the Internet Explorer Web browser capabilities through Dynamic Hypertext Markup Language (DHTML), or scripting, and builds browser capabilities into the desktop operating system itself. It includes an object model called COM+, which underlies system code as well as application code, and integrates the object model with extensive middleware support for developing transactional applications. COM+ and Windows 2000 distributed systems also underlie another initiative—Zero Administration initiative for Windows (ZAW)—designed to reduce user cost of ownership.

> In 1997, Microsoft announced the Windows DNA strategy, which encompasses the Windows 2000 distributed systems, Zero Administration initiative for Windows (ZAW), and other initiatives.

DNA Overview

Windows DNA synthesizes competing concepts at various architecture levels: structured vs. unstructured storage, object vs. transaction programming environment, mobile vs. connected mode of working, and static but interoperable Web page user presentation vs. dynamic and more powerful native code. It seeks to blend the client/server and Web worlds, provide integration between structured and unstructured storage, and offer a rich set of reusable components as building blocks to enable new applications.

> Windows DNA provides a component-based, interoperable architecture model.

For interoperability, Microsoft has built a great deal of multivendor Internet standards support into its APIs, its distributed system, its middleware, and its security models. Protocol capabilities, such as LDAP, can themselves be exposed as components, and other components can also enable interoperability by acting as proxies to non-standard heterogeneous services. APIs, such as Active Directory Service Interfaces (ADSI), use the COM or COM+ component models.

> DNA embeds Internet standards support in Microsoft's COM/COM+ environment.

Thin client and rich client   Through Windows DNA, users can make the most of native Win32 APIs and applications as well as applications laid out as Web pages for cross-platform portability; both paradigms will be supported in the Visual family of tools for

> Web-based applications (thin client) and native Win32 applications (rich client) are both supported in DNA.

Microsoft Visual Basic, VBScript, C, C++, and other programming languages. Dynamic HTML, which allows HTML itself to contain scripts, and Extensible Markup Language (XML), which allows HTML to define application constructs on the fly, have been put forward as unifying concepts between content and applications. Active Directory services and other Microsoft infrastructure elements are thus accessible through Web-based views, as well as through APIs, in keeping with DNA.

OLE DB and ActiveX Data Objects (ADO) provide an integrated view of structured and unstructured storage.

Structured and unstructured storage   Down at the storage level, Microsoft exposes ActiveX Data Objects (ADO) through the OLE DB API for universal access to both structured and unstructured information. ADO makes it possible for applications to apply relational database queries, joins, and other operations to objects or properties of objects, regardless of whether those objects are databases, documents, address books, messages, tables, or other stores or components. ADO is a bridge across logical and physical chasms that have prevented developers from creating repository-

---

Using ADO or OLE DB: Heterogeneous Join Example

As an example of combining structured and unstructured storage through ADO or OLE DB, consider a project management application whose function is to provide a list of current projects for the manager to browse and update project details and construct sophisticated queries. Suppose the list of projects is in a Structured Query Language (SQL) database, project details are in Microsoft Project files, project plans are in a Microsoft Exchange Server public folder, and information about project owners is in Active Directory services. Just viewing the information manually would take all morning! With ADO, however, the manager can issue a single query: Pull up Project Owners, Project Details, and Project Plans for all projects budgeted at $100,000 or more. The query will perform a heterogeneous join, extracting information from databases or from components acting as data.

---

spanning business applications in the past. Abstracting storage views lets applications perform heterogeneous joins across diverse information sources.

Zero Administration Initiative for Windows (ZAW)   Microsoft's many-faceted Zero Administration initiative for Windows (ZAW) is intended to reduce or eliminate the staggering desktop-by-desktop installation, configuration, and administrative workload that some studies say has driven cost of PC ownership as high as $8,000 a year. A major part of ZAW involves centralized administration of user logon, applications, security, and other resources through Active Directory services.

Zero Administration initiative for Windows (ZAW) will bring down costs of ownership.

ZAW also encompasses automatic hardware and software detection through the NetPC bus structure, replication of file shares in the Dfs, and the use of Microsoft IntelliMirror to replicate hard drives between a mobile client content and a file share. The focus is on simplicity and management, as well as designing for operations.

NetPC bus structure will play an important role in the automatic detection of hardware and software.

The Windows 2000 Server   The Microsoft Windows 2000 Server[2] is a platform for the next generation of distributed Internet and intranet applications. It includes built-in services, such as Active Directory services, Internet Information Server (IIS), Microsoft Message Queue Server (MSMQ), and Microsoft Transaction Server (MTS), that provide developers with the infrastructure to rapidly develop richer, more reliable enterprise applications. It also includes an enhanced networking and communications infrastructure, plus comprehensive distributed services, message queuing, and clustering. File system improvements and hardware advances increase the performance of applications that handle larger and larger amounts of data. Application services, such as Dynamic HTML, multimedia, transactions, and server-side scripting, enable rich clients and robust servers.

The Windows 2000 Server is a key part of DNA.

---

2. The Windows 2000 Server may be packaged in multiple flavors, just as the Windows NT 4.0 Server is packaged as Server, Advanced Server, and Enterprise. Packaging may change over time. In this book, we will refer to the basic capabilities of the product line as the Windows 2000 Server.

Putting It All Together

The Windows 2000 Server is at the core of the physical DNA architecture.

In this section, we will look at how the pieces plug into the Windows 2000 distributed systems at the conceptual level, and then go into more detail in the rest of the chapter. Figure 3-1 provides an overview of the Microsoft product-line architecture.

Figure 3-1   *The Microsoft product-line architecture.*

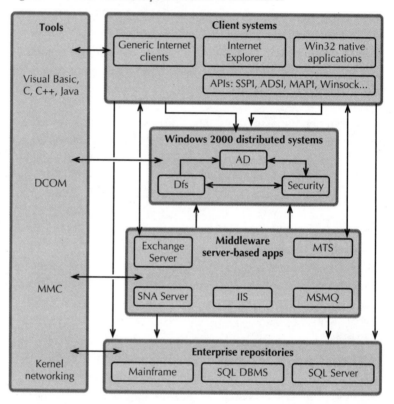

Windows 2000 is at the core of Microsoft's network architecture. Once it is fully rolled out, nothing will happen on a Microsoft network without going through Active Directory services. Generic Internet clients and the Internet Explorer will access Web pages that are maintained by the Internet Information Server in the Dfs, which in turn depends on Active Directory services.

Windows 2000 is a directory-centric environment.

Increasingly, executable files and their configuration parameters will be stored in Windows 2000 servers. Microsoft BackOffice and other server-based applications, such as Exchange Server, will use Active Directory services as the directory system. Microsoft's Visual Tools, DCOM, and development tools will allow developers to easily make use of the Windows 2000 distributed systems.

Soon, not a line of code in a Microsoft shop will run without Windows 2000 distributed systems support, and all activities will be strongly authenticated and authorized by interwoven Active Directory location and security functions. Much of this transformation will be enabled through Microsoft's client APIs, such as the Security Support Provider Interface (SSPI) and ADSI, which make it possible for developers to migrate their applications to support the new Windows 2000 paradigms without having to write a great deal of new code.

ADSI and SSPI facilitate application migration to the directory-centric environment.

An Analyst's Perspective on DNA

Putting on the analyst's hat for a minute, we note that DNA, as delivered in Windows 2000, is a vast initiative representing many million lines of code and many thousand work-years of development. Originally intended for release in mid-1998, delivery was delayed by the sheer complexity of simultaneously releasing the distributed directory and security system, a significantly redesigned Windows client with IntelliMirror and ZAW support, and an ambitious line of middleware centered on COM, COM+, and the Microsoft Transaction Server. Although parts of the DNA architecture have preceded Windows 2000, much of it must emerge together. After deployment will come the inevitable bugs and problems. However, DNA's many positive features—its standards support and well-thought-out architecture, with third-party developer resources to fill in the cracks—will provide significant benefits to customers. Many of these benefits begin with deployment of the Windows 2000 distributed system.

It will take time for Windows DNA to mature, but in the end it will bring significant benefits to customers and developers.

The Windows 2000 Distributed System

The three components of Windows 2000 that make it a distributed system are Active Directory services, Dfs, and Windows NT security. Active Directory services is the distributed, standards-based directory technology designed to enable applications, provide

Active Directory services, Dfs, and distributed security comprise the Windows 2000 distributed system.

user-friendly access to end users, and allow centralized administration of resources. Dfs adds location independence, logical naming, and improved availability to the shared file system. Windows 2000 security is based on two security models—Kerberos and public key cryptography—that allow single sign-on (an enterprise-wide logon), strong authentication, and encryption services to be used in the Windows 2000 environment and across the Internet.

Active Directory Services

Active Directory services
is used across the entire
Microsoft product line.

Chapter 1, "Introducing Active Directory Services," introduced Active Directory services as the source of many new features in Windows 2000. Chapter 2, "Active Directory Services and Industry Standards," outlined the relevant industry standards and noted that Active Directory services supports both LDAP and DNS standards. In the remainder of this chapter, we will discuss the ways in which Active Directory technology is vital to both distributed security and Dfs, and how Active Directory services is used across the Microsoft product line.

Windows 2000 Security Services

Security services are
provided through the
Windows 2000 client,
server, and security
management utilities.

Windows 2000 distributed security services are provided by three basic sources: client-based security capabilities, server-based security capabilities, and security management and administration systems. Collectively, these components provide centralized single sign-on and access control, enable public key and Kerberos encryption capabilities under most network protocols, and extend intranet sign-on and access control privileges to external users. The security service also enables delegated administration and scalability for large domains, as well as heterogeneous client authentication.

The distributed security
services take advantage
of both the Kerberos pro-
tocol and the public key
security technology.

Security model overview   Distributed security services support both the Kerberos shared-secret security mechanisms and the public key-based security services through X.509 certificates. The Kerberos protocol is used between a client, a Key Distribution Center (KDC), and Kerberos-aware applications accessed by the client. Although it might seem redundant to use both Kerberos and public key technologies, in fact, they complement one another.

Kerberos offers better performance within an intranet or a domain; verifying the cryptographic ticket conveyed between a client and an application using Kerberos secret key technology can be done efficiently with less overhead than by public key operations. On the other hand, the public key technology works without the need for an online trusted broker like the KDC, and is therefore globally scalable to users outside an enterprise or domain to provide secure Web access and secure e-mail.

The Kerberos protocol underlies the basic security and trust models within Windows 2000 domains. We will take a quick look at these models, particularly the tight coupling between Active Directory services and security services. However, there is much more going on than we can cover here; Chapter 9, "Security Overview: Kerberos, Certificates, and Access Control," will provide a more detailed discussion.

> Kerberos trusts link Windows 2000 domains.

In the Windows 2000 security model, clients access objects through services; they never have direct access to objects. To decide whether a client can access a particular object in a particular way, services map the client's authenticated identity to a security group and use group memberships to determine access control at the resource level. The client's identity is established through strong authentication that occurs at logon time under the LDAP Simple Authentication and Security Layer (SASL) protocol, as described in Chapter 2, "Active Directory Services and Industry Standards." The client is granted a Kerberos Ticket-Granting Ticket (TGT) that it uses to request service tickets as needed for application services. Application services obtain a Windows NT security identifier (SID) from the service ticket, and use it to impersonate the client for access control purposes. If the access check succeeds, the client is allowed to use the requested objects.

> Servers use Kerberos authentication and Active Directory groups to grant clients access to objects.

Figure 3-2 shows the Windows 2000 security services in operation. Note the role of the client, the Security Support Provider Interface (SSPI), the client security provider, the domain controller-based security service and Kerberos Key Distribution Center (KDC), Active Directory services, and management capabilities in providing a single sign-on to Windows NT services. The MMC's directory and

> Windows 2000 security components include the SSPI API, the KDC, the Certificate Server, and Microsoft Domains and Trusts administration snap-ins.

security snap-ins manage access controls and other security information, while the Certificate Server manages public key information.

Figure 3-2 *Single sign-on and the Windows NT distributed security architecture.*

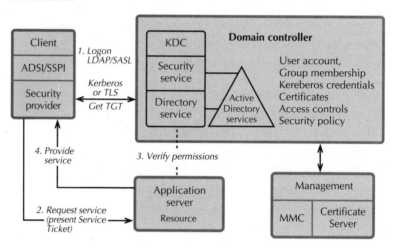

Single sign-on capabilities   The *single sign-on* in Windows 2000 is actually an enterprise-wide logon that transparently crosses domains. Again, the Kerberos protocol makes the multidomain logon possible by allowing domain controllers to establish transitive trust links up and down the domain hierarchy. Explicit trust relationships are now used only for disjoint domains or for compatibility with Windows NT 4.0, making the Windows 2000 architecture much more manageable and scalable. Because much of Windows NT 4.0's administrative overhead is associated with maintaining cross-domain trusts and groups, there are opportunities for significant cost savings and other benefits from deploying the Windows 2000 distributed single sign-on solution.

The distributed security model enables enterprise-wide single sign-ons across multiple, cooperating Windows domains.

Comprehensive integration between the Windows 2000 directory and security services underpins the entire security model. The directory service is trusted to hold the Kerberos principals (encrypted password information) that are used to verify client-to-service trust and transitive service-to-service trust. Active Directory services is also trusted to hold security policy and access control information.

Windows distributed security services trust Active Directory services to hold Kerberos security principals information.

Using the strong authentication of LDAP, the Key Distribution Center on the domain controller, and logically centralized security administration in the directory, Microsoft is closer than ever before to scaling security to the enterprise.

Public key support   Public key-based encryption is also used extensively within Windows 2000. It enables the Transport Layer Security (TLS) protocol beneath a variety of application protocols, providing a secure channel for Web access, IP security, and other application protocols. Public key technology also supports the Encrypted File System (EFS), which lets users designate that certain files or folders should be encrypted transparently to applications. In addition, e-mail users of Secure/Multipurpose Internet Mail Extensions (S/MIME) can use public key support to encrypt message information sent to other users or to apply digital signatures to message data, and to decrypt information and verify signatures.

Public key support further extends Windows security to support file encryption, secure e-mail, extranets, secure Web operations, and other capabilities.

Public key certificates can extend the enterprise single sign-on to extranet users who have TLS-capable Web browsers. For example, a user contacts a Web server from outside the firewall and requests access to an object on an intranet. The Web server verifies the user's certificate in the directory, maps the certificate to a configured account, and attempts to access the requested object using Kerberos and the privileges available to the mapped account.

Certificates can be mapped to accounts.

Public keys are normally wrapped in a certificate before they are used by an application to encrypt sensitive information or to verify a digital signature. A certification authority (CA) issues certificates for each user. With Windows 2000, any organization can act as its own CA using the Microsoft Certificate Server or a third-party product to manage certificates, certificate revocation lists (CRLs), and trust policy information—such as which CAs to trust when an application is verifying a certificate—and store the information in Active Directory services. Prior to Windows 2000, much of this public key configuration, if deployed at all, had to be managed desktop-by-desktop. Being able to configure and

Microsoft Certificate Server manages public key certificates, certificate revocation lists, and certificate usage policies in Active Directory services.

change certificate information at the domain, group, and user level—and to manage this information centrally in the directory—is a critical prerequisite for deploying public key technology.

Distributed File System (Dfs)

Dfs shares files using SMB.

The Dfs for the Windows 2000 Server is based on the server message block (SMB) file access protocol used in Windows, Windows NT, and LAN Manager. Like previous Microsoft file systems, Dfs is based on a client accessing files in a specific share (a remote directory hosted by a particular file server) using a universal naming convention (UNC) name, such as *machinename**sharename* *dirname1**dirname2* *dirname3**filename*. The client must know the machine name, the share name, and the path name (directories and files) within that share.

Dfs links file shares across multiple servers into a single volume.

Dfs overview The difference between Dfs and previous Microsoft file systems is that with Dfs, shares on multiple machines can be grouped into a single volume. To clients, everything in this volume appears to be in a single share. As shown in Figure 3-3, if a UNC name, such as *machinename**sharename**dirname1* *dirname2*, identifies a path on Dfs server A, the rest of the name, *dirname3**filename,* can be on Dfs server B. Server A contains the root of the volume, called the Dfs root, while the rest of the name is split across multiple servers and identifies a particular file in the volume.

Dfs servers refer, clients across Dfs junctions that link previously isolated shares.

The connection between the two Dfs servers is called a *junction,* and the ability to navigate across the junction is the crucial new capability in Dfs. Crossing the junction is done cooperatively by the Windows 2000 or Windows 95/98 client redirector and the server using a referral message newly added to the SMB protocol. All of this occurs transparently to the client and, as a bonus, the client can be referred to file servers accessed using Novell's NetWare Core Protocol (NCP) or Sun's Network File System (NFS).

Figure 3-3 *Dfs architecture and Active Directory services.*

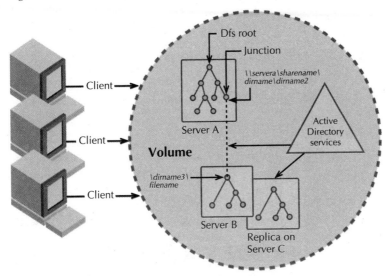

Directory-enabling Dfs Active Directory services holds information about Dfs junctions, allowing the file system to be centrally administered. Active Directory services also helps enable another new Dfs feature—the ability to replicate volumes and to direct a user to the nearest, most accessible copy—by storing information about Dfs replicas. Windows 2000 clients have built-in intelligence to select the correct replica, consulting Active Directory services using LDAP to obtain the Dfs information.

Junctions and Dfs replication features are enabled through Active Directory services.

Thus, Dfs combines diverse server-based file systems into a single namespace. Using UNC names—or links or shortcuts containing UNC names—the client can traverse the distributed file services. Dfs does for servers and shares what file systems do for hard disks: it allows customers to organize file servers and their shares into a logical hierarchy, making it considerably easier to manage and use information resources. Users no longer need to remember which server a file is on and keep track of multiple machines; the physical location of data becomes transparent.

Dfs and Active Directory services allow customers to organize file servers and shares information into a logical hierarchy.

Directory-Enabled Applications and Policy-Based Administration

COM leverages Active Directory services and the Windows 2000 distributed systems.

While the distributed systems provide a base infrastructure for client logon, file and print, security, and centralized administration, the Distributed Component Object Model (DCOM) technology allows Windows developers to build increasingly rich, componentized applications on top of the infrastructure. We will briefly introduce DCOM, then discuss the ways in which it will make use of the distributed systems and Active Directory services.

Component Object Model (COM)

COM defines a language-independent framework for invoking an object's methods through a consistent interface.

COM, on which DCOM is based, defines a framework for one software object to expose services to another software object, script, or program. COM objects can be written in any language— C, C++, Java, Microsoft Visual Basic, and others. COM objects provide access through interfaces, each of which contains one or more methods. Client software using an object acquires pointers to each interface, and uses those pointers to invoke the interface's methods. For example, an object, called File, could expose an interface, called Basic File operations, with the methods Open, Close, Read, and Write.

OLE was the predecessor of COM.

Object linking and embedding (OLE), the ancestor of COM, first brought the benefits of language-independent object-oriented computing to the Windows platform. Through OLE, for example, a user working in Microsoft Word could embed or link a spreadsheet file or a graphic object in the document, and later, by clicking that object, bring the embedded object's application to life while still inside Word.

ActiveX brings OLE and COM to the Web.

Microsoft ActiveX brings OLE and COM to the Web. Developers or publishers can paste an object's code inside a Web page and, when a browser accesses the page, it installs and runs the ActiveX object. For example, a viewer for any popular application file format can be provided to a browser through ActiveX, enabling the user to see any object accessible via the Web.

Distributed COM (DCOM)

DCOM provides generic remote invocation of COM objects. With COM, an object can be invoked and run inside an application process or in a separate process on the same computer. With DCOM, an object can be invoked on a separate computer. Figure 3-4 displays all the essential parts of DCOM.

DCOM allows remote execution of COM objects.

Figure 3-4   *DCOM components.*

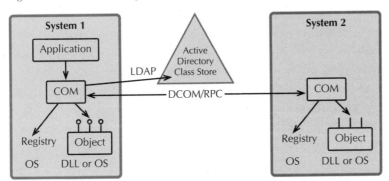

In the figure, an application on System 1 is accessing an object on the same machine (portrayed using a standard lollipop diagram meant to show object, interface, and methods) through the COM library. This local object could reside in a dynamic link library (DLL) or in the operating system (OS). However, the object could also reside at a remote location, say System 2. No problem: once System 1's COM library locates an object in the registry, DCOM does the rest. System 1's COM library calls System 2's COM library using a standard remote procedure call (RPC) connection, executes the remote object by proxy, and returns the results of the call to the client.

COM objects can physically reside in the operating system, in a dynamic link library (DLL), or on a remote system.

Scaling DCOM

Before Windows 2000, DCOM has not been particularly scalable. To find the remote object on System 2, System 1 had to have information about the remote object's location in its local registry. In a highly distributed environment, the registry approach requires hundreds or thousands of entries, all of which become invalid if

Storing distributed object location information in the registry is not scalable.

objects are moved. In an enterprise environment, the registry approach requires updating thousands of registries when a new object is brought into the network or an old object is moved.

Using the Active Directory Class Store allows DCOM to scale.

Just as the DNS made it possible for the Internet to scale to thousands and then millions of hosts, LDAP will allow scalable, distributed object-oriented computing to flourish. With Active Directory services or any LDAP directory, users can centrally administer the information required to locate and invoke objects. Active Directory services implementation contains a subtree called the Class Store, where information about COM objects and other programs is registered. Once the Class Store is implemented, client-based COM libraries will consult Active Directory services when an object requested by the application is not found in the registry, and will then use the information in the Class Store to remotely invoke the object.

COM as an Integrated Framework

COM is now the standard application/ object environment throughout the Microsoft product line.

Not only does COM provide an application/object environment for third-party products to use, it also has become an integrating framework up and down the Microsoft product line. Major Microsoft client- and server-based applications are exposing functionality through COM, basing their architecture for developer extensibility around COM, and using COM internally. As we will see in the next sections, Microsoft Exchange Server, Internet Information Server, and Transaction Server are all increasingly integrated with and around COM. The same can be said for the ADSI interface of Active Directory services. Third-party vendors will also take advantage of the Class Store to make their components more scalable. That said, though, only the COM model is supported in the Class Store. Users and vendors implementing other object models, such as CORBA and JavaBeans, will need to do their own distributed naming or invocation integration against Active Directory services or other LDAP stores.

Zero Administration Initiative for Windows (ZAW)

The key to reducing end-user cost of ownership is to simplify the use and administration of desktop systems. In Microsoft's roadmap, this will be achieved through a variety of initiatives, including NetPC, Microsoft Windows Terminal Server, Microsoft System Installer, and IntelliMirror. All the ZAW initiatives benefit indirectly from the role of Active Directory services as the repository for configuration and location data for such diverse items as load servers and class stores. In general, Active Directory services makes it possible for applications to publish the names and locations of services so that clients can locate and use them dynamically, and so administrators can reconfigure them without having to update clients. Because administrators and developers can add new types of directory objects or extend existing objects, Active Directory services can become a consolidation point, replacing or removing the need for multiple additional directory or directory-like repositories.

Zero Administration initiative for Windows (ZAW) comprises a number of features, many of which are enabled by Active Directory services.

In Windows 2000, group policies define user and computer settings for groups of users and computers. Customers create a specific profile for a group of users and computers using the Group Policy Editor (GPE) MMC snap-in to configure settings in a Group Policy Object (GPO) associated with selected directory objects such as sites, domains, or organizational units (OUs). Then, when a user is moved into an organization or added to a security group, his or her applications can be installed and configured automatically. Group policy settings include software policies that mandate registry configuration and position icons on the desktop for accessible applications, scripts (such as computer startup and shutdown, and logon and logoff), folder locations, and security settings.

Policy-based administration is directory-enabled in Windows 2000 and is a key element of ZAW.

Microsoft Middleware Use of Directories (MTS, MSMQ, IIS, and SQL Server)

Until now, ActiveX and DCOM have made their mark mainly in the client environment, but with the Microsoft Transaction Server (MTS), Microsoft is bringing object-oriented computing into its server middleware as well. MTS is a transaction-oriented system

Microsoft is bringing object-based computing to its server middleware environment.

for developing, deploying, and managing high-performance, scalable, enterprise, Internet, and intranet server applications. Through an application programming model based on DCOM, MTS is tightly integrated with the distributed systems and the Internet Information Server (IIS).

Transaction Server integrates clients and resource managers to enable two-phase commit transaction processing.

As shown in Figure 3-5, Transaction Server controls other Microsoft resource managers, such as the Microsoft Structured Query Language (SQL) Server and Microsoft Message Queue Server (MSMQ), that perform transactions on behalf of the client. An example might be a process payment transaction in an accounting system, involving updates to the accounts receivable database, the supplier database, and the cash balances database. All the updates must be committed in the event of success, or none of them in the event of an error.

Figure 3-5 *The Transaction Server environment.*

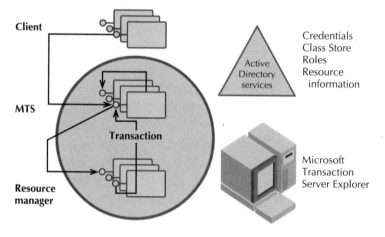

Application components that follow the MTS rules can utilize transaction services with less work on the part of the developer.

Developing two-phase commit logic is complicated; thus transaction processing monitor (TP Monitor) offerings, such as Top End or Tuxedo, tend to become complex distributed operating systems in their own right. What Microsoft has done with MTS is to build transaction processing into the server operating system. Developers can assemble transaction components using the Microsoft Transaction Server Explorer. MTS initiates transactions automatically at

Chapter Three

run time when a non-MTS-aware application creates a transactional object.

Although any Windows client running COM can already access Transaction Server applications, integration with the Internet Information Server extends the benefits of Microsoft middleware to browsers using Hypertext Transfer Protocol (HTTP) to access MTS functionality through Active Server Pages (ASP) inside IIS (as shown in Figure 3-6). HTML content deployed as ASP pages can invoke business components running in MTS. This extends Transaction Server scalability and component flexibility to Internet applications without requiring a "client footprint" other than Windows.

Transaction Server also works closely with Microsoft's Internet Information Server (IIS) to provide Web-based transaction processing.

Figure 3-6 *Integration of Microsoft Transaction Server (MTS) and Internet Information Server (IIS).*

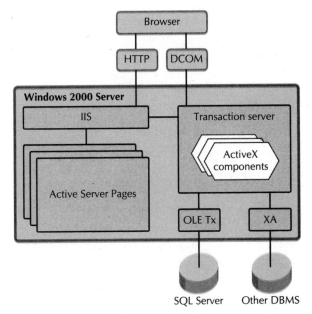

Transaction Server makes optimum use of the account, security, and other information in Active Directory services. Transaction Server components run as a system user account by default, although this account can be set to any Windows NT account (user or group). When a client tries to access the component, Transaction Server looks at the client's Kerberos session ticket (if any), impersonates

Microsoft Transaction Server leverages Active Directory services heavily, both as a user of DCOM and as a user of the integrated directory/ security services.

the client, and performs an access-control check. Transaction Server also leverages the directory to provide role-based security. From an access-control perspective, a role is similar to a group, but applies only to the Transaction Server. Administrators add users to the role, and components or interfaces then use the roles to grant access.

Transaction Server leverages the directory to sit between the client and object as a TP Monitor and Resource Broker, and to provide security services.

Transaction Server represents a natural convergence of object request brokering and TP Monitor services. In addition to orchestrating the commitment of transactions, it handles concurrency, resource pooling, security, context management, and other system-level functions. The transaction system, working in cooperation with database servers and other types of resource managers, ensures that concurrent transactions are atomic,[3] consistent, have proper isolation from one another, and, once committed, are durable. Active Directory services is an important enabler because it stores configuration information for DCOM, as well as for the IIS, SQL Server, and MSMQ resource managers.

Directory-Enabling
Microsoft Outlook and Exchange Server

Microsoft Exchange Server is a four-year-old client/server-based electronic messaging product line now enabled by Active Directory services.

Microsoft Exchange Server is yet another strategic enterprise application enabled, in large part, by Active Directory services. Exchange Server has its roots in the Microsoft Mail product line, which was originally launched in 1991 and bundled with Microsoft Schedule+ and Microsoft Office a few years later. Exchange Server, however, is a client/server-based mail system that is much more advanced than Microsoft Mail. Exchange Server uses the Microsoft Messaging API (MAPI) on the desktop (a proprietary Microsoft protocol that is based on an RPC) to access the server and X.400 or Simple Mail Transfer Protocol (SMTP) to communicate between servers.

---

3. An *atomic* transaction is defined as one or more series of actions that occur in their entirety, or not at all.

In 1996 and 1997, Microsoft made extensive changes to the architecture of Exchange Server. Exchange Server 5.5 now supports Web access, LDAP, Post Office Protocol (POP3), Internet Message Access Protocol (IMAP4), and Secure MIME (S/MIME). Microsoft has also introduced the Outlook client as an integrated Microsoft Office Suite component, bundled the Outlook Express e-mail client with Internet Explorer, and rebranded the Win16 and Macintosh-based Exchange Server clients as Outlook clients.

In 1996 and 1997, Microsoft added support for all major Internet mail protocols and brought out the Outlook product line.

Notable Outlook features include drag-and-drop capabilities for tasks, e-mail addresses, and messages; integration of address lists from Schedule+, Microsoft Exchange Server, and Microsoft Mail; and a journal for recording the user's activities. Outlook also offers groupware functions, such as group scheduling, forms, task management, and voting by e-mail. Through Outlook Webview and a collection of ActiveX Collaborative Data Objects on the Exchange Server side, browsers and other applications are able to access basic e-mail and scheduling information. Outlook Express, Outlook 98, and Outlook 2000 also support S/MIME for secure e-mail.

Outlook offers easy-to-use e-mail and basic groupware functionality, as well as S/MIME support.

Exchange Server is Microsoft's foundation next-generation messaging platform; it joins Microsoft's SQL Server, SNA Server, and other programs as key components of the Microsoft BackOffice server product line. Exchange Server is designed to support both Outlook clients and Internet mail clients, including routing of messages and information objects, address resolution, temporary storage, and the physical transfer of messages. These high-level functions are supported by an underlying directory service, an information store, and message transfer agent (MTA) connectivity options.

Microsoft Exchange Server consists of a message transfer agent (MTA), an information store, directory, and a number of connectors.

The information store contains user-created server-resident information such as e-mail messages, documents, and public folders, and it supports bi-directional replication facilities that allow all this information to be automatically distributed to multiple locations. For example, replication allows public folders to be stored

The Exchange Server information store supports bi-directional replication.

on more than one server and to be periodically updated from any of the servers. Some of the Active Directory replication technology we will discuss later comes from Exchange Server.

Microsoft Exchange Server supports the industrial standards protocols X.400 and SMTP for transferring messages.

The Exchange Server message transfer agent supports SMTP or X.400 message transfer. Administrators can configure either MIME or UUENCODE attachment formats on a per-site basis, and can select various international character sets. Exchange Server also supports reverse Domain Name System (DNS) authentication of calling IP addresses, validation of connection attempts by other SMTP servers against a configured lists of allowed hosts and addresses, and integration with server-based management and information store capabilities. Microsoft Exchange Server bundles both Web and Network News Transport Protocol (NNTP) connectors. Figure 3-7 displays an overview of Exchange Server components and interfaces.

Figure 3-7 *Outlook, Exchange Server, and Active Directory services.*

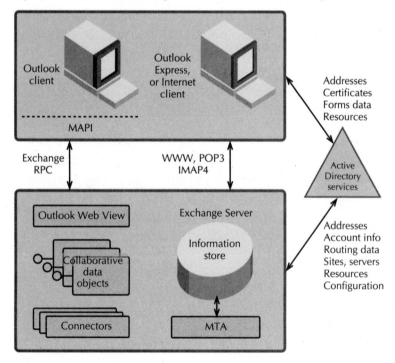

Exchange Server's X.500-like directory served as the basis for the directory that has become Active Directory services. A number of Active Directory developers came from the Exchange Server team, and Exchange Server was one of the first Microsoft products to support LDAP. Both the Exchange Server directory and Active Directory services are based logically on the LDAP/X.500 schema and physically on the Microsoft Extensible Storage Engine (ESE) database. Thus, it should not be a surprise that in Microsoft Exchange Server 6.0, the Exchange Server directory will be fully merged with Active Directory services.

The Exchange Server directory provided the basis for Active Directory services and will ultimately be replaced by Active Directory services.

An advanced e-mail client, such as Outlook, often becomes the focal point of the user's workday. From the moment the user logs on to Windows NT and is granted access to Exchange Server, almost everything he or she does is directory-enabled. Consider a typical morning consisting of coffee, reading the inbox, looking up addresses to send messages, browsing a public folder hierarchy, and pulling up a form. Many of these activities involve trips to the offline address book or behind-the-scenes directory access. Consider the dependency on directory for encrypting a message: first the user must find the recipient's name, then the recipient's certificate, then the certificate revocation lists, the trust policies, and so on.

Both Exchange Server users and system components rely heavily on the directory.

Microsoft Exchange Server management is integrated with Windows 2000 Server management. This enables central administration through the directory. The Exchange Server directory can be configured in three-level enterprise-site-server hierarchical topologies; Exchange Server defines management responsibility based on the logical grouping of one or more Exchange servers into sites and provides a single point of administration through the directory for user, site, connection, and other records. Each site contains information relative to recipients at that site, servers (MTAs, information stores, and directories), and connections (e.g., SMTP). An administrator can modify, view, or monitor recipient information, including objects such as mailboxes, distribution lists, or public folders.

For administrators, the directory constitutes the central point for all Exchange Server management.

A great many Exchange Server data items, such as distribution lists, sites, addresses, and routing information, will move into Active Directory services.

Active Directory services supports a number of functions for Exchange Server, including user directory address look-ups, certificate lookups, a forms registry, configuration management of sites and connection records, and storage of distribution lists. The data might be physically distributed, but to the user, it appears as a single directory. Synchronization between Exchange servers is supported by RPC within a single site and by messages between sites.

Internet and X.400 addresses are generated automatically in the directory when an account is created. E-mail addressing, routing, and management map cleanly onto the enterprise-site-server hierarchy of the Exchange Server directory.

Summary

Active Directory services will make Microsoft server and application environments more manageable.

Windows 2000 distributed systems and Active Directory services are arguably the most central, most critical components of the Microsoft product line infrastructure enabling Windows DNA. Active Directory technology will play a critical role in making Microsoft's networks more secure and manageable, as well as enabling a file and print environment and an electronic messaging system that are easier to use and manage than earlier offerings.

Active Directory services ties directory-enabled applications into ZAW and server-based middleware.

Active Directory services will provide payoff to customers by directory-enabling applications, reducing desktop configuration administration, and ushering in the ZAW policy-based management paradigm. Developers can also benefit from Active Directory services in working with DCOM, MTS transaction processing, and the Outlook/Exchange Server groupware and workflow platform.

Deploying Active Directory services requires significant planning and migration effort.

However, neither Active Directory services nor any other network product can offer instant nirvana. While Microsoft has worked to make Active Directory services easy to use, program, and administer, the sum of its parts is a large, complex system. Migrating to and deploying Active Directory services requires planning, training, and testing. Developing to Active Directory technology requires performance tuning and data modeling. To help customers and developers "do Active Directory services right," the next chapter provides an overview of all Active Directory services components. Subsequent chapters address each of the components in more detail and describe the best practices for development and deployment.

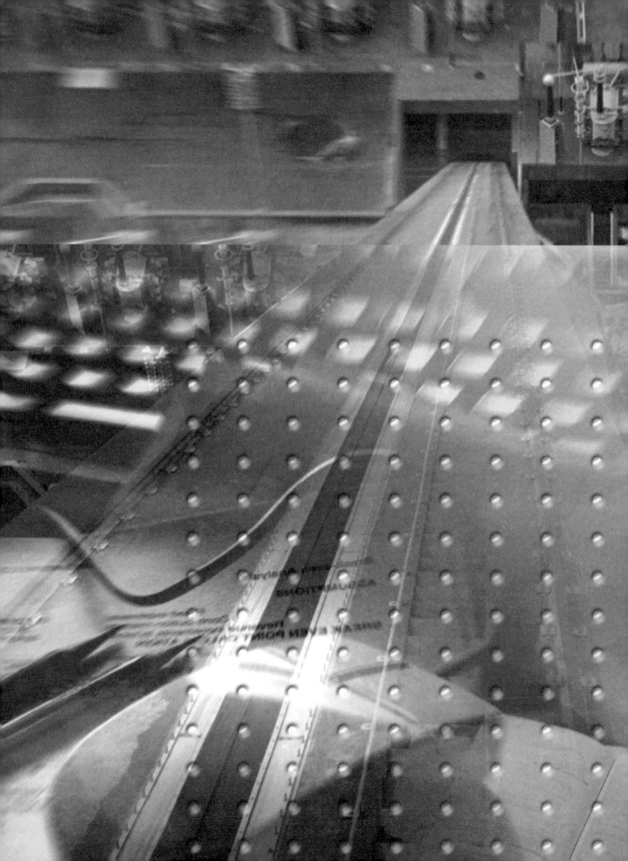

Chapter Four

Active Directory Services Architecture

Microsoft Active Directory services is designed to work as the hub for Windows 2000 enterprise network operating system (NOS) traffic, information, and services. The Microsoft Windows 2000 directory is not simply a repository for local information; it can gather and present information from other, distant domains, and organize it through the hierarchical LDAP and DNS namespaces. This information is then pulled together into Global Catalog through the process of replication, which takes place both within and across domains. Active Directory services also supports many applications, such as Microsoft Outlook, Microsoft Exchange Server, and other Microsoft BackOffice and Microsoft Office products, through its Active Directory Service Interfaces (ADSI).

Active Directory services is the hub for enterprise NOS.

It is the Active Directory architecture, which is fundamentally different from and better than the collection of Microsoft Windows NT directory repositories and programs, that allows it to do all these things and more. Active Directory technology has replaced the Windows NT directories with an integrated implementation of LDAP, DNS, DHCP, and Kerberos. With Active Directory services, administrators no longer need to set up complex trust relationships, and the registry has been replaced by a scalable database. However, managing and deploying a large, distributed system like Active Directory services and the Windows 2000 infrastructure,

Active Directory services replaces Windows NT 4.0 directories with an integration of LDAP, DNS, DHCP, and Kerberos.

although never simple, is possible with the proper resources and planning. To get an idea of how far Windows directories have come, let's first look at the Windows NT 3.*x* and 4.0 directory architecture and then compare it with that of Active Directory services.

Windows NT 3.*x* and 4.0 Network Organization

Domains are the organizational principle for Windows NT networks.

All Windows NT networks are organized into domains, or security boundaries, containing user accounts or other resources. Certain servers within a domain are designated as domain controllers (DCs). Within each domain, administrators can create, delete, and update user IDs and resource entries with a limited set of fields using the Microsoft User Manager For Domains application.

All domain security processing takes place on a domain controller.

To log on to a domain and access resources within it, users actually log on using the controller's NETLOGON program. Once connected, whenever a user tries to access a resource within the domain, the server holding that resource contacts the Security Accounts Manager (SAM) program on the controller to first verify the user's access privileges. As Figure 4-1 shows, the domain controller's Local Security Authority (LSA) contains the NETLOGON and SAM processes, makes all security and access control decisions, and houses the actual security information in the SAM Registry database.

Figure 4-1 *Windows NT 3.x and 4.0 server architecture.*

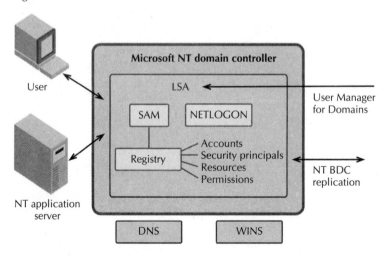

Chapter Four

Clearly, the domain controller serves a critical function in a Windows NT network. To ensure that work can continue even in the event of a DC failure, Windows NT allows multiple servers to take on the DC role. Although only one server can be the primary domain controller (PDC) to which changes or writes can be made, other servers can act as read-only backup domain controllers (BDCs) housing the NETLOGON and SAM services. Updating of these BDCs occurs through replication with the PDC.

Windows NT 4.0 supports primary and backup domain controllers, with replication to ensure consistency.

Administration of Microsoft Windows NT 4.0

Although Windows NT 4.0 directories work quite well within a single domain, enabling cross-domain access throughout a large enterprise is complex. Administrators must configure cross-domain trust relationships so that one domain controller can talk to a controller in another domain.

Enabling cross-domain access throughout a large enterprise is complex.

Let us see how this works for Bob, who works in an enterprise with domains *ntdom1* and *ntdom2*. Bob works out of *ntdom1*, which has a trust relationship with *ntdom2*. Through this trust relationship, Bob can obtain rights to access a printer or disk volume in the other domain. But first, information about his account must be configured in *ntdom2*. This information about Bob, and perhaps other *ntdom1* users who require *ntdom2* access, must also be configured in a global group held by *ntdom2* and added to the list of authorized users for *ntdom2*. And users in both *ntdom1* and *ntdom2* might require access to a third domain. It can be very complicated to track everyone who has access to other domains!

To provide access across domains, it is essential to configure complex trust relationships and groups.

Adding to the administrative complexity, all trust relationships are one-way and the global groups must be manually created in each domain. To allow cross-domain access in both directions, the administrator would have to create additional links and groups in each domain.

Trusts between domains are one-way.

The Windows Internet Naming Service (WINS) and DNS provide other directory functions within Windows NT 4.0. WINS handles NetBIOS name resolution and is required in any Windows NT

Windows NT 4.0 networks use both DNS and WINS as naming and locator services.

networks for file sharing and for some applications, even when they are operating over TCP/IP. Hosts find domain controllers and other hosts using WINS. DNS provides Internet name resolution, and its integration with Dynamic Host Configuration Protocol (DHCP) servers lets customers dynamically allocate TCP/IP addresses.

Active Directory services simplifies network administration.

Windows NT 4.0 domains are cumbersome to administer because Microsoft Windows NT Server, WINS, and DNS must be treated as separate subsystems at the cross-domain (or enterprise) level. Until now, customers have written their own administrative utilities or re-lied on products like Enterprise Administrator from Mission Critical Software, or NDS for NT from Novell to increase efficiency. Active Directory services eliminates many Windows NT 4.0 administration issues by maintaining all objects in a single database with fewer, more integrated administrative programs managing the objects.

Active Directory technology is backward compatible with Windows NT 4.0 and enables migration.

Another feature of Active Directory services is its backward compatibility and migration ability. Active Directory services can look like a Windows NT 4.0 domain controller to Windows clients while still providing a true directory service based on a database that is much richer and more scalable than the registry. Active Directory services also allows Windows NT 4.0 and Windows 2000 servers to coexist, thereby enabling Windows 2000 servers to join existing Windows NT 4.0 domains during the upgrade and migration process. During migration from Windows NT 4.0, Active Directory services can continue to support WINS; afterward, WINS is not required.

What's New in Active Directory Services?

Active Directory services provides significant enhancements compared to Windows NT 4.0.

In Windows 2000 Server, Active Directory services replaces the collection of Windows NT 3.x and 4.0 directory repositories and programs with an integrated implementation of LDAP, DNS, DHCP, and Kerberos. Complex trust relationships are no longer required; a scalable database designed to hold millions of entries has replaced the SAM Registry. Multi-master replication not only enables one domain controller to take over the logon, authorization, and access control functions from another, but also allows it to accept changes.

Other features of Active Directory services introduced in Chapter 3, "Active Directory Services in the Microsoft Product Line," are the distributed file system (Dfs), Kerberos principals, and public key certificates. Active Directory services supports the Dfs, which allows file system volumes to cross server boundaries and stores pointers to replicated volumes of shared file information. Active Directory services is also closely integrated with security services that act as trusted repositories for Kerberos principals and public key certificates. Both of these standard security services enable strong authentication at the time of Windows NT logon. These features constitute significant enhancements to both security and file sharing in comparison with Windows NT 4.0.

Active Directory services enhances Dfs and supports Kerberos and public key authentication.

With Active Directory services, Windows 2000 continues to support basic network operating system (NOS) functionality, but will also support authenticated logon and a richer Dfs. Although Active Directory services is first and foremost a NOS directory, it also provides comprehensive application-enabling through LDAP and DNS protocol support, the ability to extend the directory schema for new uses, and a class store containing application and object invocation information. To promote an understanding of how Active Directory technology for the first time positions a Microsoft NOS directory product as a general-purpose directory capable of functioning as an enterprise NOS directory, the next few sections of this chapter explore Active Directory architecture, usage, and deployment.

Active Directory technology supports advanced NOS and enterprise directory features.

Architecture Overview

To understand Active Directory technology, its critical role in the Windows 2000 environment, and the potential opportunities it creates for users and developers, we must first understand its structure or architecture. Figure 4-2 diagrams Active Directory technology from the directory architecture perspective covered in Chapter 2, "Active Directory Services and Industry Standards." Studying it carefully, we can see that Active Directory architecture has components on Windows clients as well as on the Windows 2000 Server. Note also that Active Directory services supports the LDAP/X.500 and DNS information models, as well as the Kerberos

Active Directory architecture has both client and server components and supports a number of industry standard protocols.

and public key security models at the center of its universe. It offers client access to Windows NT LAN Manager (NTLM), NetWare 3.*x,* and NetWare 4.*x* users, and backward compatibility with Windows NT 3.*x* and 4.0 networks at the server level.

Figure 4-2 *Overview of Active Directory architecture.*

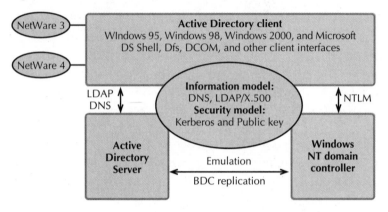

In the next two sections, we will take a closer look at the client and server components shown in Figure 4-2, and then look at Active Directory information models, security models, server architecture, domain structure, usage, and administration.

Active Directory Client

The visible Active Directory client-side components available on 32-bit versions of Windows include My Network Places, Search Assistant, and other user interfaces.

Computers running Microsoft Windows 2000, Windows 98, or Windows 95 can connect to, authenticate, and use Active Directory services on the server. To computers using previous versions of Windows, the domain looks like a Windows NT domain. Active Directory client software itself is like an iceberg; part of it is on the surface, but another part is submerged and invisible to the user. Visible client components include the Microsoft DS Shell user interface that is exposed through the My Network Places desktop icon to end users. Dfs and DCOM contain embedded logic that uses Active Directory technology to operate in a distributed manner. Other user interfaces, such as Microsoft Outlook, also contain directory logic.

Rather than building their own DNS or LDAP protocol software, directory user interfaces and applications in the Windows environment can access Active Directory services through the ADSI API. ADSI provides a layer between application functionality and system protocols, enabling enterprises to mix and match application components and infrastructure components with a greater degree of flexibility. As shown in Figure 4-3, ADSI invokes the directory-provider libraries. By emitting LDAP and other protocols, these provider libraries enable access not only to Active Directory services, but also to any LDAP- or DNS-compliant system or to proprietary NT LAN Manager and Novell Directory Services in Novell networks. In Figure 4-3, note that the client directory functionality has close ties to security; the ADSI APIs in turn enfold Security Support Provider Interface (SSPI) APIs, and the Kerberos authentication of the user takes place automatically at the same time as LDAP logon access.

All directory user interfaces and applications in a Microsoft client can access Active Directory services using directory provider libraries called through the ADSI API.

Figure 4-3 *Overview of Active Directory client architecture.*

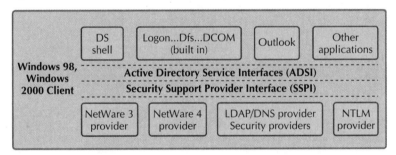

Active Directory Server

An integrated LDAP- and DNS-capable Directory System Agent (DSA) provides the server side of Active Directory services. The DSA is a collection of services (or processes) that operate over Microsoft's ESE database technology, originally developed for Microsoft Exchange Server. The DSA is built to replicate information with the other Windows NT 4.0 controllers and Windows 2000 Server DSAs, and to communicate with Windows NT 3.x and 4.0 clients, as well as with the standards-based clients. Microsoft's Dynamic DNS implementation, which integrates with

On the server side, Active Directory services provides DNS and an LDAP-capable DSA.

the DHCP server to bind host names to dynamically allocated IP addresses, provides DNS capabilities. Multi-master replication between Windows 2000 domain controllers increases the availability of information on the network.

The logon process uses LDAP and Kerberos.

In addition, as we noted in our discussion of Windows NT distributed system security in Chapter 3, "Active Directory Services in the Microsoft Product Line," LDAP is used during logon and for access control decisions by the DSA. The DSA is integrated with a Kerberos Key Distribution Center (KDC) that issues authentication tickets to clients and applications. Security Accounts Manager (SAM) functionality has been rewritten to work with the new directory and security protocols, but it continues to provide backward-compatible behavior in mixed-version Windows NT networks. Figure 4-4 shows an overview of Active Directory server architecture. In this architecture, the server exposes the LDAP, DNS, and Kerberos protocols as its primary client interfaces. It provides NTLM interfaces to older clients. A Directory System Agent (DSA) module reads or writes the ESE database storage in response to the client's LDAP requests. A Kerberos Key Distribution Center (KDC) handles client logons and requests for tickets to access resources. The DSA also supports multi-master replication with other Active Directory servers to distribute the directory, and single-master backup domain controller (BDC) replication with Windows NT 4.0 servers.

Figure 4-4 *Overview of Active Directory server architecture.*

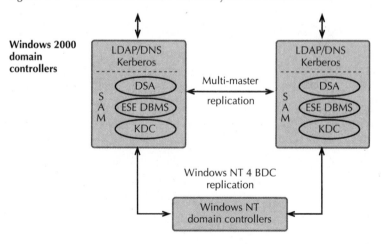

Basic Information Model

The Active Directory information model is built on the LDAP/
X.500 and DNS constructs described in Chapter 2, "Active Directory Services and Industry Standards." We saw that both X.500
and DNS define global, hierarchical namespaces. Within the DNS
namespace, there is only one type of container—the domain—
and within domains, only a limited number of data items can be
stored in resource records; such items include addresses (A),
e-mail routes (MX), services (SRV), and alias (CNAME) information. The greatest advantages of DNS are a well-established domain registration process and ubiquitous product support.
However, it is not possible to extend the DNS information model
to store fine-grained information about many different types of
network objects. DNS is pretty much limited to name-to-address
resolution functionality.

> DNS has a well-defined but limited information structure of domains and hosts.

Within the LDAP namespace, virtually any object can be defined,
but the most common containers of leaf objects are organizational units (OUs), and the most commonly found leaf objects are
variations on the organizational person object class. Within entries, one can store virtually any type of information in attribute/
value pairs. Thus, LDAP-based directories are very good at storing
fine-grained information about many different types of network
objects. Unlike DNS, however, no global domain name registration system supports LDAP.

> LDAP has a highly flex-ible, but less specifically defined structure.

Hybrid DNS and LDAP naming   Active Directory services
merges the best of DNS's global domain naming system and LDAP's
fine-grained information model. It implements a DNS/LDAP
namespace unification scheme suggested in RFC 2247. This unification scheme maps DNS domain components (DCs) into the upper part of the LDAP directory information tree (DIT). Within the
containing DNS domain structure for a Windows NT domain, additional LDAP object classes are defined—or entries created—by
administrators and applications wishing to represent fine-grained
information within domains. Chapter 7, "Planning Namespaces,
Domains, and Schema," describes Active Directory schema,
where LDAP objects and attributes are defined in greater detail.

> The information struc-ture of Active Directory services merges the best of the LDAP/X.500 and DNS worlds.

Figure 4-5 diagrams an example of an Active Directory services
information structure. In this structure, Active Directory services is
the keeper of the Windows NT domain namespace, and these domains are equivalent to DNS domains. The figure shows three
DNS/NT domains, *rapport.com, ireland.rapport.com,* and
hawaii.rapport.com, in the DNS terminology; the equivalent in the
LDAP terminology is *DC=rapport; DC=rapport,DC=ireland;* and
DC=rapport,DC=hawaii. As is usual with DNS, it is possible to contain domains as subdomains within other Active Directory domains.

Figure 4-5 *An Active Directory namespace scenario. A leaf is used to
represent objects.*

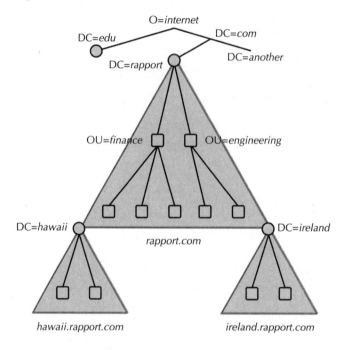

Use of LDAP organizational units or containers   Within each
domain, Active Directory uses the LDAP information structure to
introduce additional hierarchy, for example by breaking
DC=com,DC=rapport into *OU=finance* and *OU=engineering*
branches. This additional LDAP hierarchy is optional and would
let Rapport Corporation treat all objects within Finance or

Engineering as a group for access control, policy, or administration purposes. For example, the domain could delegate user administration in the *OU=finance* branch to one administrator, and *OU=engineering* to another. In addition, users in *OU=engineering* could be set up with access to resources, such as printers, in their own department, but not to resources in the Finance department.

Individual users and other objects appear as leaves in the Active Directory tree. Each leaf receives a distinguished name, such as *DC=com,DC=rapport,OU=finance,CN=daniel blum* or *DC=com,DC=rapport,DC=ireland,CN=don o'leary*. Within entries, data elements (such as e-mail address or telephone number) are held as attribute/value pairs. Users or vendors can define many different types of entries or object classes. Figure 4-6 displays a representative Active Directory entry.

A leaf in the namespace can represent a user, computer, and other objects.

Figure 4-6   *An Active Directory entry.*

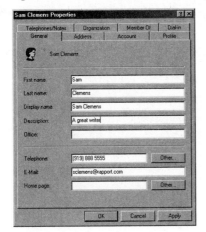

Object and attribute definitions   We have seen how LDAP embodies a naming model, or set of structure rules, using the distinguished name construct. As an LDAP implementation, Active Directory server subdivides the namespace into *naming contexts*. These naming contexts become Active Directory domains, which

The information model that Active Directory services uses includes structure-related, entry-related, and attribute-related rules.

we will discuss in the **Domains, Trees, and Forests section of** this chapter. The entries held by Active Directory services also conform to the LDAP/X.500 object-oriented model; namely, each entry belongs to an object class. Customers can create object classes for information types as diverse as users, printers, servers, and so on. In defining the rules for the structure of an entry, the *object class* specifies which attributes the entry can or must contain. The *attribute*, in turn, is the field-level definition of entry information.

Internal DSA Architecture: Security and Replication

Kerberos or TLS provides strong authentication for Active Directory users, and directory traffic can be encrypted.

Active Directory technology is part of the trusted computing base at the center of the Windows 2000 distributed system security architecture. Protection for Active Directory services itself occurs through strong authentication, encryption, and access control mechanisms. The initial authentication of a user at logon time takes place through the client's LDAP connection to the Active Directory server. Either Kerberos or public key-based Transport Layer Security (TLS) protocols running alongside the LDAP Bind operation provide authentication of all users. Once users are authenticated, their identities are mapped to a Windows 2000 account. Optionally, Kerberos or TLS can encrypt all LDAP traffic between the user and Active Directory services, and access control mechanisms can protect the directory against all operations.

Access Controls on Active Directory Services

User privileges to view or manipulate the directory are calculated through access controls that take into account user identity, the requested action, and the target information item.

Once a user is authenticated, every directory activity is subject to access controls. Access controls are stored with the object they protect as a binary value called a *security descriptor.* This security descriptor contains a list of access control entries (ACEs). Each ACE contains a security identifier (SID) that identifies the principal (user or group) to whom the ACE applies, and information on what type of access the ACE grants or denies. This is similar to the principal scheme in Windows NT 3.*x* and 4.0, but with Windows 2000, groups do not need to be manually configured in multiple domains when cross-domain access is the goal. Through the Global Catalog (GC) (described below), controllers in each domain can see any group that has been defined as a universal group.

Customers can also define access controls at the container level, where lower-level entries inherit them so that they do not need to be defined for every user. At each level of the DIT in Active Directory services, however, containers can define new ACEs for the entries within. Because each container can define new ACEs, this means is that customers can now establish administrative management at the container level. Customers can set up a different administrator for each container if necessary, instead of one group of administrators for the entire domain, as was the case with Windows NT 4.0. Customers can also create large domains with multiple administrators. They no longer need to set up all staff authorized to change user information as full domain administrators with pervasive authority (and responsibility) over large areas of the directory.

For example, a domain user might have permission to see all information about all other users in the domain, but not to make modifications. Or, a user might have permission to modify the telephone number and postal address attributes on his or her own directory entry. Customers can use access controls to assign different levels of privilege to each administrator.

Customers can define access controls at the organizational unit, container, and entry levels.

Determining Permissions to Access Other Resources

In the Windows 2000 security model, clients access objects through services; they never get direct access to objects. Controllers authenticate the user's identity at logon time using Kerberos or another method negotiated under LDAP's Simple Authentication and Security Layer (SASL). The client is granted a Kerberos Ticket-Granting Ticket (TGT) and service tickets for application servers. For access control purposes, application servers use the client security context information to impersonate the client and look up its user or group security identifiers (SIDs) in local permissions

Clients authenticate to services through Kerberos; services determine the client's permission to use resources.

tables such as the file system. If the access check succeeds, the client can use the requested objects.

Internal Server Architecture

The core server architecture of Active Directory services consists of a Directory System Agent, Dynamic DNS, and a JET database.

On any single domain controller, or server, Active Directory services has three core architecture components and a number of interfaces. The core components are the Dynamic DNS, an LDAP Directory System Agent (DSA), and the ESE database. The interfaces include the LDAP Agent, the SAM Agent (for backward compatibility to Windows NT 3.*x* and 4.0), and the Replication Agent. There is also an internal API that the interfaces use to communicate with the core DSA. Figure 4-7 diagrams the internal Active Directory server architecture.

Dynamic DNS serves as the locator service for Active Directory services.

Dynamic DNS   Dynamic DNS serves as the locator service for Active Directory services. Clients use DNS to find controllers or other types of services. All Windows 2000 services register in the DNS using only SRV RR records. With Windows 2000 DHCP, the DHCP server not only gives the client machine a TCP/IP address at boot time, but it also registers the client's backpointer <PTR> record in Dynamic DNS. The client registers its own address <A> host record. If a client's IP lease expires, the DHCP server will take the <PTR> and the <A> records out of DNS. In the Microsoft implementation, Dynamic DNS information can be stored in a DNS zone database contained within the ESE database of Active Directory services. This implementation allows DNS information to be replicated to other DNS servers on controllers using incremental changes rather than the usual full DNS zone transfer.

Customers can integrate Dynamic DNS with Active Directory services or maintain it as a separate process.

On deploying Windows 2000, an administrator can decide whether to manage the Dynamic DNS database from within Active Directory services, or to maintain a DNS separately using another product. If the administrator chooses Active Directory services, DNS is said to be "DS integrated" and the ESE database then contains DNS zones with information about hosts, addresses, services, and routes, as we discussed in Chapter 2, "Active Directory Services and Industry Standards." The Dynamic DNS process receives DNS resolver queries from DNS clients and forwards them to the core DSA; the administrator makes updates through Microsoft DNS administration directly to Active Directory services.

Figure 4-7 *Internal Active Directory server architecture.*

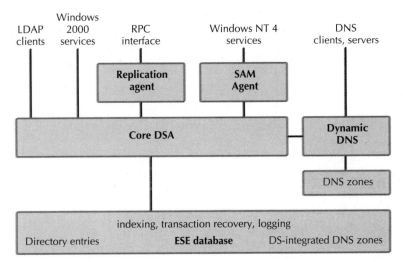

If an administrator chooses an external DNS, the Dynamic DNS process of Active Directory services will cache or copy a zone file from an external DNS system and service resolver queries, but the external system will continue to hold the master copy to which the administrator applies DNS updates.

Core Directory System Agent (DSA)   The core DSA process, through the ESE database, manages all physical storage of Active Directory services, thus isolating the storage from the many directory clients. The DSA supports a set of core operations: Bind, Add, Remove, Modify, Search, and Rename/Move Entry. Search functions support arbitrary LDAP filters, as discussed in Chapter 2, "Active Directory Services and Industry Standards," allowing applications to look up information in the directory by exact match or wildcard search using (if necessary) compound AND/OR/NOT criteria. Attribute indexing speeds response time.

The core DSA maintains the Active Directory entry structure in the JET database.

The DSA assures schema integrity and provides LDAP V3 protocol support.

Update functions maintain object identity, assigning distinguished names (DN) as external identifiers for entries, and assigning Microsoft's globally unique identifiers (GUIDs) as internal identifiers. A friendly user principal name attribute (such as *sclemens@domain.com*), usually corresponding to the user's e-mail address, is maintained as yet another domain-unique key. Active Directory update functions also maintain schema integrity, ensuring, for example, that only those attributes defined for a particular entry's object class can be added. All operations enforce access controls, regulating administrative privileges, viewing privileges, and even schema modification privileges. Finally, the DSA can refer clients to another DSA when they seek information outside its domain.

The ESE database provides storage, indexing, and transaction services.

ESE database Both the DSA and the Dynamic DNS are thus built on top of the Microsoft ESE database. The ESE database is an indexed sequential access method (ISAM) database, previously developed for and used by Microsoft Exchange Server, WINS, and DHCP. It supports simple and compound indexing and nested log-based transaction recovery.

Replication

Administrators must deploy multiple domain controllers in Windows NT domains to ensure continuous availability and to replicate domain directory changes between them.

As noted earlier, each and every Windows 2000 domain controller implements Active Directory services. A domain controller must be operating at all times, or users and applications will not be able to log on or access domain resources. Thus, within domains, administrators must set up multiple controllers. Because each instance of a domain controller must be authoritative for the domain, whenever there are changes to the domain directory (such as adding or removing users or resources), those changes must be replicated among all controllers.

Windows NT 4.0 domain controllers support only single-master replication.

In Windows NT 4.0 domains, administrators must distinguish between primary domain controllers (PDCs) and backup domain controllers (BDCs). Directory changes are made only to the PDC, which uses master-slave replication to communicate the changes to the BDCs. If the PDC goes down for any reason, BDCs can keep the domain running, but until the PDC is back online, no

one can perform any administrative actions that require a directory change.

Windows 2000 domain controllers can operate in either native
Windows 2000 mode or in a mixed Windows NT 4.0 and Windows 2000 mode. In a mixed domain, the Windows 2000 controller can act in either the PDC or BDC role. In a native Windows
2000–only domain, controllers eliminate the distinctions between
the PDC and the BDC using multi-master replication. Multi-master replication, as shown in Figure 4-8, allows changes to be
made at any controller. With no PDC as the single point of administrative (or write) failure, multi-master replication considerably improves domain-wide availability. However, replication
traffic in Active Directory domains and enterprises can be heavy
and continuous; Windows 2000 seeks to optimize replication topologies by configuring them along network site topologies.
Chapter 8, "Understanding Replication and Sites," describes this
in more detail.

Windows 2000 domain
controllers support a na-
tive Windows 2000
mode with multi-master
replication, or mixed
mode in coexistence
with Windows NT 4.0.

Figure 4-8 *Internal Active Directory services replication.*

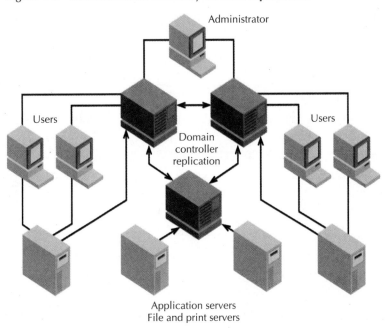

Administrator

Users

Domain
controller
replication

Users

Application servers
File and print servers

Domains, Trees, and Forests

An Active Directory namespace supports multiple domains.

Many of the advantages of Windows 2000 are a result of its ability to model the many domains in an enterprise within a hierarchical namespace. With Windows NT 3.*x* and 4.0, domains exist within a flat namespace, and administrators must manually configure trust relationships and access control groupings to enable cross-domain access. Windows 2000, however, uses its hierarchical domain structure to automatically set up Kerberos-authenticated trust relationships up and down the tree, and to automatically accomplish cross-domain replication of user, group, resource, and access control information.

Deploying Multiple Domains

An Active Directory namespace can span many domains.

An installation of Windows 2000 Active Directory services is always made up of one or more domains. Each domain can span more than one physical location or site. Every domain has its own security policies and security relationships with other domains. Multiple domains can be connected by trust relationships and can share a common schema, configuration, and Global Catalog (described below) through domain forest relationships. Thus, a domain forest is simply a collection of domains that administrators manage in the same way.

Domain Trees

A domain tree consists of one or more contiguous domains.

A *domain tree* is a set of domains that form a contiguous namespace through a set of hierarchical relationships. The example depicted in Figure 4-5 could consist be a domain tree, because *rapport.com* is the parent domain for both *ireland. rapport.com* and *hawaii.rapport.com*.

Domain Forests

A domain forest consists of one or more noncontiguous domains or domain trees.

A *domain forest* is a set of domains or domain trees that do not form a contiguous namespace. Figure 4-9 diagrams the difference between a domain tree and a domain forest. In general, an enterprise deploys a domain tree; but where trusted domains exist outside of an enterprise's domain tree, it might be impractical to merge them. Note, however, that a single domain tree is still, technically, a domain forest. Grouping Windows 2000 domains into a domain forest (or tree) sets up implicit trust relationships between the domains. These trust relationships ensure that when a client has been authenticated by a domain controller anywhere in the domain forest, other locations in the domain forest will honor its Kerberos credentials and service tickets as well.

Active Directory services always creates several partitions in a domain. These include one for the domain, one for a replica of the domain forest's schema container, and another for the forest configuration container. As shown in Figure 4-10, administrators flesh out the domain with real-world information, in the process adding containers and entries. When a once-isolated domain becomes part of a tree or forest, it begins to share information with affiliated domains through the Active Directory Global Catalog.

When Windows 2000 domains are related in a domain forest, they share a common schema, configuration, and Global Catalog.

Figure 4-9 *Domain trees and domain forests.*

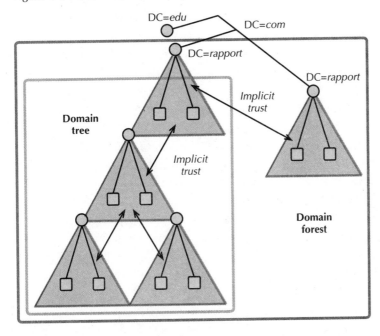

Figure 4-10 *Active Directory domain containers.*

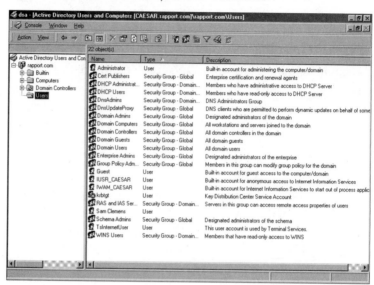

A few domain controllers must take on the role of specialized operations master for handling schema or domain name changes, as well as PDC emulation and relative ID assignment.

Multi-master replication makes equals of all domain controllers in a forest—almost. Exceptions are specialized *operations master* roles held by one or a few domain controllers. In particular, only one domain controller in a forest can serve in the schema master and domain naming master roles; the schema master orchestrates single-master schema replication to other controllers. Also, within each domain, there is only one relative identifier (RID) master that manages an RID pool for new accounts, and only one primary domain controller (PDC) emulator and one infrastructure master. Initially, these roles are assigned by default to the first controller in a forest or the first controller in a new domain. These default operations master locations work well for a small forest, but in larger environments, role assignments should be distributed across multiple controllers. Note that if an operations master fails, administrators can seize and reassign its role, but this is a drastic step and generally means the original operations master must never be brought back online.

The Global Catalog

By default, Active Directory services configures the first domain controller in the first domain in the forest as the Global Catalog. Customers can choose to configure other domain controllers as Global Catalogs. Through the usual multi-master replication service of Active Directory services, the Global Catalog replicates information with other Global Catalog servers in other domains. The information that is replicated includes a subset of the attribute information in User or other resource entries. Microsoft defines this subset, and although authorized administrators can modify it, only a single logical view for each domain forest is permissible. Figure 4-11 diagrams the role of the Global Catalog.

Domain controllers provide a Global Catalog, which contains partial attribute information for objects in a domain forest.

Figure 4-11 *Replication and use of the Global Catalog in a domain.*

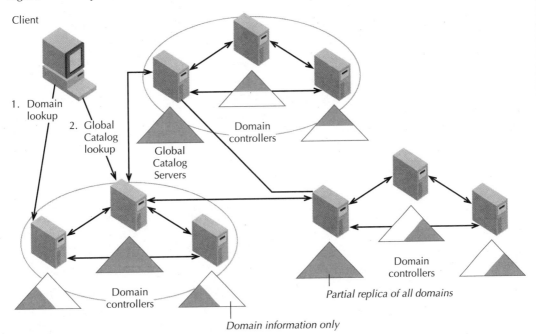

The Global Catalog servers have diverse purposes, such as enabling users to browse for the names and addresses of all other users in the domain forest, enabling users and applications to use resources and objects in remote domains, and enabling public

Global Catalogs provide a single forest search base for finding information and a repository for universal groups.

key authentication and encryption functions. Significantly, the Global Catalog provides a way to centrally maintain information about users and universal groups for access control purposes; it is no longer necessary to manually configure information about users and groups outside a controller's domain when setting up trust relationships.

Using, Developing, and Deploying Active Directory Services

Expanding the role of the directory makes network computing more functional, manageable, and cost-effective.

In a Windows 2000 network, Active Directory services starts working the moment a user activates his or her workstation. On activation, the client obtains its IP address, locates a domain controller through DNS, logs on to the domain controller, and obtains its Kerberos security credentials. Users may then request file and print services, run directory-intensive applications (such as electronic mail), browse the directory for interesting information about the network, and invoke remote, distributed objects. As noted in Chapter 3, "Active Directory Services in the Microsoft Product Line," expanding the role of the directory makes networks much more functional, manageable, and cost-effective by moving complexity off the client into the infrastructure.

Logging on

At startup, Windows clients contain logic to acquire their network identity, locate a nearby controller, log on, and acquire their security identity.

At startup, a Windows client on an intranet either has an IP address configured or it can obtain it by broadcasting on the LAN to nearby Dynamic Host Configuration Protocol (DHCP) servers. In the latter case, a DHCP server supplies the client with its initial network identity: an IP address and addresses of nearby DNS servers. The Windows client then contacts the DNS server to obtain locator information for a domain controller using a SRV RR record (in the form *service protocol.domain*, for example, *ldap.tcp.ireland.domain.com*).

To locate a nearby domain controller, the client goes through the SRV RR list to find a controller located in the same site or in a nearby site. A *site* is an area of the network where bandwidth (and therefore connectivity) among machines is assumed to be good. The software identifies site affinities by matching the sub-network identifier portion of its own IP address against the controller's address. Determining the IP subnet is a matter of con-catenating the network ID portion of an IP address with any por-tion of the host address that has been subnetted by applying a configured subnet mask. Windows 2000 equates sites to IP subnets because computers with the same subnet address are usu-ally connected to the same network segment, typically a LAN or other high-bandwidth environment, such as Frame Relay or asyn-chronous transfer mode (ATM).

Active Directory DNS directs clients to a do-main controller at the nearest available site.

The client then establishes a TCP connection to the nearby con-troller and uses the LDAP Bind operation to log on. A Kerberos authentication exchange takes place, in which the client submits its Kerberos credentials and gets back a Kerberos Ticket-Granting Ticket (TGT). The client uses the TGT to obtain Kerberos service tickets, which it caches in its Local Security Authority (LSA) for use with Windows 2000 applications.

The client logs on to the domain controller using the LDAP Bind operation and obtains Kerberos tickets.

Application Programming Interfaces (APIs)

Many Active Directory applications access the directory through the Active Directory Service Interfaces (ADSI) API. This API ex-poses layers and interfaces for ActiveX Data Objects (ADO), Microsoft Visual Basic, VBScript, Microsoft JScript, Java, and C/C++. It also enables access to Windows operating system-based directory providers capable of connecting to Active Directory domain controllers, generic LDAP servers, Windows NT 3.*x* and 4.0 LAN Manager (NTLM) servers, Novell NetWare 3 Bindery (NW3), and Novell's Novell Directory Services (NDS or NW4). Figure 4-12 diagrams the overall ADSI architecture.

ADSI is an API that com-prises layered interfaces for objects, scripts, and programs, and that makes available provid-ers for LDAP, Windows NT LAN Manager (NTLM), and NetWare.

Figure 4-12 *ADSI interfaces and layers.*

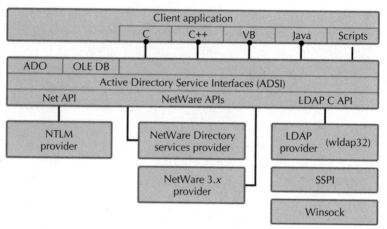

There are many ways for applications to access and use information in Active Directory services.

Applications can access and use information in Active Directory services through the LDAP protocol on the wire, using APIs other than ADSI, such as those based on a simple implementation of the RFC 1823 LDAP API or the Java Naming and Directory Interface (JNDI). ADSI, however, has been optimized for Active Directory schema, incorporating caching capabilities and the ability to perform handy functions, such as finding the local domain controller and searching its directory even if the application does not know the name of the local domain controller's naming context. ADSI also provides both LDAP-style hierarchical views of the directory and relational database–style tabular views through the OLE DB or ADO APIs.

Developing to Active Directory Services

Successful Windows developers must master Active Directory services.

Windows developers must learn Active Directory technology, and learn it well in order to make their products successful in the Windows 2000 environment. Many tasks that formerly relied on access to Microsoft's older Net APIs or registry settings will now require information from Active Directory services. For example, whenever a program wishes to bind to a service on the network or access information about a user, it must consult Active Directory services.

Based on Microsoft's Component Object Model (COM), ADSI enables C, C++, Java, and script language applications to access the directory and obtain information that might once have been configured in an unintegrated application-specific directory—or worse, in a static file on a workstation. Through COM, ADSI provides objects and interfaces for binding to the directory, searching the directory, enumerating or manipulating a list of entries or attributes, displaying information, and updating the directory. In effect, ADSI functions as an abstraction layer for the developer, hiding directory implementation details; Active Directory services, the Windows NT 4.0 registry, NetWare 3 Bindery, or Novell's NDS all look very similar to a program called ADSI.

ADSI's array of interfaces makes it easy to write directory-enabled applications in the Windows environment.

Despite the simplifying effect of ADSI, some complexities still remain. Application developers should be conservative about modifying the schema and should resist the temptation to add new attributes or entries when existing information in the directory can do the job. Because Windows 2000 currently allows only one schema per domain forest, and only one domain controller may update the schema at one time, any application that changes the schema creates a burden on administrators, particularly in large enterprises.

Developers must understand how and when to modify the enterprise directory schema.

Developers must also understand the performance characteristics of the directory and be aware that it can be highly replicated and highly distributed. The applications should be sensitive to replication latency and behave correctly in the face of information that is not yet consistent across domain controllers. In addition, massive changes that set off replication storms must be avoided. For example, in updating a human resources directory, the application developer should update only those entries in Active Directory services that have actually changed, rather than reload the entire organizational unit or domain. Later chapters, beginning with Chapter 6, "ADSI Programming and the Developer," will explore developing to Active Directory services in much greater detail.

Developers must also take care to optimize their applications for the performance characteristics of Active Directory services.

Deploying and Managing Active Directory Services

Managers must make the right resources available for each phase of Active Directory services implementation.

Windows 2000 and Active Directory services are easy enough to install and use in a small company or department setting, and customers can deploy them on a small scale from the bottom up. However, Active Directory services planning, design, migration, and deployment in a large enterprise setting are more complex, and must occur prior to bottom-up deployment. Managers must understand enough about the process to make the resources available during the appropriate point in the Active Directory services life cycle.

Active Directory services implementations require management, consultant /architect, system engineer, and administrator resources.

Figure 4-13 charts the phases of deploying Active Directory services and identifies the required resources. The resources include a consultant or architect, Microsoft system engineer, and one or more user administrators, each with a different set of job responsibilities. The figure also indicates the iterative nature of Active Directory services planning, design, deployment, and life-cycle management. Not all requirements, design or architecture issues, or deployments are static; in fact, they change over time as the enterprise deploys new technologies, expands, contracts, or enters into new relationships.

Figure 4-13 *Active Directory services planning, design, and deployment.*

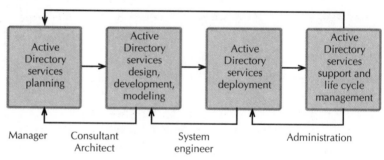

The consultant or architect must plan Active Directory services migration, interoperation, and deployment.

The consultant's or architect's primary concerns are with the up-front planning for Active Directory services. This planning stage includes developing a migration strategy for moving to Windows NT from a non-Microsoft network operating system such as Novell, Banyan, or Sun. Migration can also mean moving from Windows NT

4.0 to Windows 2000. In all cases, the consultant must address the many-faceted issues of coexistence and migration, including training, planning, interoperation, and deployment.

The consultant or architect must address requirements for heterogeneous directory information synchronization and propagation—through meta-directory software, or by using basic LDAP links—between Active Directory services and other directory applications, including human resources, network operating systems, and e-mail. The consultant must plan for interoperation between Active Directory services and other network operating systems during migration, enabling the directory to support cross-NOS logon, file access, and other functions.

Planning must address directory synchronization issues.

Finally, the consultant or architect must map out an overall deployment plan for Active Directory services, covering all phases of training, design, installation, migration, and the incremental addition of features and functions over time. Chapter 10, "Migrating to Active Directory Services," takes a close look at Active Directory services migration, interoperation, and planning considerations for deployment.

An overall deployment plan is recommended.

Consultants, architects, and Microsoft system engineers will all be needed to define the nitty-gritty Active Directory enterprise domain structure, naming design, and security and administrative architecture. These architectural blueprints must closely follow the requirements and migration issues identified earlier during the planning stage. Planners and engineers not experienced with LDAP/X.500 or an enterprise NOS with a hierarchical namespace must be aware of the complex set of design tradeoffs to be made between usability, performance, supportability, and security when defining a domain namespace architecture and schema. Many security policy and security architecture choices are also required; planners must weigh the tradeoffs between alternative security constructs (such as trust relationships) and guest accounts. They must also define access control regimes, and perhaps set up certificate authority relationships across enterprises or management domains.

Consultants, architects, and Microsoft system engineers must work together to develop an Active Directory domain structure, naming design, and security and administrative architecture.

Microsoft system engineers and administrators must install and configure the domain controllers.

A new Windows 2000 domain controller with Active Directory services might begin as a stand-alone server, or it could constitute an upgrade from a former Windows NT 3.*x* or 4.0 Server. When upgrading from an earlier version Windows NT server, Active Directory services automatically imports user accounts. In the case of NetWare and other systems, Windows 2000 includes a Microsoft Directory Service Migration Tool for both NetWare 3 binderies and NetWare 4 NDS. Over time, Microsoft and third-party vendors will provide additional, more advanced migration tools.

Microsoft system engineers or advanced administrators can then define organizational units to delegate administrative authority; lower-level administrators can handle routine user account administration.

Once installation and configuration of Active Directory services is complete, planners and engineers can, for the most part, step aside and let the administrators take over routine directory administration. Depending on the size of an enterprise, multiple administrators will be required for multiple domains. By delegating to different OU containers, it is possible to set up multiple administrators within a single large domain or within a single domain containing different departments or security policies. In all cases, administrators perform user adds, deletes, and changes; enable accounts and passwords; and perform routine monitoring of the directory. Chapter 5, "First Contact with Active Directory Services," will discuss basic Active Directory administration.

Summary

From performing basic NOS functions, to enabling advanced applications, to interoperating with existing networks and supporting migration of downlevel Windows NT domains, Active Directory services offers a sophisticated directory system. Its standards support enables interoperability and compatability in many scenarios; its interfaces are designed for applications enabling; and its internal architecture balances flexibility, performance, and security. In subsequent chapters, we will explore in greater detail the many fascinating components of Active Directory services.

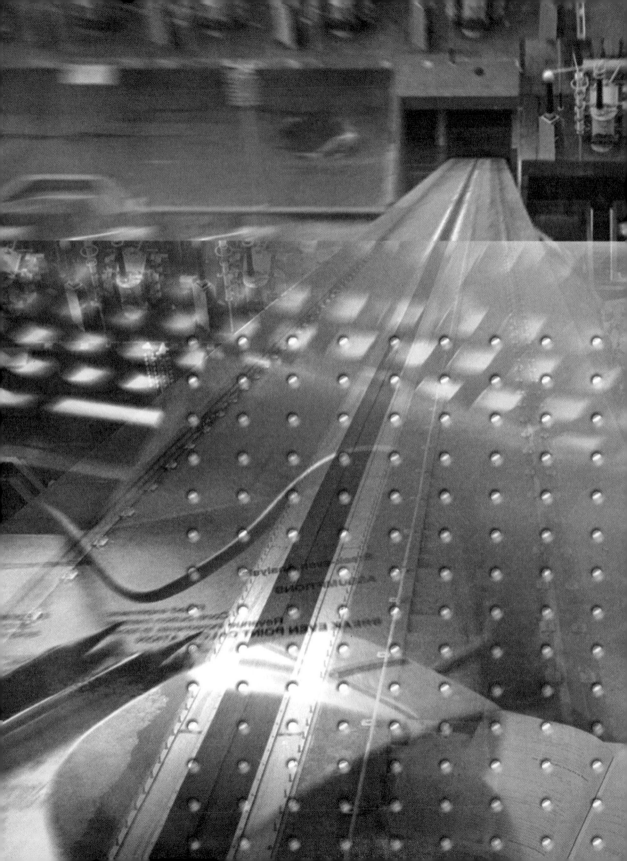

Chapter Five

First Contact with Active Directory Services

Microsoft Active Directory services is a large, multifaceted system. Much of it is easy to use, but getting acquainted with all the modes, utilities, and tools can be a bit daunting. Whereas the intent of Chapter 4, "Active Directory Services Architecture," was to give readers an overview of the structure and functionality of Active Directory technology, the goal of this chapter is to show the look and feel of the system by taking readers on a guided tour of the Active Directory client (or end user) functionality, server administration, and other features. Additionally, this chapter provides important guidance for readers who are taking a hands-on approach to learning Active Directory technology, perhaps from a home office or a lab facility in their corporate network.

Active Directory Services on the Client

Users' first exposure to Active Directory services might well come from the client side if they are logged on to a Microsoft Windows 2000 domain controller. Windows 2000 includes network client software capable of interacting with the Windows 2000 domain controller by obtaining the controller's address from the DNS and

Clients can access information published in Active Directory services.

logging on. (Recall that we discussed the whole logon process—obtaining an IP address, discovering the DNS, discovering the domain controller, and so on—in some detail in Chapter 2, "Active Directory Services and Industry Standards.") Once logged on, the client can access information published in Active Directory services.

The Windows 2000 Professional client can use all the directory-enabled functions; earlier Windows clients can be partially directory-enabled.

Active Directory clients are available on computers running Windows 2000 Professional (the Windows client) or Windows 2000 Advanced Server.[1] Active Directory clients are also available on computers running Windows 95 or Windows 98 that have add-on Active Directory client software installed from an upgrade pack into a Clients folder on the Windows 2000 Advanced Server distribution media. This upgrade permits earlier versions of clients to browse and search, but it does not enable all Active Directory capabilities; some directory-enabled features, such as group policy and automatic certificate enrollment, require the full Windows 2000 Professional client.

Users can search Active Directory services from the Start menu or browse it from My Network Places on the client.

Windows 2000 Professional and Server (Advanced or just Server) have similar functionality. Users can browse Active Directory services through familiar Windows interfaces, starting in My Network Places, can search Active Directory services (or other directories) through the Search option on the Start menu, or can see Active Directory services through one of Microsoft's applications, such as Microsoft Outlook 2000.

What the User Sees in Windows

Active Directory technology is completely—often invisibly—integrated into the client.

The primary concern of a Windows 2000 Professional user is to get the job done, which usually involves accessing and using shared files or printers. The user might also need to look for phone numbers or e-mail addresses; paper phone books are not needed once Active Directory technology is in place. These day-to-day

---

1. The instructions and procedures in this chapter are written specifically for the Windows 2000 Professional client and the Windows 2000 Advanced Server packages, but the instructions will also work for the Windows 2000 Server package.

activities are directory enabled, but the end user is generally oblivious to the directory's role. Other activities, such as searching For People and browsing My Network Places, more explicitly reference the directory but still blend in with Windows functionality.

One advantage the new Active Directory directory services has over the more limited browse lists of the Windows NT operating system, past and present, is that users can more easily find and use resources anywhere in an entire domain forest's network, not just those resources located in the small, local resource domain where Windows NT users frequently find themselves. With Active Directory services, Windows also effectively separates user information from machine information; users can sit down and work at any computer and see the same desktop with its published applications and folders. This is because the directory maintains the roles and privileges of users and computers separately from one another; it maintains a user's identity and the identity of his or her (current) machine. These identity setups determine who a user is and what he or she can do on a Windows 2000 network.

Active Directory technology allows users to find and use resources anywhere on the network, and it determines user and computer identities, roles, and privileges.

Browsing   On entering My Network Places, the user can launch searches for other users, computers, files and folders, or printers. Alternatively, a user can browse the Entire Contents of the network. Specifically, the user can browse Microsoft Windows Network, NetWare or Compatible Network, or the Directory. After right-clicking the Directory icon, selecting a domain, and choosing Folders on the Explorer bar, the user will see a display similar to that in Figure 5-1. From there, a user can browse any of the directory containers, such as users or computers or named organizational units, that he or she has access to, can bring up the property sheets for entries, and can even make changes to entries. This ability to update the directory from Windows has many uses, for example, allowing users to maintain their own phone numbers or other attributes.

From My Network Places, users can browse or search the directory.

Figure 5-1 *Viewing users of Active Directory services in Explorer mode.*

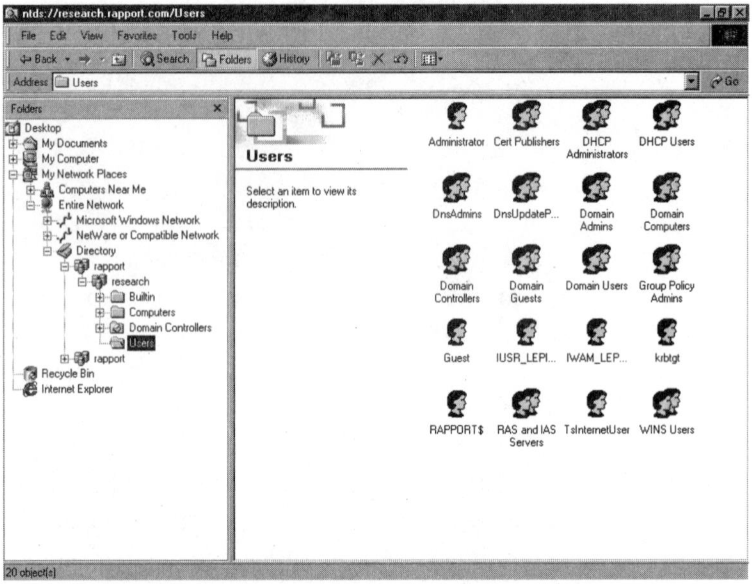

Windows 2000 provides search functionality for finding people, computers, and printers in the directory.

As we have said, Windows 2000 search functionality helps users search for files and folders, printers, people, and other computers on the network. Figure 5-2 displays the results of searching for a person in the Active Directory directory, and Figure 5-3 displays the results of searching for a printer within the Active Directory directory.

The Start | Search | For People menu option lets users search Active Directory repositories or other LDAP repositories.

There are two ways to search for people (Start | Search | For People): from the Start menu or from within My Network Places. The Find People dialog box allows users to do simple searches by name for a person within Active Directory services or, when invoked from the Start menu, within Internet Directory Services such as Switchboard. The Find People dialog box also has an Advanced tab for the purpose of searching additional fields, including Name (full name), First Name, Last Name, E-mail, and Organization, and allows filtering using the following criteria: Contains, Is, Starts With, Ends With, or Sounds Like.

Figure 5-2 *The results of searching for people in Active Directory services.*

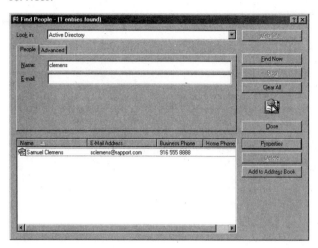

Figure 5-3 *The results of searching for printers in Active Directory services.*

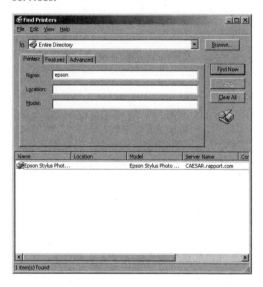

The process of searching for printers involves a different search interface than the process of searching for people. Users can specify various search criteria, for example to locate a specific printer model or a nearby color printer that will also staple pages. After conducting a successful search for a printer, users can save a

Locating printers is easy using a flexible search interface that helps users find the most appropriate printer for their needs.

shortcut (on the desktop or elsewhere) that will later rerun the search, finding perhaps the same result again or producing a new result. Users can also filter and sort printer search results on any column that appears in the results display.

Administration   Windows 2000 allows authorized administrators to manage the directory remotely from a computer running Windows 2000 Professional by installing the Windows 2000 Administration Tools. These Microsoft Management Console (MMC) snap-ins, such as Active Directory Users And Computers, Distributed File System, and other snap-ins, are included on the Windows 2000 Advanced Server CD-ROM in the ADMINPAK.MSI file. See the sections that follow for information on Active Directory administration.

Administrators can also run directory administration software from a client, which makes remote administration possible.

Other Directory Applications

The best of what there is to see in Active Directory services is yet to come. Many applications will emerge that store content in the directory. Early examples of directory-enabled applications are, of course, Microsoft Exchange Server and Microsoft Outlook 2000. Outlook 2000 exposes directory content to end users, allowing them to browse for the e-mail addresses required for basic messaging and the certificates required for secure messaging. Exchange Server exposes directory content to administrators for the purposes of defining message routes, sites, forms, and other services. Many more applications will access Active Directory services from LDAP or by using ADSI, which we discuss in Chapter 6, "ADSI Programming and the Developer." Some of these applications will create new kinds of content to store in Active Directory services by modifying the schema. See Chapter 7, "Planning Namespaces, Domains, and Schema," to learn more about using the Active Directory Schema snap-in and other mechanisms to extend directory schema, and about developing display specifiers that can extend existing directory-based user interfaces.

Applications, such as Microsoft Outlook 2000 and Microsoft Exchange Server, will also expose directory content to users and administrators.

Getting Started on the Server

This section describes the process of setting up and administering Active Directory services. Administrators should consult the help files and other more detailed resources available from Microsoft.

Setting Up Active Directory Services

To set up Active Directory services, users must install a Windows 2000 Server or upgrade a Windows NT domain controller to run Windows 2000 Server software. Note that not all Windows 2000 Servers are domain controllers; some are only member servers in a domain and have the functions of hosting shared resources, such as files, printers, or applications. However, customers can upgrade any Windows 2000 Server to a domain controller by using the Active Directory Installation Wizard.

The first step in setting up Active Directory services is to prepare a Windows 2000 Server.

Upgrade or install: that is the question   One of the first setup decisions users need to make is whether to upgrade the current operating system (assuming Windows NT version 3.51 or later) or to perform a new installation. Upgrading means installing the Windows 2000 Server in a disk partition that currently contains an earlier version of Windows NT. An upgrade automatically installs Windows 2000 Server into the same folder as the currently installed operating system and migrates users, computers, groups, and other objects into the domain's Builtin container. Installing, on the other hand, means wiping out the previous operating system at setup, or installing Windows 2000 Server on a disk or disk partition with no previous operating system.

Users can install Windows 2000 on a new server or can perform an in-place upgrade on an existing Windows NT 3.x or NT 4.0 server.

Upgrading is generally a good idea when customers need to retain their existing users, settings, groups, rights, and permissions and want to avoid recopying or reinstalling files and applications. Be sure to back up the hard drives and read the READ1ST.TXT and the Application Notes section of RELNOTES.DOC in the root directory of the Windows 2000 CD. Note that in addition to an in-place upgrade, Microsoft will support more sophisticated migration scenarios through a Domain Migration snap-in that is

Upgrading is useful for retaining existing Windows NT 3.x or 4.0 information and server-based files and applications.

planned for Web download when Active Directory services becomes generally available; we will discuss the snap-in in Chapter 10, "Migrating to Active Directory Services."

Installing Windows 2000 Server   Administrators can install Windows 2000 from a CD or from the network. The installation process includes the following steps:

Administrators can initiate the multi-step Windows 2000 Server installation from a CD or from the network.

1. Select Language preference and any advanced or special features
2. Copy basic files for Windows 2000 onto the hard disk
3. Select regional settings
4. Personalize Windows 2000 Server
5. Choose a licensing mode
6. Enter a computer name and set the Administrator password
7. Choose Windows 2000 components
8. Set the date, the time, and the time zone
9. Windows 2000 configures itself for the network
10. Allow Windows 2000 setup to automatically assign IP addresses
11. Specify a static local IP address and settings needed for DNS and WINS
12. Specify the Workgroup or Domain name
13. Windows 2000 completes its configuration cycle by configuring the Start menu, registering components, saving the settings, and finally removing any temporary files

Customers who are planning to experiment with Active Directory services should install all the networking components and the certificate services.

During installation, allow setup to assign IP addresses automatically, or specify an existing static IP address and DNS server.

Customers who are in a Dynamic Host Configuration Protocol (DHCP)–enabled network environment should allow setup to assign IP addresses automatically during installation. The computer then attempts to contact a DHCP server, lease an IP address, and obtain addresses of nearby DNS servers. Failing that, Windows

2000 determines an address in the Microsoft-reserved IP addressing range from 169.254.0.0 through 169.254.255.254, and uses this address until a DHCP server can be located. However, customers who are in a network environment without DHCP should specify a static IP address and DNS settings. Obtain the appropriate addresses from the enterprise's network administrator. Customers can also change this information later through Network And Dial-up Connections on the Control Panel.

If a user is connected to a network and specifies a workgroup or domain name, the server will prompt for an administrator account in that domain and try to join up as a member server. At this point, the server is operational and it might be part of a domain, but it is not yet a domain controller. Shortly, we will explain how to promote a server to a domain controller and configure Active Directory services.

> Users must have a valid account to join a Windows 2000 domain.

Upgrading to Active Directory services   As we have said, Active Directory services is backward-compatible with Windows NT 3.*x* and 4.0 and can function in primary domain controller (PDC) mode using the NT LAN Manager (NTLM) protocol. As a result, authorized users and computers running Windows NT, Windows 95, or Windows 98 clients without Active Directory client software can log on and access resources in Windows 2000 domains. In time, when the last Windows NT 4.0 domain controller in the domain is decommissioned, customers can change their Windows 2000 domain from mixed mode (Windows NT 4 and Windows 2000) to native mode (Windows 2000 only). Once having gone to native mode, however, returning to mixed mode is no longer possible.

> A Windows 2000 domain controller can function as a primary domain controller in a mixed domain, or can live in a native Windows 2000–only domain.

When upgrading from earlier versions of Windows NT Server, Windows 2000 automatically converts the Security Account Manager (SAM), DHCP, and WINS databases to the new database format that Active Directory services uses. This is a somewhat time-consuming process that requires enough disk space to temporarily hold both the old and new versions. After that, installation procedures differ, depending on whether the server is installing the first controller for the first domain of a domain tree, joining a

> During upgrade, Windows 2000 converts the SAM, DHCP, and WINS databases.

replica domain controller to a domain, or joining a child domain to a parent. We discuss these processes in the following sections.

Windows 2000 populates the user and computer containers during upgrade.

The Windows 2000 upgrade process places user and group objects in the users container and places machine accounts in the users and computers containers. Older Windows NT tools and APIs (such as the Net API) that create users, groups, and machine accounts continue to create them in these containers after Windows 2000 is installed.

After installation or upgrade, Windows 2000 prompts administrators to configure the server.

Configuring the server   After installation or upgrade, further configuration is possible using the Configure Your Server program. This program pops up on administrator logon, or users can invoke it using the Start | Programs | Administrative Tools menu option. Other configuration tools are also available on the Administrative Tools menu. The tools available in Configure Your Server are Active Directory, File Server, Print Server, Web/Media Server, Networking, Application Server, and Advanced.

To set up Active Directory services, customers must first promote a server to the role of domain controller.

Setting up Active Directory services   During the install or upgrade process, users will need to promote a server to the high position of domain controller. Before promoting the server, the user will need privileged administrator credentials on both the server itself and in any domain or forest that the server will join. These credentials are the logon name of a user account, the account password, and domain name. Users can promote the server by following the prompts from the Active Directory option in the Windows 2000 Configure Your Server dialog box, or by running the DCPROMO.EXE command. In either case, the Active Directory Installation Wizard will guide administrators through the promotion process. Figure 5-4 displays a screen from the wizard, in which the user specifies the new controller's domain affiliation.

Before or during the promotion, administrators must decide which type of domain controller to create from the following options provided by the Active Directory Installation Wizard:[2]

---

2. Chapter 7, "Planning Namespaces, Domains, and Schema," contains advice for domain planners.

Figure 5-4 *Active Directory Installation Wizard.*

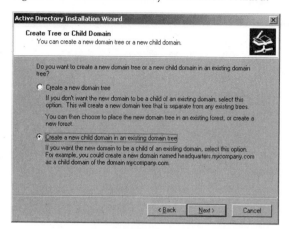

- **Additional Domain Controller In An Existing Domain.** This is a replica domain controller that will co-manage a Windows 2000 domain with at least one other domain controller. When a user selects this option in the wizard, the wizard prompts for a domain.

- **Domain Controller For A New Domain.** Select this option if the intent is not to join an existing domain. The new domain may then become a new child domain in an existing domain tree, create a new domain tree in an existing domain forest, or create a new forest of domain trees.

- **Create A New Child Domain In An Existing Domain Tree.** Select this option to set up the domain as a child domain of a domain that already exists.

- **Create A New Domain Tree In An Existing Domain Forest.** Select this option to set up the domain as a member of an existing domain forest, but not as a child of any other Windows 2000 domain. Note that this new domain tree might or might not actually acquire its own child domains; in other words, a single stand-alone domain is still considered a tree.

- **Create A New Forest Of Domain Trees.** Select this option to set up an entire new domain forest. The new domain will start the first domain tree in that forest.

Setting up DNS   Active Directory services requires the DNS to
publish Windows 2000 domain and server locations for use on
the network. Depending on how the server was installed, an administrator might already have specified the location of the DNS service
that will be used for name-to-address resolution. Otherwise, if the
Active Directory Installation Wizard cannot locate a DNS service during domain controller promotion, it installs the DNS service
automatically. Administrators can also install the DNS manually,
if need be, by using the Networking Services components under
the Add/Remove Windows Components option.

Customers can integrate
DNS zone information
into the Active Directory
database or maintain it
in a separate zone file.

Once customers have installed Active Directory services, they can
choose to use either standard zone storage or Active Directory–
integrated zone storage. Standard zone storage holds DNS information in a text file, while Active Directory–integrated zone
storage holds zone information in the Active Directory database,
which provides various performance and security advantages.
Once DNS is in place, it is normally updated automatically during the course of network operations, such as computers leasing
addresses and administrators installing new services. Customers
can update DNS manually using the DNS snap-in, as shown in
Figure 5-5, where the snap-in has a DNS zone for the domain
tbg.com, which contains a single host, *lepidus,* at the IP address
10.0.0.11.

Figure 5-5   *The DNS snap-in.*

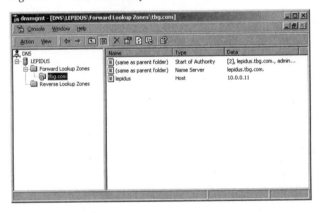

Setting up DHCP Customers who are installing Windows 2000 servers on an enterprise network can use automatic address assignment to obtain an address from the local DHCP server. However, if DHCP is not available on the network, the administrator will need to set it up to get multiple Windows 2000 machines working together. One way to do this for testing purposes is to log on to the domain as domain administrator, run the DHCP snap-in, add the current hostname (such as *caesar.rapport.com*) to the list of authorized DHCP servers, and create a new *scope*, or range of valid IP addresses that the server can lease. After this, when clients and servers on the network broadcast for DHCP service, they will get an address from the scope defined during setup. Figure 5-6 illustrates a scope in the DHCP snap-in.

Windows 2000 requires DHCP in both production and testing environments.

Figure 5-6 *DHCP administration.*

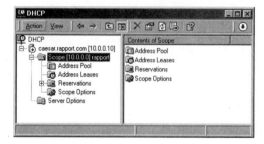

Administering Active Directory Services

The Windows 2000 Advanced Server offers four Active Directory MMC snap-ins. Customers can also create administration scripts with ADSI to automate tasks, such as making global changes to user entries.

Administrators can use designated MMC snap-ins, or they can create scripts using ADSI.

Users can invoke the Active Directory snap-ins from the Start menu or combine them in a custom MMC console. The snap-ins are:

Active Directory services provides four MMC snap-ins.

- **Active Directory Domains And Trusts:** This snap-in, described in the next section, enables domain administrators to manage top-level domain modes, trusts, and operational roles.

- **Active Directory Users And Computers:** This snap-in, described later in this chapter, enables either domain-level or organizational unit–level administrators to manage the information content of a domain. Administrators can use it to add or delete users, groups, computers, containers, or organizational units. They can also change properties of objects, such as telephone numbers, or modify group policies and access controls affecting objects or containers.

- **Active Directory Sites And Services:** This snap-in, described in Chapter 8, "Understanding Replication and Sites," enables domain administrators to manage the replication topology of Active Directory services, defining sites, subnets, and servers. It is also used to configure services such as the certification authority, which is discussed in Chapter 9, "Security Overview: Kerberos, Certificates, and Access Control."

- **Active Directory Schema:** This snap-in, described in Chapter 7, "Planning Namespaces, Domains, and Schema," permits schema administrators to add new object classes and attributes to an Active Directory domain forest schema.

Active Directory Domains And Trusts Snap-in

The Active Directory Domains And Trusts snap-in lets administrators manage both forest-level and domain-level configuration.

Active Directory Domains And Trusts is the snap-in for managing the relationships between Active Directory domains. On startup, the snap-in displays a screen similar to the one in Figure 5-7. The left pane shows the Active Directory Domains And Trusts snap-in at the top of the console tree and the managed domains beneath it. To navigate within the tool, select the console entry and click the Action menu, or right-click the console entry and select Properties or other options. Administrators can also select any domain in the console tree and expand or collapse its child domains by clicking the plus or minus signs to the left of the domain name, and can invoke functions by clicking the console's Action menu, or right-clicking to get a domain's context menu. We recommend consulting Microsoft's Windows 2000 Help system or administrators' manuals for more detailed instructions; here we will discuss basic domains and trusts functionality.

Figure 5-7 *Active Directory Domains And Trusts management tool.*

Administrators can use the Active Directory Domains And Trusts snap-in to manage two forest-level configuration items: the user principal name (UPN) suffixes and the operations master role definitions. Administrators can define UPN suffixes from the properties of the Active Directory Domains And Trusts console root. Here, they can add alternative UPN suffixes. Later, when administrators add or modify user entries, they can select the appropriate suffix for that user from a drop-down list containing those options that the domain administrator defines. Thus, for example, Suzan Fine in the domain *tbg.com* could be set up with the suffix *rapport.com*. Based on her UPN value, her e-mail address and certificate subject name might be *sfine@rapport.com* rather than *sfine@tbg.com*. Another forest-level configuration item is the operations master role definitions. As described in Chapter 4, "Active Directory Services Architecture," designated domain controllers in a forest serve in the operations master roles of schema master and infrastructure master. These or other domain controllers can serve as relative identifier (RID) pool master and primary domain controller (PDC) emulator master in a domain.

> The Active Directory Domains And Trusts snap-in allows administrators to manage UPN suffixes and operations master roles.

From the top level of the Active Directory Domains And Trusts snap-in, administrators can connect to another domain controller and—given the right credentials—can fully administer modes, roles, and trusts for that domain. Administrators can also make a one-time domain-wide change from Mixed Mode (Supports Both Windows NT 4 And Windows 2000 Domain Controllers) to Native

> Administrators can also set up explicit trusts with external domains, connect to domain controllers, and change a domain to native (Windows 2000 only) mode.

Mode (No Pre-Windows 2000 Domain Controllers), and they can add explicit trusts with other domains outside the forest. Unlike the automatic trusts set up between domains in a forest, these explicit trusts are one way and intransitive. Administrators can also view or repair any trusts already in place.

Active Directory Users And Computers Snap-in

The Active Directory Users And Computers snap-in makes basic administration in a domain possible.

Active Directory Users And Computers is an MMC snap-in designed for daily administration of users and computers. It supports adding, deleting, and moving users and their computer accounts within organizational units and groups in the directory. Administrators can also modify directory object properties, such as security properties of user and computer accounts, groups, organizational units, and shared network resources.

The snap-in user's privilege level determines what kinds of administration he or she can perform.

To use the Active Directory Users And Computers snap-in, administrators must have sufficient privileges to perform a specific operation. Ordinary users, by default, have some privileges, such as the ability to modify certain fields in their personal entries, while members of other groups have additional privileges. Members of the Account Operators group can create and delete user accounts. Members of the Administrators and Domain Admins groups can reset user passwords, disable accounts, and perform many other heavy-duty actions.

The Active Directory Users And Computers console tree lets users browse the directory hierarchy and offers many options.

Diving into Active Directory Users And Computers snap-in for the first time, customers will find that the left pane of the snap-in window contains the hierarchy of the domain, which generally comprises the Builtin, Users, Computers, and Domain Controllers containers created by default, plus any other containers or organizational units that domain administrators have added (Figure 5-8). Snap-in users can expand or collapse each container; they can also right-click any container to bring up an option-loaded context menu. As is common with MMC snap-ins, the right pane of the window depicts a selected container's children.

Figure 5-8 *Active Directory Users And Computers snap-in.*

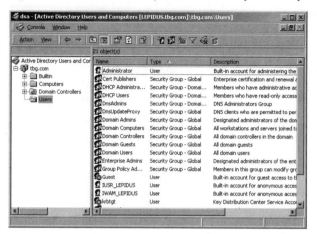

Active Directory Users And Computers container options on the context menu always enable domain administrators to delegate control over a container to less privileged administrators; find users, groups, or contacts in the directory; add new users, groups, contacts, or computers; or add new universal naming convention (UNC) links to printers or shared folders. When the selected container is an organizational unit, administrators can also use its context menu to move the container, delete the container, or add its children as members of a group in the directory. Similar context menus are available for the Domain and Domain Controllers containers, but the Domain container also lets administrators change domain-level parameters, such as the controller to which they are connected, the operations master, the default domain policy object, or the mixed/native mode.

Active Directory Users And Computers snap-in has context-sensitive menus for users, groups, computers, domains, and other objects.

In addition, administrators can access a container or organizational unit's property sheet through the context menu of the object in the left pane of the Active Directory Users And Computers snap-in. Containers only allow administrators to modify the description attribute, but organizational unit property sheets include a General tab with the ability to modify the OU's description and postal address attributes; a Managed By tab with the name, phone, fax, and postal attributes of the OU's administrators; and a

At the property-sheet level, administrators can set an organizational unit's description, postal address, and other attributes, and can define the group policy for members of the organizational unit.

Group Policy tab to manage users and computers within the OU. (See Chapter 7, "Planning Namespaces, Domains, and Schema," for more detail on group policy.)

Administrators can also run the New Object Wizard to add more information to Active Directory services.

Remaining functionality in the Active Directory Users And Computers snap-in includes adding, deleting, and changing directory objects, such as organizational units, users, computers, and groups. Administrators can add new objects by selecting the New option on the context menu of the appropriate container. This invokes the New Object Wizard, which obtains the initial information required. For users, the New Object Wizard asks only for first name, last name, logon name, downlevel (NT) name, and password parameters.

Administrators can make changes to the property list for user, group, computer, or other leaf objects.

Once an object is created, administrators can do many things to it through the context pane of the Active Directory Users And Computers window. From here, administrators can make changes to the full property list of an object (or to whatever subset they have access to). Property lists can be quite rich; for example, by default, the User object has eight tabs, containing general, address, account, profile, telephones, organizational, group membership, and dial-in privilege information. Privileged administrators can also call up a user object's context menu in the right pane to add it to a group, reset its password, disable its account, move it, send mail to it, or open its home page.

Summary

To make first contact with Active Directory services, customers or developers must install the Windows 2000 Advanced Server from the CD or the network. Next, customers must promote the server to the lofty rank of domain controller and use the Active Directory Installation Wizard to determine whether the server should join a domain or start a new domain, domain tree, or domain forest. Administrators then use the Active Directory Domains And Trusts, and the Active Directory Users And Computers snap-ins to configure and administer the enterprise's domain. Once the domain is operational, customers find that from the Explorer-style directory view in My Network Places, to the Can Print Color or Can Staple checkboxes in Find Printers, to the rich, context-sensitive menus of Active Directory Users And Computers snap-in, Active Directory services weaves directory-enabled tools and functionality deep into the fabric of the Windows 2000 client, as well as into the server. And there is more to come; Microsoft Outlook 2000 and Microsoft Exchange Server releases subsequent to version 5.5 are just the first of many Active Directory–enabled applications.

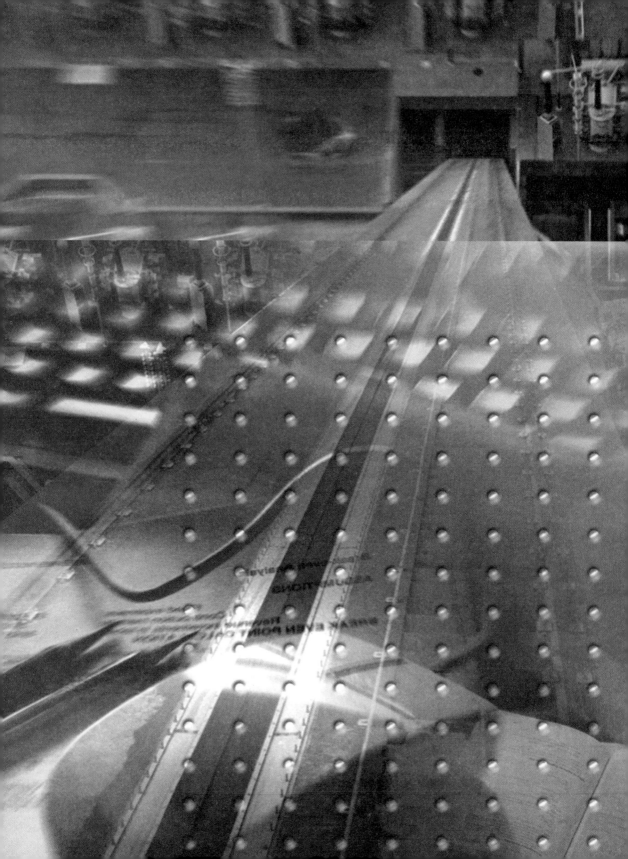

Chapter Six

ADSI Programming and the Developer

Microsoft Active Directory Service Interfaces (ADSI) is a published application programming interface (API) specification and a set of software libraries that developers can use to access various directory services. Developers can access ADSI at either the application level or the provider level. This chapter will focus on developer considerations for programming directories using ADSI, and will provide a high-level overview of common directory programming tasks and Active Directory services interfaces and internals.

ADSI is an API for developers who want to access directory services.

What Is ADSI?

ADSI is one of four Windows Open Directory Services Interfaces (ODSI). Other ODSI interfaces are Network Provider Interface for supporting automatic logon to multiple namespaces, Windows Sockets Registration and Resolution (RnR), and RPC OLE DB for rich query. These APIs work in conjunction with ADSI.

ADSI is part of the ODSI family of APIs.

Much like an application can call the Windows printing APIs to print documents, an application can call ADSI to interact with directories. Much like a printer vendor can supply drivers that plug in to the Windows printer driver APIs, a directory vendor can

ADSI provides interfaces both to client applications and to system provider libraries.

ship a directory driver that, once installed on a computer, can communicate with that vendor's specific directory. An ADSI-enabling software library sits between the application and the provider. Figure 6-1 diagrams its sandwiched position between client and provider interfaces.

Figure 6-1   *ADSI communicates with both clients and providers.*

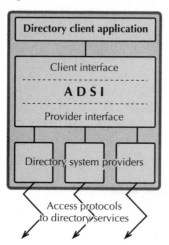

ADSI is based on COM, works with multiple programming languages, and enables access to Active Directory services, other LDAP directories, Novell NetWare, and Windows NT.

Based on Microsoft's Component Object Model (COM), ADSI can run multiple programming languages, such as C, C++, Java, and Microsoft Visual Basic. Together with ADSI, Microsoft ships directory system providers for Active Directory Global Catalog, LDAP, Novell's Novell Directory Services (NDS), Novell's NetWare 3.*x* Bindery, and earlier Windows NT directories. In addition, ADSI supplies its own OLE DB provider, so that any client already using OLE DB, including those using ActiveX Data Objects (ADOs), can query directory services directly.

What Information to Store in a Directory

Applications should use directories to store information that is globally interesting.

Directories contain location and configuration information for many different kinds of objects on a network. Because directories are designed to make the most up-to-date information readily available, the type of information that developers store in a directory is limited to relatively compact, non-volatile information that is of global interest to multiple applications or multiple distributed instances of applications.

Many enterprises using Active Directory services will have a fairly distributed topology with at least some relatively slow WAN links. For this reason, the stored information should be stable, non-volatile, relatively compact, and insensitive to problems related to replication. To accommodate the worst-case network situations, attributes in the directory should change less frequently than twice the replication cycle, for example, less than once a day on average in many networks. In addition, attribute values should be of an appropriate size, or not much more than 10 KB.[1] Applications should also be, by design, relatively insensitive to replication-induced inconsistency. To maintain consistency, keep information structures simple, and avoid storing information that requires total consistency within or between replicas. For more design tips, see Chapter 8, "Understanding Replication and Sites."

> Information in the directory should be relatively stable, or non-volatile, reasonably small in size, and relatively insensitive to replication-induced problems.

Selecting an API

During the directory Stone age, every application had to ship its own directory. Thankfully, that age is coming to an end, and today all system, application, or internal corporate developers should consider using a general-purpose LDAP directory, such as Active Directory services, for information that is relatively stable, compact, and globally interesting. Often, customers already have a general-purpose directory other than one based on Active Directory technology (such as Novell or Netscape), a meta-directory, an X.500 directory, or something else. In these situations, developers have to fit in with the customer's directory systems by using an available API, a compatible protocol, and a provider implementation that operates well with the target server.

> Developers should make their applications work with as many existing directories as possible, given their customers' environments, by using standard APIs.

---

1. These are rough guidelines only. As Active Directory services enters the marketplace, developers should stay tuned to actual user feedback to find out where the thresholds for directory information size and volatility are.

Depending on the type of application, developers might use ADSI, the Internet's RFC 1823 C API, Java Naming and Directory Interface (JNDI), or other APIs.

As shown in Figure 6-2, developers can use ADSI for accessing directory information held in Active Directory services or in another directory by implementing LDAP, Windows NT 3.x or 4.0, NetWare 3.x, or NetWare 4.x protocols. In general, C/C++ with either ADSI or RFC 1823 (and successor APIs from the IETF)[2] offer better performance than Java-based or script-based implementations, but Visual Basic and other scripting languages over ADSI or other APIs are the easiest to program. ADSI is available only on Windows, whereas RFC 1823 is available on all major platforms. IETF Java APIs or JNDI offer the most portable approach within client-based or server-based Java applications. There are many cases in which it makes sense for developers to use ADSI, but be sure to investigate the target customer base and performance characteristics carefully before committing to one approach or another. For example, a developer should not use ADSI—at least not exclusively—if the application needs to run on platforms where ADSI is not available, such as Macintosh, UNIX, or old Windows clients.

Figure 6-2 *Directory mix-and-match possibilities.*

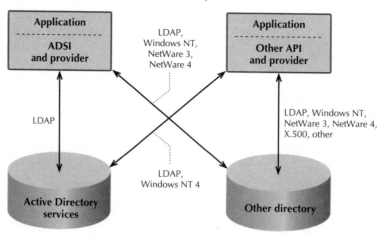

---

2. RFC 1823 is an informational RFC from the IETF specifying a 'C' API for LDAP that has been widely implemented in the industry. The IETF is updating RFC 1823 to reflect new functionality in LDAP V3.

Types of Directory Applications

As ADSI proliferates along with Windows 2000 and service pack releases for older Windows client and server operating systems, many developers will use the API to gain access to Active Directory services or another directory service that an ADSI provider supports. Many types of applications will use Active Directory technology and other directory systems to browse the network and locate or manipulate objects. These types of applications include directory-enabled applications, directory-enabled networks, and directory-enabled management packages.

Directory-enabled applications, networks, and management packages will implement ADSI.

Directory-enabled applications   Directory-enabled applications may use ADSI to enable user-directed browsing, profile user-specific security roles, provide user-specific functionality, locate user-specific resources, or store application-specific configuration and routing information. Typical chores include binding (or authenticating) the user to a service running under Windows 2000, searching the directory for information matching diverse criteria, manipulating attributes, and publishing information to help clients find services—such as user profiles—in the directory. At times, directory-enabled applications must also update the directory schema to add new application-specific data definitions.

Directory-enabled applications require ADSI to handle user information in many different ways.

Directory-enabled networks   Network management systems supporting resources, such as devices, operating systems, management tools, and applications, can use the directory to publish information about resources, discover resources, and obtain policy directives. The Directory-Enabled Networks (DEN) specification now undergoing standardization by the Desktop Management Task Force (DMTF) defines models for a policy-based network. Through the directory, network resources can obtain user-level or application-level information that enables policy-based routing or quality of service decisions. For example, suppose a user wants to access a high-fidelity video application on an intranet server. To obtain the desired functions, the user must reserve 1.5 Mbps of bandwidth through a particular set of switches and routers. To deliver consistent levels of service—as

Directory-enabled networking devices and management tools use ADSI to add user-level or application-level granularity to services, and to store configuration information.

specified by enterprise policies—however, the network must have access to the user's privileges and other information as defined in the directory.

Network infrastructure improves due to the directory's manageability, access control, and performance features.

Network resources can also store network configuration information or map profiles and policies. As with management applications, the network infrastructure benefits from the directory's manageability, access control, and performance features.

Directory-enabled management tools use ADSI to access, update, and manipulate directory information.

Directory-enabled management   Directories are becoming the central paradigm for administering network information. Management applications can manipulate system information in the directory or be governed by that information. For example, a particular administrator might be granted access rights to all the printer configuration entries in Building 1, but not to those in Building 2. Similarly, asset management or billing systems can generate sophisticated reports using directory information, such as a list of all users, by cost center, enabled for a high-end licensed workflow application. Other directory management tools construct and maintain directory information in a consistent up-to-date state. These management tools might enable directory synchronization with an e-mail system directory and might store copies of e-mail users' names and addresses in Active Directory services. Meta-directory tools might also support the loading of all entries from a Human Resources database, and the merging of certain attributes (such as postal address) into Active Directory services.

ADSI Architecture Overview

MSDN Library and the Windows 2000 SDK are valuable resources that describe ADSI exhaustively.

While a programmer's manual is beyond the scope of this book, the following sections will give readers an appreciation for both the ADSI architecture and common ADSI programming tasks. Developers who are familiar with the Microsoft Component Object Model (COM) will benefit from this overview of what directory programming can accomplish. The Microsoft Developer Network (MSDN) Library and Windows 2000 software development kits

(SDKs) are two sources that describe ADSI exhaustively. Even developers who are not COM experts will benefit from this more general discussion of the architecture, but we recommend a basic understanding of COM before diving deeply into ADSI.

ADSI has its basis in Microsoft's Component Object Model (COM). ADSI defines a directory service model and a set of COM interfaces that enable client applications to access directory services. COM itself acts as the generic model for Microsoft software programs to expose objects, or interfaces and methods, to one another. Some of the most important generic benefits of COM are that it supports multiple languages, including C, C++, Java, and Microsoft Visual Basic, as well as scripting languages such as VBScript and Microsoft JScript. It enables pairs of objects to communicate with one another, regardless of whether they are located in the same computer process, in different processes, or even on different systems, using Distributed COM. ADSI inherits some of these benefits from COM.

ADSI is based on Microsoft's Component Object Model.

Supported Language Interfaces

ADSI supplies both high-level and low-level interfaces to COM. Languages, such as Java, Visual Basic, and VBScript, which access COM through function names that bind to code at run time, use the high-level COM automation interfaces, also known as Automation-compliant interfaces. ADSI also supports non-automation, or direct interfaces, for language environments like C and C++ that can access COM interfaces directly through pointers, which optimize performance.

ADSI supports both high-level COM automation interfaces, such as Visual Basic, Java, and JavaScript, and low-level direct COM interfaces for languages, such as C/C++.

Developers can embed scripts that access ADSI in Web pages, thus making it possible to invoke ADSI through a Web browser or a Web server. Also, OLE DB or ActiveX Data Object applications abstract data into a row-and-column format. Applications can view directory data in a convenient tabular fashion, because ADSI supplies its own OLE DB provider, which enables a subset of the OLE DB query interfaces.

ADSI also provides indirect interfaces that make it possible to use the directory in Web-based applications or to view it as a database.

Directory Objects Interfaces

As a COM-based API, ADSI exposes functionality through objects. ADSI objects represent computers, users, files, servers, printers, and print queues. ADSI first defines objects as elements. Each defined object supports one or more COM interfaces (called *meta-interfaces*) through which developers gain access to information about the object itself and information about what the object represents.

All ADSI objects have certain properties, regardless of whether they physically exist as entries in an Active Directory directory, another LDAP directory, a NetWare directory, or some other directory. The basic properties of ADSI objects do correspond fairly closely to the LDAP/X.500 information model detailed in Chapter 2, "Active Directory Services and Industry Standards." Thus, all ADSI objects contain a relative name (or a relative distinguished name in LDAP), a schema class (or object class), and an ADsPath string. *ADsPath* is a COM display name appearing in either OLE or URL format; it uniquely identifies a directory entry regardless of directory service implementation. In the case of LDAP, the ADsPath contains the X.500 distinguished name, such as *cn=daniel blum,ou=consulting,dc=rapport,dc=com.*

IADs and IDirectory Interfaces

The lollipop diagram in Figure 6-3 represents ADSI directory objects as they appear through COM. The IUnknown interface is required for COM Object Management; its QueryInterface method passes the application pointers and identifying information about the other interfaces, while the *AddRref* and *Release* methods increment and decrement reference counts to objects so that the operating system will know whether the resources represented are in use. The IDispatch interface is required on all automation objects for type library and method invocation information. Thus, with IUnknown and IDispatch interfaces handling the housekeeping through the methods discussion, the IADs, IADsPropertyList,

Side notes (left margin):

ADSI exposes directory information through COM objects, which represent directories.

All COM directory objects have a relative name, an ADsPath name, and a schema class.

ADSI and COM provide various interfaces to directory objects. These include IADs, IDirectory, and COM's IUnknown interfaces.

and IDirectoryObject interfaces provide the functionality of ADSI. These will be discussed in the following text.

C/C++ applications have access to direct, or non-automation, COM interfaces, which ADSI identifies using the naming convention IDirectoryXXX. Both the C/C++ applications and applications written in other languages have access to automation COM interfaces using the naming convention IADsXXX.

COM automation applications use the IADs interfaces; non-automation applications use the IDirectory interfaces.

As the fundamental interface required to access ADSI objects, the IADs interface implements identifiers for the name and type of objects; binding information to uniquely identify an object instance in a directory tree; and methods to retrieve a pointer to an object's parent container, set, retrieve and cache its property values, and retrieve its schema definition. Client applications use IADs methods—such as *get_name, get_schema, getinfo, setinfo* in Visual Basic—to communicate with directory objects. Provider implementations must implement the IADs interface to support directory client access to the namespaces (such as a Novell NDS tree) they expose.

IADs is the fundamental interface that all ADSI objects supply.

Figure 6-3 *ADSI object interfaces.*

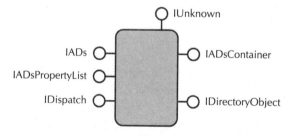

Basic Binding, Searching, and Object Manipulation

There are a number of programming tasks that most or some directory applications must undertake. These include binding to an object in the directory, searching, querying, updating objects, updating attributes, and managing groups and collections of entries.

Binding to Objects in the Directory

Binding makes a directory object available to a program.

Binding to an object is the first step toward using the directory with ADSI. At the time of binding, Active Directory services verifies the user's credentials and, subject to access rights, allows the user to access the data in the object. Programs use a binding string that is similar or identical to the LDAP URL introduced in Chapter 2, "Active Directory Services and Industry Standards," as their way of specifying the desired object. Binding with ADSI is flexible enough to allow the program to access a specifically named object, without knowing a server location in advance, to locate the directory contents on a specific server, or to access a Global Catalog. The sidebar, *Binding to the Directory with ADSI,* shows a number of examples. Developers should be aware, however, that only the standard approach of binding to a specific server and a specific object is guaranteed to work with a generic LDAP server, although all approaches should work with Active Directory technology.

Using IADs interfaces, clients can bind to entries and enumerate their properties.

Clients access, or bind to, a directory entry using its ADsPath. Once the client accesses an object through Visual Basic or another automation client, ADSI retains the properties of the object in a property cache. With the IADsPropertyList interface, the developer can count or enumerate the list of properties belonging to an object, add and remove properties, or even purge the entire list in one step. The developer can also retrieve a single property from an entry very simply. The following VBScript code sample shows the use of the IADs interface in binding to the Mark Twain entry in the domain *rapport.com* on the *rapport* server using both LDAP and Windows NT providers. Readers can become familiar with ADSI by experimenting with this and other examples in this chapter.

```
Dim Entry1
Dim Entry2
Set Entry1 = GetObject("WinNT://rapport/mark twain,user")
Set Entry2 = GetObject( _
  "LDAP://rapport/CN=marktwain,CN=users, DC=rapport,DC=com")
MsgBox Entry1.Name
MsgBox Entry2.Name
```

Binding to the Directory with ADSI

The following are examples of binding strings used to accomplish various binding scenarios with ADSI:

- Binding to a server and an object

  ```
  LDAP://rapport/CN=daniel blum,DC=rapport,DC=com
  ```

- Serverless binding

  ```
  LDAP://CN=daniel blum,DC=rapport,DC=com
  ```

- Binding to the domain

  ```
  LDAP://DC=rapport,DC=com
  ```

- Binding to the default naming context on a specific server (where *caesar* is the hostname)

  ```
  LDAP://caesar.rapport.com
  ```

- Binding to a persistent globally unique ID (GUID)

  ```
  LDAP://<GUID=48560110f7e1d111a6bfaaaf642b9cfa>
  ```

- Binding to a persistent Windows NT security ID (SID)

  ```
  LDAP://<SID=43560190f7e1d111b6bfaaaf842c9cfa>
  ```

- Binding to the Global Catalog

  ```
  GC://CN=daniel blum,DC=rapport,DC=com
  ```

- Binding to the rootDSE, or the root of the information tree on any LDAP server, to discover the server's defaultNamingContext

  ```
  LDAP://rootDSE
  ```

The Visual Basic GetObject interface and the C/C++ ADsGetObject interface use the current user's default credentials, which in many cases is exactly what a program should do. However, in other cases, developers will want to explicitly supply credentials through the IADSOpenDSObject or ADSOpenObject

Programs can specify credentials and other security options when binding.

interfaces. The user principal name, LDAP distinguished name, or downlevel Windows NT name can all be used. Other options include SSL, Secured Authentication, and Anonymous Binding.

ADSI also supports binding to multiple namespaces.

ADSI namespaces   Notice that the code example featured a GetObject WinNT and a GetObject LDAP. These alternative forms of binding reflect the fact that ADSI organizes objects within namespaces. The IADsNamespaces interface provides access to the IADsNamespaces object, which contains one Namespace object for every ADSI provider implementation installed and enabled for use on the current system. Each Namespace object is itself a container for whatever object a particular directory service defines as the root. Windows NT and Novell's NDS are the other two namespaces that Active Directory technology supports out of the box.

ADSI also supports binding to multiple namespaces.

Developers can use the ADsPath *ADS://* or *@ADS!* and the IADsNamespaces method to start browsing through the entire directory structure. Another option is to go directly to a particular namespace by using its name prefix, for example, *LDAP://*. Developers should not assume anything about the content of Active Directory services or other LDAP installations. Each program should be written to configure itself on the fly as it explores its environment. Also note that within namespaces or directory systems, ADSI supplies a uniform set of methods for interacting with predefined objects and interfaces. However, not every namespace implements all possible objects, nor does ADSI support all the objects and methods of all possible namespaces.

Key points about binding   The following points provide guidance for developers on which namespaces and binding techniques to use.

- The ADSI LDAP or Global Catalog are the best providers of access to Active Directory services, although the Windows NT provider yields Windows NT 4.0 backward compatibility for user, group, and computer information that is available in Windows NT only.

- Bind to the Global Catalog service for fast search. The Global Catalog service contains selected properties for all objects within an Active Directory tree or forest.

- Never hardcode server and domain names. Use serverless binding and rootDSE to eliminate specific location and namespace dependencies.

- Access objects using the object's GUID to protect the program from consequences arising from object renames or moves. Cache GUIDs in the registry or other local stores.

- When possible, bind using the security context of the currently logged on user.

- Use the encryption option to use an SSL-encrypted channel to communicate between the application under development and Active Directory services.

Searching and Querying with ADSI

Almost all directory-enabled applications require some type of searching capability. Examples of the heavily used Search operation in action include finding people or finding printers in a directory.

ADSI search capabilities allow programs to explore a directory namespace using either the ADO/OLE DB or the IDirectorySearch interface. ADO/OLE DB support both the LDAP search syntax and a database-oriented Structure Query Language (SQL) search syntax. IDirectorySearch is available for C/C++ languages, supports only the LDAP syntax, and reduces some of the OLE DB programming overhead.

> ADSI search capabilities allow programs to explore LDAP and other directory namespaces.

Recall that we discussed the LDAP syntax in Chapter 2, "Active Directory Services and Industry Standards," in the section titled *Mastering the Lightweight Directory Access Protocol (LDAP)*. The basic ADSI search process for all applications is to construct a command, execute the search, and manipulate the results. During the construct command phase, the ADSI client marshals its search parameters into an LDAP or SQL query string. The LDAP query string has the format of an LDAP URL. During the execute search

> An ADSI client performing a query must construct a command, execute the search or query, and then manipulate the results.

command phase, the client invokes a Query operation against ADSI, binding to the underlying directory service (to establish a connection, authenticate, and so on) if necessary. During the manipulate results phase, the client acts on data returned by ADSI from the underlying directory service or the property cache, perhaps displaying or otherwise processing the information.

ADSI clients construct a query string made up of search constructs based on the LDAP/X.500 model.

ADSI search building blocks ADSI supports multiple providers and essentially passes a search query string in a command through to the provider for execution against the native directory service. Executing the command includes binding to the directory if necessary. While there are multiple ADSI providers, they are mostly loosely based on the LDAP/X.500 data structure, enabling ADSI to use the following search constructs, or parameters, consistently:

- **Base distinguished name (DN):** The Base DN parameter names the entry to which the query will initially direct itself.

- **Scope:** The Scope parameter defines whether the query acts on only the Base DN, or on the Base DN and its immediate child entries, or on all the Base DN's descendants in the directory hierarchy. These Scope parameter values are called Base, OneLevel, or SubTree, respectively. The Base scope picks a single entry. The OneLevel scope is often useful when enumerating or processing an entry's direct subordinates, and sometimes for searching. The SubTree scope is useful for deep searching.

- **Filter:** The Filter parameter is a string that specifies the criteria to be met by the objects that a query returns. This string is in LDAP search filter format. It allows single exact-match, phonetic match, or wildcard search terms. It also allows combination of single search terms through the use of AND, OR, and NOT constructs, which can be nested. RFC 2254 fully and formally describes the search filter.

- **Attributes to return:** The search filter returns the specified attributes from matched entry or entries.
- **Search preferences:** A search preference set allows programmers to indicate limits on the query, such as the maximum size of the query result, overall time limits, whether to chase referrals during the search, or whether to cache results.

ADSI search examples   Query strings based on the foregoing concepts and complying with RFC 2255 specifications for an LDAP URL and RFC 2254 specifications for a search filter take this general form:

<BaseDN>; Filter; Attributes[; Scope]

An example of a search command based on this syntax is:

<LDAP://cn=users,dc=rapport,dc=com>;(cn=mark*);
ADsPath,cn,mail;subtree

As shown in Figure 6-4, this search would find entries named Mark Twain and Mark Hanson anywhere beneath the Users container.

The search syntax, or query string, format is based on the LDAP URL.

Figure 6-4   *Example of a search.*

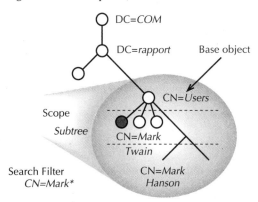

The following Visual Basic code implements an ADSI search.[4]

```
Dim con As New Connection, rs As New Recordset
Dim con As New Command
'Open a Connection object
con.Provider = "ADsDSOObject"

'Open the connection
con.Open "Active Directory Provider"
con.Properties("User ID")  = "jsmith@xyz.com"
con.Properties("Password") = "pa*ssw?ord"
'Set connection to as an active connection
Set Com.ActiveConnection = con

'set search preferences
Com.Properties("Page Size") = 1000

Com.CommandText = _
  "<LDAP://DC=ArcadiaBay,DC=Com>;" _
  &"((objectCategory=Person)(cn=andy*));" _
  &"ADsPath,cn,manager,telephone,;" _
  &"subtree"

'Execute the query
Set rs = Com.Execute
...
```

Developers can also use SQL dialect to search the directory.

The SQL dialect in ADSI's OLE DB provider could incorporate the SELECT statement in the form:

SELECT *attrlist* FROM *'ADsPath'* WHERE *conditions* ORDER BY *attr*

One could use a sample SELECT statement to build an Active Directory query as follows:[5]

```
SELECT cn, ADsPath
FROM 'LDAP://DC=ArcadiaBay,DC=Com'
WHERE objectCategory='person' AND sn='H*'
ORDER By sn
```

---

4. Source: Microsoft

5. Source: Microsoft

Once search results are collected, OLE DB provides a consistent method of manipulating search results, or Recordsets, as follows:[6]

```
rs.MoveFirst
While Not rs.EOF
  'Multivalue attr
  if (rs.Fields(i).Type = adVariant)
      ... rs.Fields(i).Value(j)
  else 'single value attr
      ... rs.Fields(i).Value
  end if
  rs.MoveNext
Wend
```

> ADSI provides a method of manipulating search results, or Recordsets, in a tabular (row, column) manner.

In addition to the search capabilities supported by the ADSI OLE DB provider, ADSI supplies the IDirectorySearch interface to query directory services directly for non-automation clients. IDirectorySearch requires search information similar to that of the methods of the OLE DB interfaces. It reduces the OLE DB programming overhead while sacrificing some of the richer navigation features supplied when using OLE DB queries.

> C/C++ and other non-automation language programmers can use the ADSI IDirectorySearch interface to obtain much of OLE DB's flexibility with slightly reduced programming complexity.

Every ADSI object supports IDirectorySearch when a provider implements it. The developer uses the SetSearchPreferences method to define the preferred settings for the query, and ExecuteSearch method to initiate the query. As with OLE DB, query results are expressed in the form of a table.

Recommendations for searching   The following lists some recommendations to follow when searching with ADSI.

- **Use the right names:** Most objects have CN (common name) as their naming attribute. However, a few, such as DC (domain component) and OU (organizational unit), have other naming attributes. Use of the Name attribute (holding the full distinguished name) is also possible.
- **Search by class:** Often, a developer might want to search for a particular class of objects—printers with location

---

6. Microsoft Corporation provided the search example codes in this section.

equal to Building 12, for example. However, with Active Directory technology, developers should use Microsoft's proprietary objectCategory attribute, which is indexed, in place of objectClass, which is not indexed. Use objectClass primarily when the desired end is to examine the schema and retrieve an entry's full inheritance tree. Note that when accessing non-Microsoft directories, objectCategory might not be present, but objectClass might be indexed.

- **Look in the right place:** Use the Global Catalog to perform a fast search (with no interdomain referrals), search the entire forest, or search the schema and configuration containers. Use the domain directory to access attributes that are not in the Global Catalog, to obtain highly current and highly available information, or when needing to modify as well as query the directory.

- **Use the right dialect:** Developers should generally use the LDAP dialect, reserving the SQL dialect for writing database-oriented applications that just happen to be using the directory. Save SQL for when it is necessary to use the full power of SQL to perform heterogeneous joins of directory information—for example, joining Active Directory data to data in the SQL Server or the Index Server.

- **Search efficiently:** Query filters should contain at least one indexed attribute, or more if OR terms are used. However, indexing does not help if wildcards are in the middle or at the beginning of a string. Also, assume that a subtree search will return a large result set and use paging to conserve network resources and avoid overloading the client. Restrict queries to retrieve only what is necessary, but note that one search of an object that reads two attributes is cheaper than two searches of the same object, each returning one attribute. Bind to an object once and hang onto the binding handle. Do not create many connection objects. Test searches against large Active Directory installations and, if necessary, against a sampling of non-Microsoft directories.

- **Be move-and-rename safe:** Use persistent references to objects, such as GUIDs, if it is important for a program to be able to access an object many times, even after it is moved or renamed.

- **Know the available options:** You can set Search Scope, Paging, Result Caching, Sorting the Search Results, Referral Chasing, Size Limit, Server Time Limit, Client Time-Out, and Returning Only Attribute Names parameters. These options are available in C/C++ through IDirectorySearch.

Manipulating Directory Objects

The IADsContainer interface enables an ADSI container object to create, delete, and manage subordinate objects. Container objects represent the hierarchical nature of directory trees in Active Directory namespaces or in other supported hierarchical namespaces. One can use the IADsContainer interface to count, enumerate, filter, create, delete, copy, or move the child objects of the current object. The following VBScript code enables a client to navigate a Container object.

The IADsContainer interface enables developers to deal with hierarchical relationships among entries.

```
Dim Child
Dim Container
On Error Resume Next
Set Container = GetObject("LDAP://" _
  &"CN=users,DC=rapport,DC=com")
If Err = 0 Then
   For Each Child in Container
       MsgBox Child.Name
   Next
End If
```

Manipulating Directory Attributes

The IADs interface provides several methods that allow developers to get a specific property by name: the IADs::*Get* and IADs::*GetEx* methods. The *GetEx* method, unlike *Get*, handles multi-valued properties as an array. Developers can also enumerate all properties on the object using IADsPropertyList and obtain special properties using IADs::*get_Name* to return an object's

The IADs interface provides methods that enable developers to access attribute values of directory entries.

relative name, IADs::*get_Class* to return the object's class, and IADs::*get_Parent* to obtain ADsPath to the object's parent. The code that follows provides an example of using the *Get* method in Visual Basic.

```
Dim MyUser as IADs
Dim MyCommonName as String

' Bind to a specific user object.
set MyUser = GetObject("LDAP://CN=Daniel" _
    &"Blum,DC=rapport,DC=com")

' Get property
MyCommonName = MyUser.Get("CN")
MsgBox MyCommonName
```

The IDirectoryObject interface provides C/C++ clients with direct access to directory entries with low performance overhead.

The IDirectoryObject interface provides clients written in C and C++ with direct access to directory entries. It enables access by means of a direct on-the-wire protocol, rather than through the ADSI property cache. In place of the properties supported by the IADs interface, IDirectoryObject callers can get or set any number of attributes with one method call. Unlike the corresponding automation methods, which are transacted, IDirectoryObject methods are executed as soon as they are called, and do not require creating an instance of a directory object in memory. Thus, their performance overhead is very low.

Managing Groups and Collections

ADSI Collection objects enable aggregation of security groups, distribution lists, and other information.

ADSI uses Collection objects to represent any arbitrary set of items in a directory service that are of the same data type. Collection objects can represent both persistent information, such as groups, and volatile information, such as print jobs in a print queue. Collections are important in helping developers and administrators manage directory information; for example, without the use of groups, defining access control lists (ACLs) is often impractical.

ADSI provides the IADsContainer, IADsMembers, and IADsCollection interfaces. Group memberships are special collections of IADsMembers interfaces supported by IADsGroup. ADSI also supplies the helper functions ADsBuildEnumerator and AdsEnumerateNext, which simplify enumeration in C and C++ programs. Automation clients use enumeration implicitly when they call Next in a For loop, as shown in the VBScript code below.

ADSI provides IADsContainer, IADsMembers, and IADsCollection interfaces and the ADsBuildEnumerator and AdsEnumerateNext helper functions.

```
Dim Group
Dim Member
Set Group = GetObject("LDAP://" _
   &"CN=Administrators,CN=Builtin,DC=rapport,DC=com")
For each Member in Group.Members
   MsgBox Member.Name
Next
```

Other interfaces on the IADsGroup object include IADsGroup::*Add* and IADsGroup::*Remove* to add or remove members. There is also an IADsGroup::*IsMember* method that returns TRUE if the specified object is a direct member of the group. IADsContainer::*Delete* deletes the group, and IADsContainer::*MoveHere* moves the group.

Active Directory technology supports security groups and distribution groups with universal, global, or local domain scope.

Developers should use Active Directory security groups to control access to resources in many cases, but it is important to understand groups well, because they can cause problems if customers use or implement them improperly.[7] Developers should use distribution groups only for e-mail distribution lists or other non-security related grouping purposes. Also, define universal groups as functional groups that span domains, but nest global groups within universal groups to help minimize Global Catalog replication traffic during membership changes. Use global groups for domain users that need to access resources across the enterprise, and local

---

7. For example, having too many groups increases administration efforts, time needed to replicate across domains, and bandwidth needed for replication. Also, putting an ID into too many security groups can slow down the logon process. Rather than creating hardcoded groups to go with a program, it is sometimes better to create extended access rights for program-specific objects in the directory.

groups for access confined to a single domain. Store groups at the root of the domain, within an organizational unit, or within a container.

Advanced Security, Schema, and Service Publication

Advanced directory programming often requires more than just binding, searching, and updating objects and their contents. These advanced programming tasks, which are more complex than the basic ones, involve manipulating access controls or other security objects, installing application-specific information types into the schema, or publishing information about services.

ADSI and Security

ADSI security incorporates access control, authentication, and encryption.

Directory applications must interact with ADSI security to authenticate users and manage access controls on directory information. Therefore, ADSI enables applications to submit various kinds of credentials to a directory service. This section provides a brief discussion of ADSI and security for the developer. For general information on Active Directory security, see Chapter 9, "Security Overview: Kerberos, Certificates, and Access Control."

An application can submit credentials consisting of a name and password to ADSI.

In ADSI, credentials consisting of a user name and password allow system software to authenticate the identity of a user during the initial system logon. Developers can employ the IADsOpenDSObject to establish a user's credentials for a directory service, or let ADSI use default credentials associated with the current user. Once the system authenticates the user, the user is free to make requests for system resources, access file shares, and be granted file permissions, to the extent that the underlying directory service's security requirements support these.

ADSI also enables strong authentication and encryption.

Developers can also use the binding options of the OpenDSObject method to set the ADS_SECURE_AUTHENTICATION flag, in which case one of the Windows 2000–supported secure authentication methods (Kerberos, SSL/TLS, or NTLM authentication) will be used. Developers can also set the ADS_USE_ENCRYPTION flag to enable encryption of the directory traffic during the connection. Note that underlying provider-specific directory services might override these flags, or in some cases not support them at all. For example, the Microsoft ADSI provider for Novell Directory Service (NDS) always uses strong authentication.

Access control for Active Directory services works through Windows NT security descriptors attached to every directory object or property. Each security descriptor contains a discretionary access control list (DACL) and a system access control list (SACL). The DACL is a set of access control entries (ACEs), each having a security identifier (SID) that represents the *security principal* (user, group, or computer) to whom the ACE applies, and permissions, which allow or deny users and groups rights to particular actions. An example of a permission attached to an object is Read permission on the mail attribute. The DACL determines who can see the object and what actions they can perform on the object.

ADSI allows applications to manipulate various access control objects in directory services through ADSI security descriptor interfaces.

To manipulate access controls on directory objects or properties through ADSI, developers use a set of low-level APIs provided with Windows NT and Windows 2000 for the purpose of manipulating security descriptors. Developers must understand, however, that other directory service provider implementations, such as Novell's NDS, might handle access control definition and management functionality differently.

ADSI models itself after Windows NT security, and different directory service providers might not offer all the ADSI security functionality.

It is possible to set up multiple ACEs in such a way as to leave security loopholes. Developers must be careful to check the cumulative logic of all the ACEs in the ACLs they define, and then to test access from a variety of accounts. Developers must also be sensitive to the performance implications of ACLs. Active Directory entries inherit security descriptors from both their parent object class and their parent container entry. Changing access controls on a container might cause rewriting of all the subordinate entry security descriptors, which could create performance issues in large containers.

Developers must also be cautious about security and performance problems that can arise from manipulating access controls.

ADSI Schema Model

The basic ADSI schema model derives from the LDAP/X.500 concept of object classes as abstractions of real directory information objects, such as people, applications, and printers. ADSI provides a way for directory applications to access the formal definitions of object classes, attributes, and attribute syntaxes. Moreover, ADSI enables applications to extend the directory. Smart directory browser programs can look at the schema to decide what to display to users, and applications might make run-time decisions based on what is installed in the directory schema. The ability to express and modify the on-line schema is a powerful tool for making new functionality available to client software, while still supporting older versions. For more information on Active Directory security in general, see Chapter 9, "Security Overview: Kerberos, Certificates, and Access Control."

ADSI enables developers to access and extend directory schema information.

The root-node container objects found within each provider Namespace object include an ADSI schema container object. This object contains the definition of all the functionality for that provider. An Active Directory schema container object is a partition within the Configuration container, and there is only one schema per forest. This makes extending the schema a significant step for the large enterprise, and for that reason, schema extension functionality must be reliable, robust, flexible, in accord with the latest IETF standards at the time, and in accord with prevailing industry best-practices for the definition of LDAP information. In fact, before even thinking about changing the schema, developers should study what is already defined and determine whether they can use existing object classes and attributes.

The root node of each provider namespace contains schema definitions, and there is one schema per Active Directory forest.

As we said, installing new schema information is not a trivial matter. Not only is there just one schema per forest, but also, once made, schema changes cannot be fully reversed without reinstalling the Active Directory forest. For this reason, Active Directory technology puts some safeguards in place, ensuring that before the ADSI schema can be extended, someone must designate one domain controller as the temporary schema operations master for the domain forest. All programs performing schema extensions

Handle extensions to the schema with caution.

must run within an account defined as a member of the Schema Administrators group.

With these cautions in mind, developers who need to program the Active Directory schema should refer to Chapter 7, "Planning Namespaces, Domains, and Schema," for more detailed information. Active Directory services exposes schema class definitions and schema attribute definitions for a forest as directory entries within the schema partition. These may be found, for example, under *cn=schema,cn=configuration,dc=rapport,dc=com.* If given sufficient privileges, developers can modify these definitions using the same interfaces as those designed for modifying any directory content.

Developers can update the Active Directory schema by changing appropriate directory entries that represent object classes and attribute types.

Publishing Information About Services

Network application developers require the ability to publish information about their services in the directory. This ability enables clients to rendezvous with one or more instances of the service on the network. Publishing a service in Active Directory services involves creating and maintaining service connection point objects. Publishing not only requires ADSI, but also could involve using Win32 APIs, the RPC name service (RpcNs), Winsock Registration and Resolution (RnR), and the COM+ Class Store. Services use one or more of these mechanisms to advertise themselves. Clients find an object advertised by the service, then use binding information in this object to connect to the service.

Developers need to publish information about services on the network.

Service objects contain binding information that applications use to connect to instances of the service without needing to know its host computer names or addresses. A client queries Active Directory services for an object representing a service connection point (SCP) and uses the binding information from the object to connect to the service. Examples of binding information published in services are File Services UNC Names, URLs for Web services, port numbers, or specially coded RPC bindings. Note, however, that services using sockets, RPC, or COM+ do not need to publish a connection point.

Binding information in service objects enables clients to find and connect to services.

Services can publish themselves using the serviceConnectionPoint object or a subclass.

Services that are not using existing means of binding, such as RPC Name Service, Winsock RnR, or COM+ mechanisms, need to publish a serviceConnectionPoint (SCP) object in the directory. The SCP contains keywords identifying the source vendor and product, a serviceClassName (such as SqlServer), service binding information, and the service's DNS name. Services might need to extend, or subclass, the base SCP object class to define additional usage parameters for clients. Note that clients of the service must have previous knowledge of how to interpret and use the binding attribute. A service that uses an SCP should also provide an API for clients to access and use its binding information. Figure 6-5 illustrates an example of a client accessing the SCP for MyService, and then connecting to MyService.

Figure 6-5 *Client binding to a published service.*

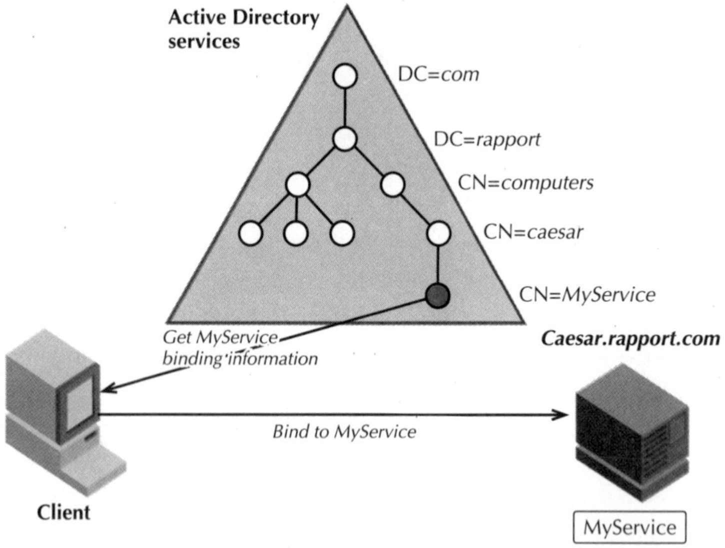

Usually, developers should initially publish service connection points under the computer object where the service is installed in the directory, but allow them to be moved.

A service should publish its connection point information in the domain hierarchy—not in the configuration hierarchy where it would cause unnecessary replication traffic, nor in the existing user, group, or computer hierarchies where it might confuse administrators. Usually, the best location to initially create a service is the computer object in the domain where the service is installed. However, services should enable their configuration entries in such a way that an administrator can later move them into an organizational unit or other container. Because services are moveable, developers should provide clients with a way to find a service through search queries. Any program caching the name of a service (such as the client or the service configuring itself) should refer to the SCP by its GUID, or by a reliable search query that can always locate it.

The Directory Services Provider

ADSI providers are COM interfaces that wrap native directory service objects using ADSI to make them accessible to ADSI clients. ADSI supplies the building blocks necessary to represent the features and services of most directory services and directory service objects. In addition, the ADSI meta-interfaces can make native objects and properties usable by native directory administrators through an ADSI client, and mapping to the ADSI schema representation can make the namespace accessible to directory service browsers. Developers can write ADSI providers in many languages, because the ADSI COM interfaces are defined as dual interfaces that allow both run-time and compile-time name resolution. Both Automation-compliant languages (such as Visual Basic and Java) and C and C++ can call ADSI interfaces.

> ADSI providers are COM interfaces that expose native directory systems to higher-level programs.

Functional ADSI providers should support the ADsPath strings, a top-level Namespace object, and the IADs and other interfaces. These interfaces should enable developers to search their directory, manipulate objects and attributes, and (in some cases) provide online schema support. They should also map specific directory service names for the appropriate attributes to the ADSI property names, enabling client applications to display directory service objects in a uniform manner across all directory services. In addition, the provider or developer can supply custom components to provide access to custom properties not modeled in ADSI to represent native features of the directory service.

> ADSI providers should support ADSI conventions and can also extend ADSI using custom objects.

Summary

ADSI enables developers to use most Active Directory services features.

ADSI is Microsoft's published interface to Active Directory services. Other APIs, such as Messaging API (MAPI) or LDAP's C API, will provide some level of directory access, but nothing short of an appropriate ADSI client implementation will enable applications to take full advantage of the power of Active Directory services.

ADSI provider interfaces allow customers and developers to mix and match directory clients and servers.

Like other Windows APIs, ADSI serves as an abstraction layer between directory clients and directory service providers. Riding above ADSI, the client ignores the internal details of the underlying directory service. Below ADSI, the provider need know nothing of the client. To a significant extent, ADSI enables diverse directory clients and servers to mix and match. Already with Active Directory services, Microsoft ships multiple providers of diverse directories, including LDAP, Global Catalog, Novell NDS, Novell Bindery, and Windows NT. In the future, independent software providers might ship additional ADSI providers.

COM interfaces permit developers to use multiple languages to accomplish basic directory functions.

ADSI client application developers can leverage ADSI's COM interfaces to work in both scripting languages and system programming languages, such as Visual Basic, Java, VBScript, C, or C++. These interfaces allow developers of directory-enabled applications to perform routine directory tasks, such as browsing, searching, and end-user authentication, and advanced tasks like administration and service publication.

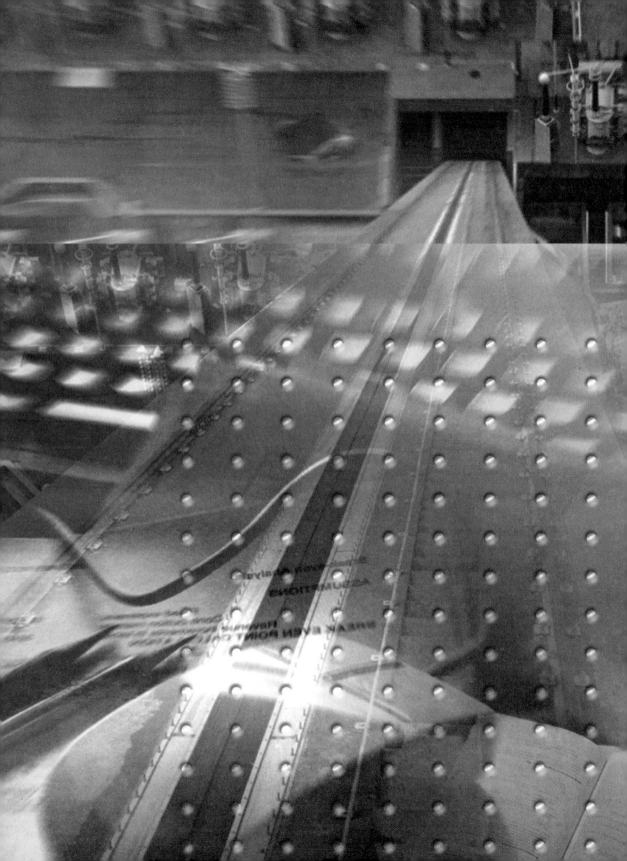

Chapter Seven

Planning Namespaces, Domains, and Schema

Microsoft Active Directory directory services supports a distributed and replicated information model, with a structure based on Domain Name System (DNS) domains and the Lightweight Directory Access Protocol or LDAP/X.500 schema. A *schema* is a structured framework or plan; in computing terms, it describes the organization of information in a database—or, in our case, a directory—by defining such aspects as attributes, parameters, or domains. These schema definitions specify the content of directory entries and attributes within Microsoft Windows 2000 environments. Customers can change the schema to add new information types to Active Directory services.

Active Directory services are based on DNS domains and on an LDAP/X.500 schema structure.

What Is a Schema?

The Active Directory schema holds the *directory metadata,* which is the formal definition of all object classes representing entries that the directory can store, the rules governing hierarchical naming

A schema is the formal definition of a directory's information model and structure.

relationships among those entries, and the attributes that make up the entries. Active Directory architecture includes a default schema that defines naming constraints and content for many object classes, such as users, groups, computers, domains, organizational units, and security policies.

The Active Directory schema models DNS domains and merges them with LDAP information.

The default Active Directory schema combines the DNS and LDAP/X.500 information models. DNS domains define the initial hierarchy of the Active Directory namespace, it is the LDAP/X.500 information model that defines the lower levels of the hierarchy and the contents of the Active Directory directory. (For a more detailed discussion, see Chapter 4, "Active Directory Services Architecture."

Customers or developers can dynamically extend the Active Directory schema.

Because of its LDAP/X.500 roots, the Active Directory schema is dynamically extensible; developers and customers can modify the schema in a number of ways to suit particular needs. Developers can customize the enterprise namespace, define new object classes, or define new attributes for new and existing object classes. Customer administrators typically extend the schema with the Microsoft Active Directory Schema snap-in tool, whereas developers use programming tools, such as Microsoft Visual Basic.

Active Directory domains, trees, and forests use a common schema.

A significant limitation on Active Directory technology in the initial release of Windows 2000 is that each Active Directory forest is restricted to using one schema throughout. This means that large-enterprise customers must deploy either a single forest (significantly restricting the autonomy of internal administration domains) or several forests (with significant integration efforts necessary to achieve the full enterprise-wide benefits of Active Directory services). Note, however, that a future release might remove the Active Directory schema restrictions and the tradeoffs they impose. Meta-directory technology acquired from the former ZOOMIT Corporation could figure significantly in future releases that enable multiple forest coexistence, or multiple schemas in future forests.

At the domain level, however, Active Directory technology increases flexibility by enabling customers to define domain-level policies or to subdivide domains into organizational units where new access controls or other policies can be defined. Replication schedules, limits on password lengths, and access controls are examples of policies that customers can determine at the site, domain, or organizational unit levels, respectively.

Policy definition can take place at the Active Directory domain, organizational unit, or site level.

Why Is a Schema Important?

At the namespace structure level, the schema is important to customers because the structure of the directory determines many administration (policy), performance (replication), and security (access control) issues. Schema management at the object and attribute level is also important to maintain an orderly data model for the company and to ensure that applications do not conflict with one another or confuse end users.

The schema is important to both customers and developers.

The schema is important to developers because they must use the schema to model information needed for their products or extend the schema to publish new information. Deploying applications on complex intranets is not cost-effective unless sufficient information is shared in the directory.

Planning Namespaces

Active Directory technology holds content within a *namespace*—a structure for naming distinct entries of directory information. The Active Directory namespace is both an LDAP and a DNS namespace. Each Active Directory namespace (tree or forest) has a single Global Catalog, a single configuration, and a single schema or set of logical data definitions of object classes and attribute types that govern the directory content. Examples of object classes are users, computers, and groups. Examples of user-class attributes are common name, telephone number, and description.

Active Directory namespaces consist of trees (multiple domains) and forests (multiple trees).

Structure of Active Directory Namespaces

Active Directory architecture holds its content within a namespace, which can take the form of a tree or a forest structure.

Because Active Directory technology is based on the hybrid LDAP/DNS namespace, administrators are able to group entries, domains, organizations, users, and resources into a single logical namespace, across which domains share information and enable cross-domain access rights. Domain groupings can take on either a tree structure or a forest topology in which the trees do not share a single root. We will use the term *domain forest* to describe an Active Directory enterprise or department-level installation.

Domains have a tree-like structure with a root, containers, and leaf objects.

Each Active Directory domain (or group of contiguous domains) has the structure of a directory tree. Directory trees have several properties. At the most basic level, a tree is made up of multiple directory objects, or entries. These entries include a root entry, leaf entries, and container entries that hold leaf entries as subordinates.

Each Active Directory domain consists of a naming context or zone, controlled by a different group of domain controllers.

Enterprises can define an Active Directory forest as a single domain or as a single domain tree, or it might truly exist as a forest of domains and domain trees. The *root* of the forest is the first domain to be installed. Each domain forms a *naming context* or *zone* within that global namespace. Thus, if a company's forest consists of the domains *na.rapport.com*, *europe.rapport.com*, and *uk.europe.rapport.com*, a different set of domain controllers manages each domain, even though they are all part of the same tree.[1]

Customers must plan their Active Directory namespaces up front, or face costly consequences.

Note that an enterprise cannot rename or delete the forest root domain without completely reinstalling the forest. The Active Directory namespace requires planning up front, before customers install any Windows 2000 domains or servers. Otherwise, when customers do get around to planning the namespace, unplanned Active Directory domains or forests will probably require reinstallation, and users will face significant difficulties, such as having to reload all user accounts, reconfigure servers—and perhaps even rebuild servers—to fit the new domain into the trees or forests.

---

1. A Windows 2000 domain controller acts as an LDAP/X.500 Directory System Agent (DSA).

Caution: Register Active Directory Domains Properly

Running Active Directory services in a properly registered namespace is critical, particularly in the event of an enterprise merger, acquisition, divestiture, or other organizational change that brings the customer in contact with the outside world. An Active Directory namespace should usually exist within a registered domain; this means that customers either register their top-level Active Directory domains (for example, *rapport.com*) directly, or locate the domain beneath an existing registered domain (for example, *na.rapport.com*). In the end, all Active Directory domains should derive from *.com, .edu, .uk,* or another top-level ancestor. Note also that properly registering the Active Directory domains under the global DNS is one thing; making them globally visible is another. In general, Active Directory domains should be hidden behind a firewall to protect the security of Windows 2000 systems and accounts.

And although Microsoft's planned Domain Migration snap-in will enable or improve functionality for pruning, grafting, or renaming domains, these kinds of tree operations can cause administrative headaches or disruptions. It is important to minimize the need for such operations.

Trees and terminology The following technical terms and definitions relate to namespaces:

- **DNS domain:** The administrative and security area within the DNS namespace.
- **Directory information tree (DIT):** The global tree structure comprising the LDAP/X.500 namespace.
- **Container:** An entry in the DIT that contains other containers or leaf entries.

- **Relative distinguished name (RDN):** A set of attribute values that describes an entry uniquely within the scope of its immediate container (parent or superior) entry in the DIT.

- **Distinguished name (DN):** Used in Active Directory services and all LDAP/X.500 systems as the naming path to uniquely identify an entry in the DIT. Concatenates the entry's own RDN with the RDNs of all superior containers.

- **Partition, naming context, or zone:** Conceptually equivalent to a domain, and comprising a region of a DNS or LDAP tree extending down from a root container to a lower boundary of leaf entries or containers that another administrative authority controls.

- **Domain** (Windows 2000): Administrative and security area within both the LDAP/X.500 DIT and the DNS namespace, controlled by a group of Windows 2000 domain controllers.

Forests and Domains

Namespace planning is complex.

Because namespace planning is complex, we will examine some scenarios, including a single forest and multiple forests and some basic domain planning considerations. Refer also to Chapter 10, "Migrating to Active Directory Services," for namespace planning when a migration is planned.

An Active Directory forest contains the configuration and schema for a group of domains.

As we discussed, in Active Directory architecture, the top-level naming contexts start with a domain, domain tree, or forest. As such, the top-level naming context (or forest of contexts) defines a forest root as a single configuration and a single schema container, which are both replicated to all subordinate domains. Each forest root contains a schema and a configuration for the forest. It also defines transitive trust relationships among domain controllers, and the searchable Global Catalog. Figure 7-1 shows a typical Active Directory domain forest scenario. In this figure, *dc=rapport* is the forest root; as the first domain installed, *rapport* holds the configuration container. Other naming contexts include the domains *dc=domain.rapport.com, dc=consulting.rapport.com,* and *dc=education.rapport.com.*

Figure 7-1 *A domain forest scenario.*

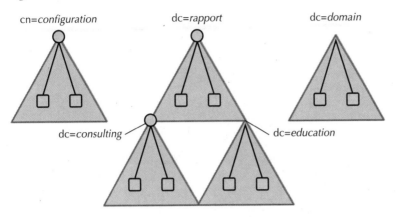

There are always at least three naming contexts: a schema context, a configuration context, and at least one domain-naming context. Beyond that, enterprise scenarios can be as simple as a single domain for all information or as complex as a forest of domain trees, or even multiple forests. In the case of multiple forests, there are also multiple enterprise roots and multiple schemas. But Active Directory technology does not automatically share information or trusts across forests, which makes the multiple forest environment more complex than the single forest.

An enterprise might require one or multiple forests.

Organizations that do not want to use a single common schema should create separate forests, such as the structure shown in Figure 7-2. Note that *dc=subsidiary, dc=rapport,* and *dc=rapportrd* have separate configurations and Global Catalogs; to share any information between these forests, directory synchronization and explicit trusts are needed. Customers with multiple forests give up the Global Catalog capability of creating a single searchable namespace for the entire enterprise within Active Directory schema. They also lose the automatic, transitive trusts that exist within a forest.

Working across multiple forests requires special directory synchronization processes and explicit trusts.

In some cases, the integration, information sharing, and administrative benefits of a single domain or forest are high enough to warrant forming the largest possible forest. Even if customers cannot form a single forest or tree, they should design their separate namespaces and environments in a way that will not preclude a

Some customers deploying multiple forests should still design the namespaces for a forest merge in the future.

Figure 7-2 *A multiple forest scenario.*

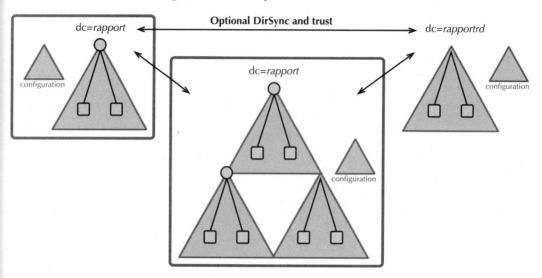

forest merge in the future, if enterprise requirements change, or if Microsoft or a third-party vendor provide capabilities and tools to allow multiple schemas in a forest.

Planning forests Because of the complexity of sharing information across forests, why would customers not use a single domain forest or domain tree for the entire enterprise? The problem is that Active Directory forests can have only one schema, and only one domain controller at a time can make changes to that schema. But many Active Directory–enabled applications developed by Microsoft, third-party developers, or customers themselves will change the schema to add new types of object classes or new types of attributes. To agree on a single forest, or schema, all business units, sites, and organizations within the enterprise must also agree on common schema administration procedures, common application accreditation and certification procedures, and even on coordinated procedures for adding new Microsoft service packs or other releases that change the schema. Many customers simply will not tolerate that degree of centralization. It is also possible that performance issues in large-enterprise environments could constrain the size of forests.

The need for schema diversity and other factors will drive some large enterprises to deploy multiple domain forests.

A good general planning methodology is to first determine which parts of the enterprise are willing to share a given domain tree or domain forest. For each forest, set up the Active Directory domain structure as a single domain, a domain tree, or a mix of both. The next problem is to determine how to link Active Directory namespaces with existing DNSs, which could be UNIX-based implementations that support heterogeneous applications. The choices are to put the forest at the top level of the enterprise as shown in Figure 7-1 or to define the domain forest beneath existing enterprise DNS domains.

Begin by determining which parts of the enterprise can share a schema or live together in a forest.

Deciding how to integrate Active Directory services with an existing DNS is a complex matter in itself. In many cases, there will be significant tradeoffs between meeting the needs of existing applications (Windows NT 4.0, UNIX, mainframe, or Novell) and the needs of Windows 2000. Chapter 10, "Migrating to Active Directory Services," describes additional considerations for defining Active Directory and DNS integration strategies. For now, Figure 7-3 shows a multidomain integration scenario. Suppose Domain Corporation is a large multinational corporation with the following root domains, *domain.com, domainrd.com, domain.fr,* and *domain.uk,* and that the organizations operating the *domain.com* and *domain.com* domains decide to define Active Directory domains named *ntdom1, ntdom2, ntdom3,* and *ntdom4* in a single forest positioned beneath (and therefore not affecting) their existing DNS. In this topology, the DNS for rapport.com and rapportrd.com is not affected by Active Directory services, except as required for zone replication and referral. However, the organizations operating the domains *domain.uk* and *domain.fr* want to have their own independent forests. In the case of *domain.fr,* the Active Directory domain will become the sole DNS domain. On the other hand, *domain.uk* will add its domain forest (*ntdom5*) under the existing DNS. All these deployments are perfectly legitimate.

Customers must decide how to integrate forests into or under existing DNS domains.

Basic domain planning After the units of schema, or the scope of forests, have been established, customers will need to determine the domain structure within a forest. Using a single domain, or just a small number of domains, will simplify planning, administration,

Start with the smallest number of domains and add new ones as they are justified.

Figure 7-3 *Multiple domains in a forest.*

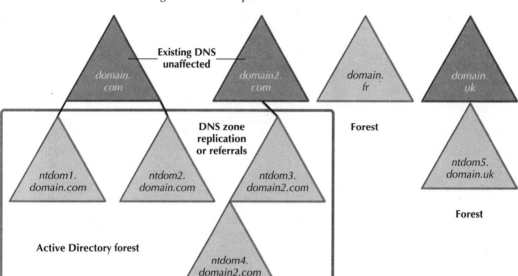

 = non-Active Directory domain

 = Active Directory domain

and deployment. Active Directory domains have been tested with millions of objects, and Active Directory technology also supports delegation of administration rights and some policies within the domain. Start by putting all objects into a single hypothetical domain and add new domain trees or domain branches to the forest if, and only if, additional domains are justified.

Create new domains to localize security policy or to reduce the amount of replicated traffic over wide area networks (WANs).

The domain is the unit of replication partitioning, administrative scope, authentication, and account management policies (such as password rules). Customers should create new domains if they need to localize replication or security policies to different parts of the forest. A remote site connected to the WAN over a dialup or other low bandwidth link might not be able to support full replication within a large domain. Business units might demand ownership not only of the update rights to entries representing their users and resources, but also over the policies for assigning administrative personnel, external Kerberos domain trusts, password policies, and logon policies. A group of systems set up along the enterprise firewall to serve an extranet of trading partners should generally have its own separate domain. Or, the R&D department of a large manufacturing company might run its network computing infrastructure on quite different lines from the rest of the enterprise.

In the Microsoft Windows NT 4.0 environment, customers frequently created many resource domains to localize administration of different kinds of resources, such as Microsoft Exchange Server or other applications. In many cases, the ability of Active Directory services to delegate administration and some policies even within a domain makes many older Windows NT 4.0 resource domain subdivisions unnecessary. Customers should review their Windows NT 4.0 resource domains to see whether they, in fact, contain software or hardware that might not work well in a Windows 2000 environment, or whether it is possible to collapse them into larger Windows 2000 domains.

Customers migrating from Windows NT 4.0 should be able to reduce the number of domains.

Enterprises often require multiple Active Directory domains. These domains can be set up in a tree topology or in a forest topology. Consider choosing a forest topology when there are distinctly different organizational brand identities (such as the TV sports network ESPN and its parent corporation, Disney) within an enterprise that should be exposed in top-level domain naming. Also, if there is the possibility of divestiture for a given division, that division should be set outside the main domain tree. In other cases, a domain tree topology might prove desirable.

Define domains in a forest topology to reflect different organizational brand names; otherwise, consider using a domain tree topology.

Other domain planning considerations   For domains that will contain people entries, customers should emphasize stability in choosing domain tree structures. Renaming or moving any domain in the future will create administrative disruptions. The effect will extend to end users, who might experience e-mail address changes and other disturbances. In perhaps the worst-case scenario, if customers use Active Directory services as a public key infrastructure (PKI) repository for advanced electronic commerce authentication systems (such as those provided by Entrust Technologies or Verisign), it might be necessary to revoke and reissue every user certificate (and smart card!) in the changed domain.

Consider the stability of the organization when defining domains.

Name the forest root domain with special care. It is not possible to move, rename, delete, or reassign the enterprise or forest root once it has been named.

Customers can define domains along geographic or organizational lines or a combination of both.

Customers can set up domain trees along organizational or geographic lines. Although organizational domain structures can facilitate definition of some hierarchical policies (such as access controls) and allow users to browse the organizational structure in a convenient way, they can be unstable, change with reorganization, neglect physical network boundaries, complicate replication, and lead to duplication of equipment in sites that house more than one division of the company. A safer approach is to organize top-level domains by world area, country, or large physical sites, and then set up OUs within domains so that organizations can control some aspects of policy and administration. Before going too far with geographic domain partitioning, however, note that Active Directory architecture provides optimized site-sensitive replication features to make at least some of the topology more transparent. See Chapter 8, "Understanding Replication and Sites," to learn how to factor replication into namespace design.

Domain planning cannot be overly generalized; every customer has a unique environment to consider.

Figure 7-4 shows an enterprise domain tree that breaks up the large Domain Corporation along major lines of business and then subdivides the multinational chemicals business into two geographic domains. Be aware that Figure 7-4 is only an example; every customer has its own unique circumstances to consider when planning domains.

Containers, Policies, and Naming

Active Directory architecture supports a configuration-naming context for each forest and a domain-naming context for each domain.

Active Directory technology supports a configuration-naming context for each forest and a domain-naming context for each domain. The configuration-naming context is sometimes called the *enterprise-naming context,* and it is replicated across all domains in the forest. Much of the information in the domain-naming context, however, is not replicated outside the domain.

Figure 7-4 *Organizational and geographic domains for Domain Corporation.*

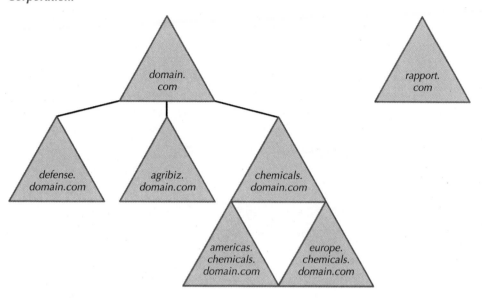

The Configuration Container

The root domain in a forest is the first domain installed. For example, *dc=domain,dc=com* is the root domain for Domain Corporation. Active Directory architecture creates the configuration container as a child of the root domain, *cn=configuration,dc=domain,dc=com*. Schema is a child of the configuration container, *cn=schema, cn=configuration,dc=domain,dc=com*. Therefore, the only writable copy of the schema and the configuration container is in the root domain, but the schema- and configuration-naming contexts are both replicated to all domain controllers in the forest.

The enterprise configuration container holds schema, sites, services, display specifiers, and other branches. The schema and display specifiers containers hold the forest definition and display characteristics of Active Directory object classes and attributes. The schema has a naming context of its own. Customers can manage the information in the schema branch using the Active

The configuration container holds the schema and other information.

The configuration container also holds information about sites, services, and other parameters.

Directory Schema snap-in. Developers can manipulate stored schema definitions through programming.

The enterprise configuration container holds schema, display specifiers, and other branches.

Active Directory technology also uses the information in the sites branch to optimize replication and logon; we will discuss this subject in Chapter 8, "Understanding Replication and Sites." Customers can influence the sites configuration through Active Directory Sites and Services Manager. The services container holds parameters for those applications that are invoked as Windows 2000 services (from Microsoft or third-party developers).

Domain Containers

An Active Directory domain defines containers for computers, users, and many other objects.

An Active Directory domain is created with a number of containers that form its domain-naming contexts and exist only within that domain. These containers are:

- **Computers:** This container holds domain member workstations and servers. Customers can also store computer objects in customer-defined OU containers (see below).
- **Users:** This container holds domain member workstations and servers. Customers can also store user objects in customer-defined OU containers (see below).
- **Builtin:** This container holds a number of groups, including administrators, account operators, backup operators, print operators, and others. The function of these groups is to control privileges and permissions for resource administration at the domain level. (Note: user-defined groups are stored in the computers, users, or other containers.)
- **System:** This container holds domain-level configuration for IP security, policies, RPC services, Winsock services, file links, meetings, and other system functions or applications.
- **Foreign security principals:** This container holds information about explicit trusts to foreign Kerberos servers.
- **Domain controllers:** This container holds the computer objects for those servers that act as domain controllers within the domain.

Naming Active Directory Entries

As we will see, customers and developers have considerable flexibility to customize information within the framework that the Active Directory architecture creates at the time of installation. For example, customers can define OUs to contain user or computer objects. Customers can also determine the naming of many objects, both user-defined and system-defined. Entries that customers must name include the domain itself, users, computers, and others. This section presents guidelines for naming the customer-defined entries.

Individual Active Directory entries must be named.

In choosing a domain name (*dc=*), it is best to stick to the Internet standard DNS conventions, using the characters *A-Z, a-z, 0-9,* and -. Although Microsoft DNS does allow additional characters from NetBIOS, their use is not recommended because they can be incompatible with non-Microsoft systems. DNS names can be up to 253 bytes long and up to 63 bytes per dot-separated label.

Domain names should strictly follow DNS conventions.

Within domains, customers must define naming conventions for other objects. In this regard, it is important to understand that Active Directory architecture actually supports several types of names or ways to identify users. Table 7-1 describes the way Active Directory architecture names and identifies objects.

Active Directory architecture uses many forms of names for most objects.

Containers and Policies

Once customers have defined and laid out domains, they can further subdivide large domains into OU containers to group information more logically, to make it easier to find, and to set more granular policies. As discussed earlier in the *Planning Namespaces* section of this chapter, the forest maintains a common schema, and the domain is the unit of replication partitioning, account policy, and authentication. Thus, customers cannot change the replication, account policies, or partitioning characteristics of Active Directory deployment at the OU level. However, customers can delegate administrative rights to groups of administrators representing various organizations at the OU level, or they can define group policies at the OU level.

Use OU subdivisions in domains to define access controls and other policies.

Table 7-1   Active Directory naming examples.

Type of name or identifier	Example	Notes
Common name	Daniel Blum	Creates the LDAP relative distinguished name (RDN). Generally consists of first name/last name. Must be unique in its OU or domain container.
ADsPath (or LDAP distinguished name)	*LDAP://cn= daniel blum, ou=consulting, dc=rapport, dc=com*	The full pathname of the user; the way LDAP applications retrieve it. Contains the LDAP distinguished name.
SAMAccountName (logon id)	*djblum*	The logon name must be unique in the domain.
User principal name	*djblum@ rapport.com*	The logon ID concatenated with an @ symbol and the domain or some other administrator-defined suffix.
Canonical name	*rapport.com/ consulting/Daniel Blum*	A friendlier version of the pathname, used by some applications that require user input.
Display name	Blum, Daniel	Can be identical to common name, a variation for creating a sorted list, or a unique nickname that an end user creates.
Object globally unique identifier (GUID)	[16] x7c x12 xa9 xb4 xdd xc4 xd2 x11 x8f xba xa2 x3b x6b x26 x56 x55	The unique database ID of the user. Acts within Active Directory services as an internal identifier.
Object security identifier (SID)	[28] x01 x05 x00 x00 x00 x00 x00 x05 x15 x00 x00 x00 x9e x40 x7e x14 x67 xfd x7c x30 x8a xa7 x32 x3f x58 x04 x00 x00	The security ID of the user, for backward compatibility with Windows NT 4.0 and in Active Directory Kerberos authorization information.

Customers can use access controls at the OU level to define which attributes of objects are visible, and to create special administration policies. For example, a particular OU might designate a number of contained users and resources for administration by a special functional department or facilities support group. Alternatively, domain administrators might remain the primary managers of the OU, but the administration of telephone numbers or some other attribute could be a task for a secretary or facilities support person. Customers could aggregate a Windows NT 4.0 resource domain into a new, larger domain, using an OU to keep local administrators in control. Chapter 9, "Security Overview: Kerberos, Certificates, and Access Control," discusses Active Directory OUs, delegation, and access controls in greater detail.

OU access controls determine user rights to modify or display various attributes of the OU and its subordinate entries.

Windows 2000 makes extensive use of policy-based management, and the directory is generally the policy repository. For example, the domain's system container holds a domain policy object. The domain policy object contains a variety of configuration items governing account management policies, such as password length and change frequency, as well as policies for built-in system services, such as the Microsoft certificate authority, Internet Protocol Security (IPSec), and the Encrypted File System (EFS). System services define these policies in the directory at installation and enable management of them through appropriate administrative snap-ins.

Windows 2000 stores domain policies, group policies, and other kinds of policy information in Active Directory services.

The Group Policy Editor   Customers can use Microsoft's Group Policy Editor (GPE) tool to configure multiple objects. GPE can help the administrator to manage the following settings: system services behavior, desktop look and feel, and application settings; software installation parameters; security settings; file deployments to the desktop or locations such as the Start menu; redirection of folders such as My Documents; and scripts to run at startup and shutdown or logon and logoff. Computer configuration settings start applying when users start up or reboot. User configuration settings take effect when the user logs on. Each type of setting applies to any user or computer in the site, domain, or OU to which the policy applies.

The Group Policy Editor allows customers to attach policies to domains, sites, or OUs.

Group policies are stored in complex Group Policy Objects (GPOs).

Group policies are stored in Group Policy Objects (GPO) which, in turn, have associations with Active Directory container objects (site, domain, or OU). Application of group policy occurs hierarchically from the least restrictive group (site) to the most restrictive group (OU), and the settings are cumulative. None, one, or multiple GPOs may be set for any container. Despite the power of GPOs, customers should minimize the number of GPOs associated with users in the domains or organizational units until they fully understand the tradeoffs inherent in these tools. For example, the larger the number of GPOs that are applied to a user, the longer it takes to log on, and the more complex the policy is to manage.

Understanding Object Classes and Attributes

Entries belong to an object class, which specifies their attributes and naming characteristics.

Active Directory entries and attributes follow the information model originally defined in X.500 and used for LDAP. In LDAP, every entry belongs to an object class and consists of a collection of attributes. Using attributes in its own directory configuration entry, each object class specifies the following:

- Which attributes in an entry are mandatory (mustContain)[2]
- Which attributes in an entry are optional (mayContain)
- Which attributes name an entry (rDNatt)
- The position of an entry of this class in the hierarchy (possSuperiors and possInferiors)
- An access control template that will create the initial template for the default security descriptor for new objects of this class

User and computer are examples of Active Directory object classes.

Every entry, or object, in the directory is an instance of one or more object classes defined in the schema. For example, every user account on the network has an object of the user class to represent it, and every computer tracked by Active Directory ser-

---

2. Phrases such as mustContain or any other phrase beginning in lower case, containing no spaces between words, and capitalizing all words except the first, reflect the distinctive syntax used for attribute descriptions in LDAP and Active Directory. We retain it for clarity.

vices has an object of the computer class to represent it. Attributes hold specific information about an object. For example, the schema includes a common name attribute, which is found in user, computer, group, and other types of entries. An attribute-definition object also specifies the *syntax,* or structural rules, of the attribute, such as whether it can be an integer or string, and whether the attribute can be multi-valued.

The definitions of object classes and attributes are themselves objects stored in the directory under the *cn=schema,cn=configuration* naming context. By using the directory itself as the schema store, developers can manipulate the schema with the same operations available for managing the directory itself. The following are some of the objects commonly found in Active Directory architecture:

Active Directory architecture stores its object class and attribute definitions in the schema container.

- **Domain object:** The root of a Windows 2000 or DNS domain in Active Directory architecture.
- **Organizational unit object:** A specialized container within a domain, used to delegate administration and policy.
- **Container object:** An object that customers can create under many different kinds of objects, which can itself contain other objects.
- **User object:** A user with a Windows 2000 account. Contains the attributes of an organizational person, a mail recipient, and a security principal. These classes define a rich backdrop of contact and context information about the user. The user's object can occur in the tree beneath domain or organizational unit objects.
- **Group object:** A group in Windows 2000 used for administration and setting permissions. Group objects can occur in the tree beneath domain, container, or organizational unit objects.
- **Computer object:** A computer running Microsoft operating systems in a Windows 2000 network. Can also contain any

of the attributes of a user. Computer objects can occur in the tree beneath domain, container, or organizational unit objects.

- **Foreign security principal object:** Intended for foreign entities outside the Windows 2000 forest to which permissions can be assigned. Foreign security principal objects can occur in the tree beneath container objects.

- **Volume object:** A disk partition or volume named by the uNCName attribute. Volume objects can occur in the tree beneath domain or organizational unit objects.

- **Group policy container object:** A container of policy directives that can apply to domains or organizational units.

- **Class store object:** A container of COM or COM+ location and invocation information for remote objects.

- **Server object:** A Windows 2000 computer acting in the role of a server.

Object Class Inheritance

Object class definition uses an inheritance model.

Following the LDAP/X.500 information model we discussed in Chapter 2, "Active Directory Services and Industry Standards," object classes use an inheritance model that allows definitions to first be packaged or grouped and then inherited by lower-level subclasses from the higher-level classes to ensure consistency of definitions. Figure 7-5 describes a partial map of the inheritance relationships among the object classes shown.

In the figure, the object class hierarchy begins with the Top object. A number of classes, such as domain, container, and organizational unit, are defined as subclasses of the Top class, but other classes, such as user, group, and computer, are more complex. The user class, for example, obtains attributes through the mail recipient, security principal, and organizational person classes.

Note that some object classes are defined as *structural* in nature, meaning that they define naming rules for entries of their type. Structural object classes are shown boxed in Figure 7-5. Other object classes, shown without boxes, are defined as *abstract* or *auxiliary*, meaning that no entries of their type should ever be created directly; rather, abstract object classes (like Top) exist as placeholders in the hierarchy, and auxiliary object classes (such as mail recipient) combine with other classes (such as organizational person) to enrich a structural class (such as user). Because Active Directory object classes are complex, customers and developers should be cautious in modifying them.

Structural object classes determine an entry's content and its position in the namespace; auxiliary classes determine only the content.

Standard Attributes

In many cases, customers or developers will not need to modify the Active Directory schema. The schema ships with many objects and hundreds of attributes, embodying a great deal of expected contact information for the user. Other (non-Microsoft) LDAP systems recognize many of these attributes. Although the terminology of the standard object classes seems cryptic, it should

Active Directory technology already supports many standard attributes.

be feasible to deduce their purpose and use these attributes—and the standard user and other object classes—as much as possible before creating new attributes or classes.

Some LDAP attributes and descriptions available in the Active Directory entry are:

assistant	c (or country)
department	description
directReports	division
employeeID	facsimileTelephoneNumber
generationQualifier	givenName
homeDirectory	homeDrive
homePhone	homePostalAddress
initials	ipPhone
locality or site	language
mail	mailNickname
manager	middleName
mobile phone	organization
otherFacsimileTelephoneNumber	otherHomePhone
otherIpPhone	otherMailbox
otherMobile	otherPager
otherTelephone	organizationalUnit
pager	personalTitle
physicalDeliveryOfficeName	postalAddress
postalCode	postOfficeBox
seeAlso	surname
st (state)	street
streetAddress	telephoneNumber
thumbnailLogo	thumbnailPhoto
title (job title)	url
certificates	userPassword
common name	

Modifying Object Classes and Attributes

Directory-enabled applications often need to modify the schema.

Although customers and developers should first use the shipped attributes and object classes, sometimes they will need to modify the schema. Customers might need to store new information about people, or to develop and deploy new applications that require enterprise-wide access to directory objects within the Windows 2000 environment. Chapter 6, "ADSI Programming and the Developer," discusses general considerations for using or not using Active Directory services as the repository for application data. Although customers should not misuse the directory by storing large or volatile objects in it, directories will become more dynamic over time. The remainder of this chapter shows how customers and developers can update the schema.

Only a designated group of schema administrators can manage the schema. Two additional safety measures restrict and control modifications to the schema. First, the customer must select the The Schema May Be Modified On This Server option in the Active Directory Schema snap-in. Second, only one domain controller at a time can write to the schema; that domain controller is the operations master for schema, or the schema master. The administrator, or a program running under a privileged administrator account, must be connected to the schema master to manage the schema. Although not necessary, the administrator should take the schema master offline until the schema changes have been made and verified.

Active Directory technology protects the schema from casual modification through access controls and registry settings.

Administering the Schema

The Active Directory Schema snap-in allows schema administrators to manage the schema by creating or modifying classes, creating or modifying attributes, and specifying which attributes the Global Catalog indexes or catalogs. The Schema snap-in is a Microsoft Active Directory Domains and Trusts snap-in available on Windows 2000 servers. Figure 7-6 shows the administrator adding a new auxiliary object class called contractor, through the Schema snap-in.

Active Directory Schema Manager provides a graphical interface for administrators to update object classes in the schema.

Figure 7-6 *Schema snap-in adding a contractor object class.*

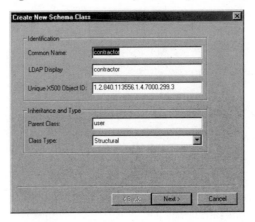

The Schema Manager tool can also add new attributes.

Having created the contractor object class, the administrator can then right-click its definition to bring up tabs for the object classes, general, relationships, attributes, and security. In Figure 7-7, we see the administrator adding two new attributes—contractorIdent (an alphanumeric ID, such as a badge number) and contractorSponsorPerson (the distinguished name of the individual who authorizes the contractor's access) as mandatory attributes. Through attributes and settings in the other tabs, the administrator can radically change the behavior of existing classes. However, customers should be careful about making any changes to built-in classes, because such changes can negatively affect Active Directory behavior .

Administrators must configure attribute name, ID, syntax, and other criteria when creating a new attribute.

Before administrators can add attributes to a new object class (contractor in our example), they must define the attributes through the Schema snap-in. Figure 7-8 shows the Create New Attribute screen. Through this screen, the administrator defines the name of the attribute, its object identifier, a syntax (such as distinguished name, case insensitive string, integer, and so on), optional minimum and maximum values, and whether or not the attribute can be multi-valued. Most of these definitions are straightforward, but the object identifier requires further discussion.

Defining Object Identifiers
for New Object Classes and Attributes

Active Directory architecture follows the LDAP/X.500 standards in labeling all attribute and object class definitions with a globally unique object identifier (OID). This use of OIDs is perhaps the core of what makes LDAP's information model extensible: nothing is hard-coded. The OID itself is a hierarchically formatted numeric string made up of many branches, each separated by a period. Thus, for example, the numeric string *1.2.840.113556* has four branches, where *1* designates ISO, subsequent branches *2* and *840* designate an identified organization registered by ANSI, and *113556* is reserved for Microsoft. Microsoft is then free to create additional branches and register OIDs to its heart's content. Individual customer or developer organizations should register their own OID branch through *http://www.ansi.org* in the United States, or through their own national registration authorities, a list of which can be found at *http://www.iso.ch*. Customers are also able to obtain an OID through Microsoft consulting, or possibly through a Microsoft reseller, such as Compaq Corporation. Obtaining an OID through a vendor can be quicker, more convenient, and less expensive than obtaining it through ANSI (which entails a $2,500 fee), but it does tend to tie customers a little more tightly to the vendors. The key point is to register all classes or attributes using a valid OID to avoid the possibility of future conflicts with another user's schema.

Figure 7-7 *Schema snap-in configuring the contractor object class.*

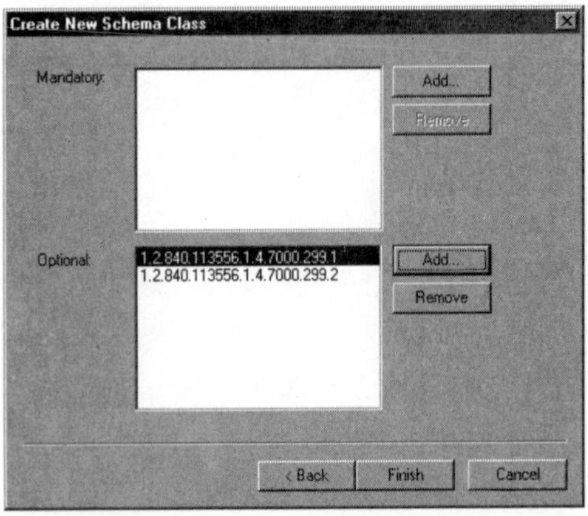

Figure 7-8 *Schema snap-in creating an attribute object.*

Developing the Schema

Developers need to manipulate the Active Directory schema in certain cases.

Developers will need to manipulate the Active Directory schema in certain cases. Some developers will simply implement smart directory browsing functionality that understands the schema already resident in an Active Directory installation. Other developers, seeking to create new applications and to publish services in the directory, might need to define new object classes to represent those services, or extend existing object classes, such as user or computer, to add new functionality.

Smart directory browser programs can look at the schema to decide what to display to users, although applications typically deal with the schema at install time. Applications might also make run-time decisions based on what is installed in the directory schema. The ability to express and modify the on-line schema is a powerful tool for making new functionality available to client software while still supporting older versions.

Customers can use the schema to discover information in a namespace, or to make it easier to install new functionality.

For all the extensible schema's potential, installing new schema information is not simple with Active Directory technology or, for the most part, with other directory services accessible through ADSI. Before customers can use any of the schema extension methods of ADSI with Active Directory, administrators need to designate (or change) one domain controller as the temporary schema master for the enterprise.

Handle any extensions to the schema with caution.

Because modifying the schema for an enterprise is a weighty matter, a company's applications should first seek to use previously created object classes and attribute types of the Active Directory schema. Such types might have come from the X.500 or LDAP standards, from industry efforts such as the Directory Enabled Networks (DEN) consortium, or from collaboration between Microsoft and the third-party vendors themselves.

Tools and Techniques

Because classes and attributes are represented in the directory as objects, to add a new class or attribute, administrators need only add a new class-schema object or attribute-schema object with the necessary attributes. Similarly, modifying a class or attribute means just modifying the class-schema object or attribute-schema object. These objects are generally found under the *cn=configuration,cn=schema* container for the forest.

Because Active Directory schema definitions are themselves directory objects, updating the schema is similar to updating the directory itself.

Administrators can program modifications to the schema by using
Visual Basic, C++, or Java, employing the same types of API function calls discussed in Chapter 6, "ADSI Programming and the
Developer." Another way to modify the schema is to use the LDAP
Data Interchange Format Directory Exchange (LDIFDE) batch
loading tool (discussed further in Chapter 8, "Understanding Replication and Sites") or any other tool that can generate LDAP updates. Some developers might prefer the high-level language
approach, because it offers more control. On the other hand,
some customers might prefer the LDIFDE approach, because with
LDIF they can potentially see the precise updates to be made before authorizing the process to continue.

Schema Modification Examples

A minimal definition of a new class could consist of just the cn,
objectClass, and governsID attributes. However, a useful class
also requires some combination of mustContain, mayContain,
and possSuperiors attribute definitions. Any attributes specified
when adding a new class must already exist. Also, as we discussed above, the OID of a new class specified in the governsID
attribute must be unique, not only in the enterprise in question,
but throughout the world.

The following code reproduces the contents of the file INPUT.LDF
containing attribute-adding directives for the contractorIdent and
contractorSponsorPerson attributes from the example above. The
code is in LDAP Data Interchange Format (LDIF). The command
ldifde -i -s SERVERNAME -f INPUT.LDF initiates the LDIF import
of this part of the schema. (The example assumes that the class-
schema entry for contractor has already been added.)

```
dn:
 cn=contractorIdent,cn=schema,cn=configuration,cn=rapport,cn=com
changetype: add
objectclass: Attribute-Schema
cn: contractorIdent
```

```
Attribute-Id: 1.2.840.113556.1.4.7000.299.1.1
Attribute-Syntax: 2.5.5.6          #Syntax value for
                                   #numeric string
Is-Single-Valued: TRUE             #store exactly one value

dn:
 cn=contractorSponsorPerson,cn=schema,cn=configuration,cn=rapport,cn=com
changetype: add
objectclass: Attribute-Schema
cn: contractorSponsorPerson
Attribute-Id: 1.2.840.113556.1.4.7000.299.1.2
Attribute-Syntax: 2.5.5.1          #Syntax value for
                                   #distinguished name

dn:
 cn=contractor,cn=schema,cn=configuration,cn=rapport,cn=com
changetype: modify
add: mustContain
mustContain: contractorIdent
mustContain: contractorSponsorPerson
```

Display Specifiers

Not only administrators and end users, but also developers, should take part in populating with actual values any new attributes and classes configured through the schema. In another nifty Active Directory feature, Microsoft has made its user interfaces extensible so that, in many cases, developers need not burden customers with whole new user interfaces to deal with new directory schema information. Instead, for many applications, developers can use the new directory-based display specifier classes to configure the appearance of both directory management snapins and the context menu items and property pages that directory objects use. Once in place, these display specifiers manifest new attributes or classes (such as our contractor information) in the user interface. Display specifier objects are stored in the configuration namespace of a forest under a container that corresponds to a local ID. For example, developers should store display specifiers for the US English language under the container *cn=409/ cn=display specifiers/cn=configuration.*

Display specifier classes define context menus and property pages for new schema items.

Summary

Considerable effort goes into customizing the Active Directory namespace for a customer installation and preparing the Active Directory class-schema object and attribute-schema object to act as a repository for a new application. The challenge of providing scalable multidomain access and replication in a large enterprise is considerable, and demands rigorous planning. In addition, both customers and developers might need to use the Active Directory Schema snap-in or programmatic tools to extend the directory schema—with caution.

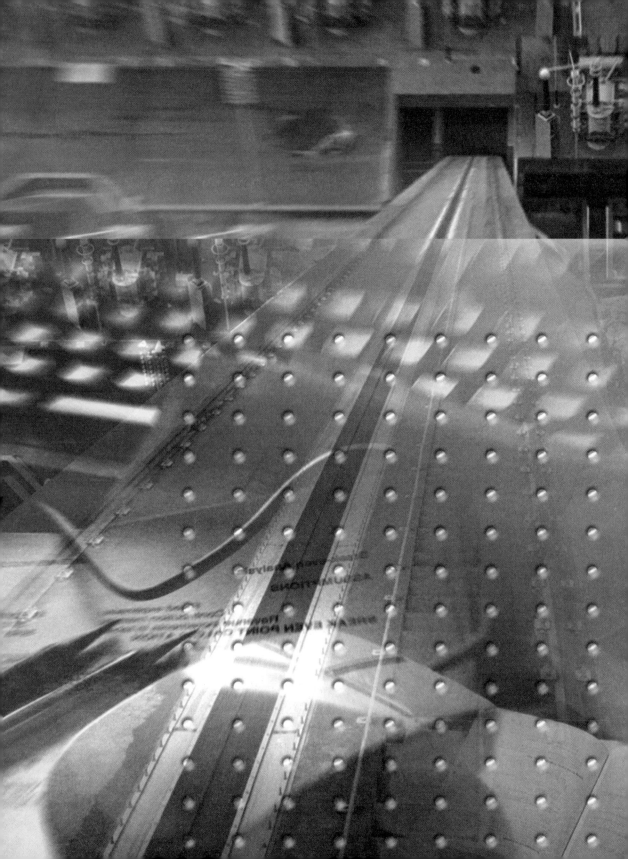

Chapter Eight

Understanding Replication and Sites

Microsoft Active Directory services gives users, applications, and services high availability and access to resources across the enterprise. It does so by orchestrating replication of domain user, resource, and configuration information across many domain controllers, even when those servers are located in disparate sites with varying network bandwidth topologies. It also conducts replication across domains to create the Global Catalog for domain trees or domain forests.

Active Directory replication makes domain user, resource, and configuration information highly available across the network.

The flexibility built into Active Directory replication makes life easier for everyone involved. Administrators can make directory changes to any domain controller, and Active Directory multi-master replication algorithms take care of the rest. Architects or planners can create domains that span multiple network sites, and then optimize the replication topology. Developers can build directory-enabled applications that become ubiquitously available, thanks to Active Directory replication.

Flexibility built into Active Directory replication benefits customers and developers.

Be forewarned, however, that this increased efficiency, flexibility, and accessibility to resources comes at a price. Active Directory replication consumes network resources and requires optimization over complex networks. Effective planning and design practices,

Implementing replication in large enterprises requires effective planning and design.

as well as good development practices, are necessary to ensure that products peacefully coexist with Active Directory technology, and that customers' money is well spent. And because standards for LDAP replication do not yet exist, customers and developers must also consider using directory synchronization and meta-directory tools for exchanging directory information beyond the borders of Active Directory forests.

Distribution and Replication Perspectives

This section discusses the need for directory replication and notes that there are many forms of replication. It distinguishes replication from synchronization and discusses the role of each in enterprise directory coexistence and migration. This information becomes valuable as customers and infrastructure developers position proprietary Active Directory replication and synchronization tools into an overall enterprise directory implementation context, and as developers plan their migration toward LDAP replication standards over time.

Why Replicate?

Replication is necessary to maintain a directory that is consistent, up to date, high-performance, and highly available.

The more customers come to depend on the directory for directory-enabled networks and directory-enabled management, the more critical directory availability and performance become. If developers follow my advice, The Burton Group's advice, Novell's advice, and Microsoft's advice, their applications will consult a general-purpose LDAP directory constantly rather than create new special-purpose directories, configuration files, or registry settings. At startup alone, applications might consult the directory a half dozen times to locate executable files, user profiles, user credentials, persistent stores, access controls, and other information. Smart application programming interfaces, such as Active Directory Service Interfaces (ADSI), try to help by caching reasonable quantities of information; but even so, references to the directory will come fast and furious as the user navigates the enterprise, launching new programs, invoking new objects, seeking new resources, or communicating with others. If customers and developers do not optimize directory performance—and this is where replication comes in—new directory-intensive systems, like public key infrastructure (PKI), will give a whole new meaning to the term "killer app."

If directory response time slows, users feel the delay. If the directory becomes unavailable, users cannot work at all. The overloading or failure of one server must not bog down the entire network. Replication helps prevent network gridlock by moving multiple copies of directory information close to the user. But since directory information is constantly changing with each addition, deletion, or modification to user, application, or machine information, the copies must also be constantly updated. Enter internal Active Directory replication and heterogeneous directory synchronization, the services that automatically synchronize multiple copies of directory information.

Replication improves directory performance by moving information closer to the users.

Single-master and Multi-master Replication

Over time, vendors and standards committees have developed two main types of replication: single-master and multi-master. With single-master replication schemes, each Directory System Agent (DSA) is said to own a portion of the directory information tree (DIT) and to be able to replicate with other DSAs. Microsoft Windows NT 3.*x* and Windows NT 4.0 both support single-master replication from primary to backup domain controllers.

Directory replication can be single-master or multi-master.

The problem with single-master replication is this: if one server goes down, the directory in use becomes a read-only repository. Administrators cannot add new users; directory-enabled applications cannot be reconfigured. Clearly, a read-only state that lasts more than a few minutes is unacceptable in a large, dynamic enterprise networking environment. To ensure that directories remain writable, many systems, such as Novell's NDS and Active Directory services, support multi-master replication. In multi-master replication schemes, a single DSA server does not own an entry; rather, any server can process and replicate updates. As long as

Use multi-master replication for highly distributed, mission-critical directories.

one or more servers remain in operation, administrators and applications can make updates and continue with business as usual.

Replication and Partitions

Advanced directory systems distribute, or partition, their namespace between servers.

Directory implementations based on X.500, LDAP, DNS, and most other models use a hierarchical namespace. This namespace determines distributed directory topology as customers divide information among multiple DSAs, or servers, along the lines of the namespace. Different standards or models use different terms for these namespace partitions; DNS standards call partitions *zones* and LDAP/X.500 standards call them *naming contexts*. In general, a *partition* is the information area beginning at a branch of a directory tree and continuing to the bottom of that tree and/or to the edges of new partitions controlled by subordinate DSAs.

Replication takes place on a partition-by-partition basis.

Since each DSA is responsible only for its own partition, replication occurs along partition lines. Each DSA in an enterprise could own a partition and replicate it to all the others. Or there could be just one partition replicated among many DSAs. There are many scenarios; Active Directory implementation makes some decisions out of the box but leaves other decisions to customers and developers. As we will see later in this chapter, proper directory partitioning and namespace design is critical to optimizing directory replication design.

Replication Options

Replication can have complete or partial granularity and can be direct or indirect. Both suppliers and consumers can initiate it.

Depending on the whim of the customer, replication can work in different ways. Replication granularity could be complete or partial. For example, Microsoft Exchange Server 5.5 replication requires mail servers to replicate all the directory information in a site, and to send the entire entry or record, even if only a single attribute changes. Active Directory replication, on the other hand, replicates all information in a domain, but conveys the changes at the attribute or field level. Replication can also be direct (always coming from the master DSA) or indirect (forwarded through multiple DSAs from the source to the destination). Finally, either the supplier (push model) or the consumer (pull model) can initiate replication. These choices affect the efficiency of the process, as well as the completeness and reliability of the replicated data.

Multivendor Replication

In the early 1990s, X.500 standardized a form of flexible, single-master replication; but it was not widely adopted by vendors, and to date, there is still no standard for LDAP replication. Currently, the IETF's LDAP Duplication/Replication/Update Protocols (LDUP) working group is deliberating LDAP replication, and we will eventually see RFCs emerge. However, multivendor directory replication is a very hard problem, and Microsoft's Active Directory architects are not convinced it will be useful or achievable. Instead of full replication between multivendor systems, Microsoft advocates using a looser form of integration called *directory synchronization*.

As yet, there is no industry standard for replication between servers that support LDAP.

In the absence of standards, products support almost every conceivable form of replication, and directory synchronization is used between products. Directory synchronization tools typically use a published interface to extract change information from a pair of directory implementations, and then perform either unidirectional or bidirectional updates. Sometimes, directories and directory synchronization products use existing LDAP tools, such as LDAP Data Interchange Format (LDIF), to import and export bulk information. Active Directory synchronization tools support bulk LDIF import/export and a mechanism for obtaining all the changes that have occurred to the directory since a specified time.

To enable replication between various products, many vendors support directory synchronization using LDAP tools (such as LDIF or change notification services), as well as proprietary mechanisms.

Although Active Directory synchronization tools and those of other vendors have some degree of flexibility, it is not enough to manage complex multivendor customer directory environments. Synchronization tools can be unidirectional or bidirectional, they can support full or partial attribute interchange, they can even be programmable to map the divergent namespace designs found in multivendor scenarios, but they do not provide advanced meta-directory services. Meta-directory services include the ability to

Beyond directory synchronization, complex directory deployments require meta-directory services.

join information about people who are scattered throughout multiple directory systems, synchronize passwords, automatically create accounts in multiple applications or systems when administrators add a person to the directory, and provide many other critical multivendor integration requirements that go well beyond synchronization or replication. Material presented in the section, *Synchronizing Heterogeneous Directories,* later in this chapter and in Chapter 10, "Migrating to Active Directory Services," helps customers and system developers to define strategies for integrating Active Directory services with meta-directory services.

Active Directory Replication Characteristics

Active Directory technology features a distributed directory, partitioned by administrative domain, with flexible and granular multi-master replication capabilities.

As Chapter 4, "Active Directory Services Architecture," explained, Active Directory services partitions directory information into administrative domains. These domains are identical to DNS domains, and they get mapped into the LDAP/X.500 DIT framework. Customers can define domains along geographic, functional, or organizational lines, depending on how their IT departments organize and support the enterprise network. Within a domain, Active Directory services supports multi-master replication of all directory information among domain controllers. Between domains that have links to one another in an enterprise domain tree or domain forest, Active Directory replication copies a subset of domain information to read-only Global Catalogs that provide enterprise-wide directory visibility. Active Directory technology can also provide directory synchronization between domains that are not part of the same forest, or to multivendor directories. Finally, it is possible to link Active Directory services to other directory products, using meta-directory services to meet more sophisticated integration requirements. Table 8-1 characterizes Active Directory replication and partitioning capabilities.

Table 8-1   Active Directory replication capabilities.

Replication characteristic	General replication options	Active Directory implementation
Partitions	DNS zones, LDAP/X.500 naming contexts	LDAP/X.500 naming contexts mapped to DNS domains
Replication protocols	X.500, IETF LDUP drafts, proprietary	Proprietary
Replication models	Single-master or multi-master	Multi-master in general; single-master replication for certain information, such as schema changes
Replica granularity	Full naming context, selective entries, selective attributes	Full replication within domains, partial between domains
Update granularity	Full replica update, entry-level update, attribute-level update	Entry-level or attribute-level update
Replica update method	Consumer initiated, supplier initiated, scheduled	Consumer initiated after supplier notification within a site; account lockouts, other urgent replication events communicated through immediate notification
Replication data transports	SMTP, FTP, proprietary	Proprietary RPC over IP transport, SMTP in certain cases
Multivendor directory integration	Basic directory synchronization, highly configurable directory synchronization, meta-directory services	Basic directory synchronization

Replication, Domains, Sites, and WANs

Low-bandwidth links demand flexible replication systems.

The low-bandwidth links often found between physical network sites can be a source of replication problems. Frequent, heavy replication traffic could interfere with other uses for the bandwidth and cause the network to become unresponsive. Depending on how a customer organizes its IT department, DNS, LDAP, or Active Directory domains can be arbitrary administrative concepts, bearing little or no relationship to the underlying network topology. Domain controller servers and their users, however, exist in the physical network site topology. Look, for example, at Figure 8-1, where in the domain forest, the domain *D2.rapport.com* crosses two sites, and Site 1 crosses three domains.

Figure 8-1 *Active Directory domains, sites, and domain controllers.*

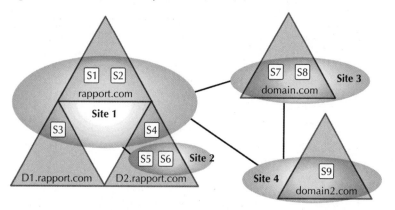

Active Directory technology optimizes its domain replication for site topologies.

Active Directory technology takes pains to accommodate site topologies in the interdomain and intradomain replication algorithms. Domain controllers determine whether potential replication partners are in the same site or in a well-connected network area. They then automatically calculate replication topologies, set schedules, and determine replication transport protocols to make the most of the available bandwidth. In Figure 8-1, for example, Active Directory services handles intradomain replication between S5 and S6, which are in the same site, differently from replication between S4 and S5, which are in different sites.

Likewise, it manages replication between *rapport.com* and *D1.rapport.com*, which are both in Site 1, differently from replication between *rapport.com* and *domain.com*, which are in different sites. Also, the Active Directory DNS will look at a client's IP address to determine its machine site affiliation before returning the address of a domain controller.

Understanding Multi-master Replication

Active Directory services performs multi-master replication on a granular basis for all controllers in a domain, domain tree, or domain forest. The system builds separate topologies for naming contexts in use within a single domain and for naming contexts in use throughout a domain forest. Each controller automatically calculates the replication topology according to a set of consistent heuristics that automatically factors in site bandwidth considerations. It is also possible for administrators to tailor replication for a particular customer environment. In this section we will discuss the Active Directory multi-master replication protocol and its basic operation; in the following major sections, we will first describe Active Directory replication within the domain-naming context, and then replication within the enterprise-naming context (or domain forest). Next, in the *Planning Replication Topology* section of this chapter, we will discuss those aspects of replication topology that customers can influence. Finally, we will explain how customers and developers can deploy synchronization techniques between Active Directory services and external systems.

> Active Directory services replicates among all domain controllers.

The Basics

Multi-master replication occurs automatically within Active Directory domains and domain forests. Customers and developers need only to understand that the protocol is robust enough to run on auto-pilot, and that they (usually) cannot inadvertently damage it. However, multi-master replication generates a significant amount of traffic in return for its high availability benefits.

> Active Directory replication occurs automatically.

The replication process is incremental and relays only the changed information.

In a domain, Active Directory services automatically links controllers into a replication topology. As information changes on any controller, it notifies its replication partner. The replication partner then initiates, or pulls, the updates. The replication operations are Object Creation, Object Manipulation, Object Move, and Object Deletion. Once initiated, these operations propagate, directly or indirectly, through chains of domain controllers until all of them have been brought up to date.

Keeping Replication Up to Date

Active Directory entries and attribute values store update sequence numbers, version numbers, and time stamps showing where and when they changed.

Each domain controller keeps a counter called an update sequence number (USN) and increments it with every initiated Active Directory update transaction. Every Active Directory entry stores the USN existing at the time of its creation and the USN of its most recent modification; every Active Directory attribute value stores the latest USN. Attribute values also store the globally unique identifier (GUID) given them by their originating directory database, the USN relative to that originating database, an update version number, and a time stamp. Active Directory multimaster replication uses the sequence numbers to determine when to propagate changes to replication partners and which changes to propagate.

Within a site, domain controllers notify each other of replication updates.

Within the same site, if a change occurs in a domain controller's database, the domain controller waits through a pause interval before it notifies its replication partners. This pause interval is 5 minutes by default, but customers can change it through a registry setting. The pause interval will batch update processes if many updates happen in a short period. If there are no changes on a domain controller, replication partners still try to get changes after 6 hours, just to make sure they remain synchronized. Between sites, no notification mechanism is used, but the administrator fully schedules replication.

High-water mark USNs and up-to-dateness tables minimize redundant replication update propagation.

Domain controllers maintain a high-water mark USN for each replication partner. This high-water mark USN represents the update state of that partner as of the last replication. Domain controllers also maintain an up-to-dateness table that lists the most recently obtained USN for every originating domain controller. Replication partners use the up-to-dateness table to determine what information needs to be replicated. Note that because domain controllers have multiple replication partners, it would be possible to receive the same originating update from more than one replication partner source. Thanks to the up-to-dateness table, however, a domain controller should only receive a particular update once, regardless of the high-water mark USN conditions.

Resolving Replication Conflicts

Occasionally, update conflicts occur. For example, two administrators might add the same logical user entry using the same distinguished name, or change a telephone number for a user on two different controllers. Or, an administrator might add users under an organizational unit branch that has been moved. Active Directory multi-master replication can referee these and other kinds of conflicts.

Multi-master update conflicts can occur with entry creation, entry deletion, and attribute value modifications.

Active Directory technology resolves attribute value modifications in the order of attribute version number, which is incremented with each update. If the version numbers are the same, time stamps determine the winner. If the update time stamps are the same, Active Directory services arbitrarily picks the value with the highest originating database GUID. Other conflicts occur and can be resolved. For example, if someone adds or moves an entry under a deleted parent, the DSA stores the contents of the entry in the lost and found container. Or, if two administrators create two objects with identical relative distinguished names (RDNs) on two domain controllers at the same time, one of those objects receives a (different) system-wide unique name.

Active Directory technology automatically resolves replication conflicts.

Urgent Replication

The Security Account Manager (SAM) and the Local Security Authority (LSA) use *urgent replication*—a push mechanism—to immediately update domain controllers of any newly locked-out accounts, relative ID (RID) pool changes, and changes to domain

The SAM and LSA processes of Active Directory technology use urgent replication of security-related items.

controller machine account information. Urgent replication causes an immediate notification to all replication partners, without waiting until the pause interval is over.

Replication in the Domain

Domain controllers in the same domain replicate the complete domain-naming context.

Domain controllers in the same domain replicate all the branches of the domain-naming contexts, including default branches, such as *cn=users* or *cn=computers*, and custom ones that customers create. By default, controllers use RPC replication over IP within domains. However, controllers handle replication within sites (intrasite replication) differently from replication between sites (intersite replication).

Sites and Replication

A site is a well-connected area with plentiful bandwidth. Intrasite replication is cheap.

For the purposes of Active Directory technology, a *site* is a well-connected area with plentiful bandwidth. This typically means a LAN, several bridged LANs, or a very high-capacity campus network. In such environments, bits are cheap and users expect rapid response times. Thus, within a site, Active Directory services replicates information frequently and does not bother with CPU-intensive compression operations designed to conserve bandwidth. The Active Directory DNS will also point network clients to a nearby domain controller in the same site when they log on.

Windows 2000 organizes servers into sites automatically, but users can tweak the definition of a site.

As mentioned earlier, customers should base domain definitions on administrative considerations. However, domain controllers and users physically exist within sites. When customers first set up a Windows 2000 network, Active Directory services assigns the domain controller to a first default site. When new domain controllers are promoted, Active Directory services looks at the subnetwork portion of their IP address to determine whether they are in a previously configured site or in a new site. If the new domain controller's subnetwork ID does not match that of an existing site, Active Directory services stores the domain controller's server object within the same site as the domain controller that authorized its promotion (through Active Directory Installation Wizard).

If the subnets are well connected by high-bandwidth network connectivity, customers can tweak the site topology by grouping multiple subnets into a site. These changes to the topology, and other changes we will discuss, are administered through Active Directory Sites and Services snap-in module, as shown in Figure 8-2.

Figure 8-2 *Active Directory Sites and Services Manager.*

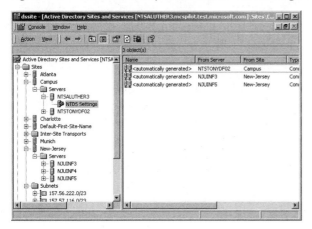

Intrasite replication   The Active Directory Knowledge Consistency Checker (KCC) service on each domain controller monitors the site's container in the enterprise configuration and the list of domain controllers in the domain controllers container. Observing the sites in the domain, it calculates intersite and intrasite domain replication topologies every 15 minutes. The KCC expresses these topologies by storing a connection object under each destination server object's NTDS Settings object in the enterprise configuration container. This connection object defines incoming replication from the replication partner, and there is a single connection object per replication partner. Because the KCC runs as a service, it automatically adapts to changes in the topology. Figure 8-3 displays an example of a replication ring serving domain controllers DC1, DC2, DC3, and DC4 within the NYC site of *rapport.com*.

Active Directory's Knowledge Consistency Checker (KCC) service calculates and configures replication topologies.

For intrasite replication, Active Directory services uses RPC replication configured in ring topologies.

The intrasite replication heuristics calculated by the domain controllers converges on a series of bidirectional ring topologies configured to ensure that no domain controller in the site is more than three hops from any other. The rings are ordered by the domain controller's server GUIDs to ensure convergence on a single deterministic topology by KCCs running on multiple controllers. This speeds replication at the cost of extra CPU cycles, disk reads, and replication traffic. Although an administrator can tweak intrasite replication by adding extra connection objects to reduce the hop count between controllers to two or one, in general, customers do not need to modify intrasite replication.

Figure 8-3 *Replication ring within a site.*

The KCC creates a spanning tree topology to link sites and attempts to minimize replication traffic. Administrators can also tweak intersite replication topology.

Intersite replication   The KCC creates a spanning tree topology to link sites, and associates a replication schedule with the connection objects between controllers in different sites. As shown in Figure 8-4, intersite replication of the domain-naming context uses RPC transport over IP. Replication is fully scheduled across sites and the traffic is compressed. Thus, for intersite replication, Active Directory technology optimizes for reduced network traffic at the cost of increased CPU utilization and replication latency. Controllers conduct intersite replication on a scheduled pull (that is, recipient-initiated) basis only; there are no controller-to-controller update notifications. In addition, domain administrators can tweak intersite replication by designating one controller in the site as the preferred bridgehead server. This causes replication updates to go through the designated controller rather than other servers in the site.

Figure 8-4 *Replication between sites.*

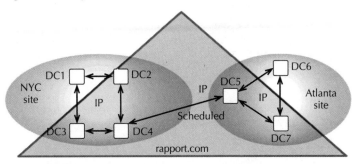

Replication in the Enterprise

Enterprise-naming, or domain forest–naming contexts include *cn=schema* and *cn=configuration* and a partial view of all domain contexts that together create the Global Catalog. Active Directory services replicates the configuration and schema containers to all controllers, and replicates the partial domain information to controllers configured as Global Catalog servers. It is possible to configure any domain controller as a Global Catalog, and any domain controller can participate in partial replication. However, Global Catalog replication works somewhat differently from schema and configuration replication. Essentially, the Global Catalog tries to use as its source a nearby domain controller or the Global Catalog that carries the requested naming context.

The enterprise-naming context replication comprises configuration information, schema information, and the partial replication of all domains to Global Catalogs.

In a single domain, replication of the configuration and schema containers is necessary, and it basically follows the same topology as the domain replication. Figure 8-5 illustrates what happens when the *rapport.com* domain adds a child domain, *research.rapport.com*, that happens to cross sites. The solid lines in Figure 8-5 denote the continuing domain-naming context replication, which occurs entirely within the NYC site for *rapport.com* but crosses the NYC and Atlanta sites for the *research.rapport.com* child domain. The dashed lines denote the enterprise-context replication, which rings the NYC and Atlanta sites and crosses between them.

Configuration and schema container replication cross domains.

Figure 8-5 *Intersite and interdomain replication.*

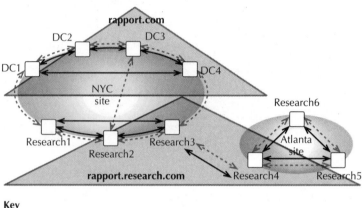

Key

Domain context replication   ⟵————————⟶

Enterprise context replication   ⟵- - - - - - - - -⟶

Planning Replication Topology

Complex, large-enterprise topologies must be carefully planned.

Replication must occur smoothly and quickly in customers' networks, or overall network reliability and performance will suffer. Although a small office with just a few domain controllers generally requires no administrative intervention for replication to work well, customers must carefully configure larger, more complex enterprise network replication topologies. We noted that as the network expands, Active Directory services discovers more sites. Customers can group, or not group, subnets together to control the creation of sites as they see fit. They can also create new connection objects to customize the intrasite topology. The real work begins, however, as administrators grapple with multisite, multidomain configurations across a varied LAN topology.

Site Links

Active Directory services creates a number of tools to help administrators fine-tune replication.

Recall that Active Directory replication topology in an enterprise is actually defined as a set of connection objects associated with servers. The KCC creates these connection objects automatically, and users can add them manually. In complex topologies with dozens or hundreds of sites, Active Directory services creates simplifying abstractions that make it easier for administrators to define and manage a topology that corresponds closely enough to existing LANs and WANs to result in proper routing performance.

The Active Directory Sites and Services snap-in module supports a site link abstraction. A *site link* is a group of sites that can communicate at uniform cost via some intersite transport. A typical site link would connect just two sites through IP and corresponds to an actual WAN link. Another site link connecting more than two locations might correspond to an ATM backbone connecting clusters of buildings on a large campus, or several metropolitan offices connected through leased lines and IP routers.

Administrators can create a site link for an intersite transport (IP or SMTP) by specifying two or more sites, a numeric cost, a replication frequency, and a schedule of time periods when the sites might be unavailable, such as during business hours or other times of high rates for a dial-up line. Typically, between sites, replication should be set up to occur one to four times per hour.

Active Directory services will calculate the optimal communication paths within site links using the minimum spanning tree replication topology between sites, as we discussed earlier in this chapter in the *Intersite Replication* section. Similarly, Active Directory services orchestrates communication between site links. The value of the numeric cost parameter is that it allows automatic adjustment of topologies as the network changes. For example, in Figure 8-6, Active Directory services would replicate from New York to Zurich to Tokyo. However, if the enterprise installed a dedicated line from Tokyo to New York, a reduction in the cost associated with that link would ensue, causing the replication pattern to adjust automatically. New York would then replicate directly to Tokyo without traversing Zurich.

Administrators can create site links to properly channel and schedule replication traffic flows across a WAN.

A site link contains a group of sites, a numeric cost of communication, and an availability schedule.

Active Directory services calculates replication topologies between site links and adjusts them automatically when administrators change configured costs to reflect network upgrades.

Site Link Bridge

Administrators can define a site link bridge to force Active Directory services to calculate optimum paths between site links.

If appropriate, administrators can further control the replication topology by disabling automatic (or transitive) replication routing between site links, and instead grouping site links into an administrator-defined site link bridge. A Site Link Bridge object represents a set of site links, typically corresponding to an intranet linked by router, or a set of routers. Each site link in a bridge should have some site in common with another site link in the bridge; Active Directory services then uses the numeric costs associated with each site link in the bridge to calculate an optimal intersite link replication topology and schedule. Figure 8-6 shows an example site link and site link bridge topology, with site links New York SL, Atlanta SL, Boston SL, Zurich SL, Frankfurt SL, London SL, Tokyo SL, Hong Kong SL, and Singapore SL. Administrators define additional site links to express the cost of communicating between New York and Atlanta (NA), Zurich and Frankfurt (ZF), and so on. Finally, three site link bridges are used, one for each world area (APSLB, NASLB, EUSLB) to regionalize the replication traffic.

Figure 8-6 *Site links and site link bridges.*

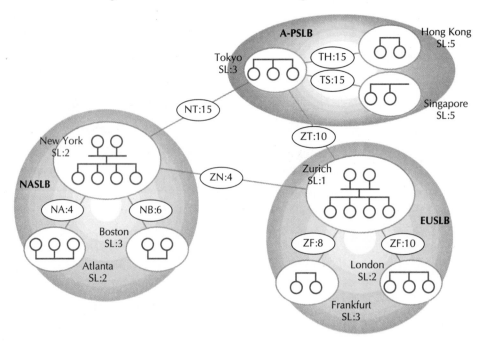

Exchange Server Sites vs. Active Directory Sites

Before the development of Active Directory services and Windows 2000, Microsoft Exchange Server messaging environment also supported sites, and much of the site-based replication technology in Active Directory services got its start with Exchange Server.

However, customers who have deployed Exchange Server 5.5 or earlier versions should not simply translate Exchange Server sites to Active Directory sites, because Exchange Server (a messaging system) and Active Directory services (an infrastructure resource for all kinds of applications) have different usage and performance characteristics. Exchange Server customers should review the *Customer Site Planning Methodology* section of this chapter and follow the steps that it describes. In general, Active Directory services will require more sites than will Exchange Server.

Customer Site Planning Methodology

To plan an Active Directory replication topology, follow these steps:

- Obtain a network map detailing network sites and connections between sites
- Obtain statistics or estimates of WAN speed and topology, including existing traffic levels between sites, and actual network reliability and performance between sites where public networks (Internet or dial-up connections) are used
- Group subnets into sites in pockets of LAN bandwidth (the fewer sites, the better; it is easier to break them up later than to regroup)
- Create low-cost site links between sites that are well-connected through high-speed network backbones
- Create medium-cost site links between sites that are connected with a comparable IP transport forming a full

Large-enterprise customers should obtain a network map and plan their sites, site links, and site link bridges to optimize the replication topology.

mesh, such as frame relay clouds, or Metropolitan Area Networks (MANs) with a T1 connection

- Create a high-cost site link for each pair of sites that cross a WAN link
- Let the Active Directory KCC do the routing between the site links or, if necessary, create site link bridges for groups of site links on different sides of a low-speed WAN connection

Replication and Domain Planning

Customers should design domain namespaces with replication in mind.

Although administrative considerations should form the basis for setting up Active Directory domains, replication and geography still play a role. Notwithstanding the best efforts of Active Directory technology to handle multisite replication transparently and efficiently, regardless of domain topology, customers should still consider the network as well as the political topology when designing the domain structure. In some cases, a low-speed, unreliable WAN cannot handle replication traffic well at all. If a domain is too big and an enterprise network too weak and distributed, the large domain will create more traffic than desired, take bandwidth from other deserving applications, and will perform unreliably. Customers should also take naming stability into account when designing their namespace; domain names that are likely to change with frequent reorganizations will lead to major restructuring, massive replication spasms, and many other problems that are best avoided. For these reasons, even customers wishing to minimize the number of domains in their environment might consider deploying one or more domains per world area.

Designing Applications with Replication in Mind

Developers must build applications to be resilient in the face of transient inconsistency that replication introduces.

By its very nature, replication introduces transient inconsistency in Active Directory services. That is, at any moment in time, not all copies of an object, a set of objects, or an attribute are consistent. For example, an application might create a group object containing the distinguished names of several member objects. After replication to a particular server, an application might find that the group has been created, but some of the members have not. The application might fail if its code cannot deal gracefully with this error condition. In general, transient inconsistency is a time bomb waiting to blow up on applications that are not programmed to deal with it. And when disaster strikes, the causal transient conditions could be unrepeatable, complicating the lives of developers charged with tracking down the problem.

Developers must internalize the notion that Active Directory services is constantly replicating information. They must prepare themselves to deal with states induced by latency or multi-master replication. These states can be update version skews, where one replica has new values and another has old values. Or they can be partial update situations, where one replica has new values, but another has some new and some old values. Partial update situations can even, for a time, allow inconsistent information (as in our groups and members example) to exist.

> Replication latency can cause directory information to appear inconsistent to an application at a particular moment in time.

Simply put, the directory application developer's motto should be: Less is best. When possible, developers should use a single attribute or object to store application information. Also avoid using attributes that are interrelated. Design and code defensively, taking replication-induced inconsistency into account in error messages, retry procedures, and problem diagnostics. For complex applications that must store multiple objects and attributes in the directory, Microsoft recommends using an *object set,* which is defined as a contiguous subtree with child counts on the container entries, and GUIDs stamped on each object in the set. Object sets could allow developers to detect both partial update and version skew—if developers use them properly.

> Developers should design and code defensively, avoiding overly complex structures.

Finally, as we discussed in Chapter 6, "ADSI Programming and the Developer," in the section, *What Information to Store in a Directory,* developers should take care not to cause replication problems for customers by storing very large attribute values in the designated Active Directory directory or by updating information too frequently. Remember that directory changes equal replication equals bandwidth equals money. Also, customers might

> Developers should also take care not to cause high levels of replication.

have optimized their domain structure to create smaller domains in isolated, slow WAN-linked areas. However, if developers create large volumes of new Global Catalog attributes or universal groups, such information will be replicated enterprise-wide, potentially annoying the cost-conscious (and the response time–conscious) customer.

Synchronizing Heterogeneous Directories

Active Directory services must coexist with other vendor directories in customer environments.

Sharing directory information across diverse computing and application environments is necessary so that users can locate and access enterprise-wide information and resources, and systems can properly authenticate and authorize users. Customers will therefore need to make Active Directory technology synchronize with other directories in heterogeneous computing environments. In some cases, Active Directory services might replace an existing directory; interoperation then requires a migration tool, such as the Microsoft Directory Service Migration snap-in aimed at NetWare users. In other cases, customers will require a long-term coexistence between Active Directory services and other systems, such as Lotus Notes messaging and collaboration directories. Bidirectional directory synchronization tools can address such coexistence. In large enterprises, however, many directories must coexist; often a meta-directory environment best satisfies customer needs.

Migration Tools

Directory migration tools provide a one-time, one-way export of directory contents into Active Directory services.

Directory migration tools are designed for a one-time transfer, or replication, of the contents of one directory into another. At times this can be as simple as exporting the user entries from the source directory and importing them into the destination directory. But in many cases, migration must also encompass import and export of organizational structure information, groups, and access control data. Engineers must then understand the original directory environment, security, and access controls before migrating the information.

The Microsoft Directory Service Migration Tool makes it possible for customers to create a model of the NetWare environment in a special subtree of Active Directory services. Customers can adjust the model before actually installing any migrated users, groups, or access controls in Active Directory services. However, the Microsoft migration tool is unidirectional, not bidirectional, so it does not enable directory synchronization for the purpose of co-existence with NetWare. Since coexistence with NetWare will be required during (and perhaps after) migration, there is an opportunity for third-party developers to add on directory synchronization utilities and to develop value-added Windows 2000 and NetWare migration and coexistence solutions.

The Microsoft Directory Service Migration Tool is made for simple, one-time migration scenarios.

Directory Synchronization

Directory synchronization enables bidirectional replication of changes to and from a pair of established directories. For example, Microsoft will provide bidirectional synchronization between Active Directory services and Exchange Server 5.5 messaging environment's directory for customers to use until they can migrate to the next version of Exchange Server, which will use Active Directory services natively. Microsoft has also released a basic, general-purpose bidirectional synchronization tool that customers and third-party developers can use to communicate with other environments.

Directory synchronization tools enable coexistence.

Figure 8-7 displays an example of directory synchronization between Microsoft Exchange Server and Lotus Notes. This directory synchronization ensures that all Lotus Notes e-mail users in the enterprise appear as custom recipients in Exchange Server and Active Directory services, and that all Exchange Server recipients appear in the Lotus Notes directory. To accomplish this basic directory synchronization, a directory synchronization utility would copy user adds, deletes, and changes to each respective directory. The utility would only copy partial attribute information from entries, at a minimum, the user name and e-mail address.

Directory synchronization is often used between e-mail environments, such as Microsoft Exchange and Lotus Notes.

Figure 8-7 *Microsoft Exchange Server and Lotus Notes directory synchronization example.*

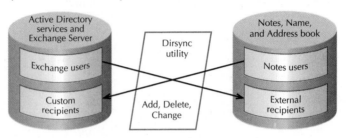

LDIFDE or Visual Basic scripting can be useful for simple migration and basic directory synchronization.

Third-party developers and customers themselves can build migration utilities as import and export scripts or basic directory synchronization utilities using Microsoft's LDIFDE tool, or they can write Visual Basic script programs. Chapter 6, "ADSI Programming and the Developer," provides some Visual Basic examples; here we will focus on LDIFDE. LDIF (the LDAP Data Interchange Format) is an IETF RFC for the batch update of LDAP directories. Customers and developers can invoke LDIFDE on the DOS command line from within a batch file. For a full description of LDIFDE's options, customers can type in the command from the DOS prompt (without parameters). A few examples are shown in the *Using LDIFDE for Import/Export* sidebar. Another tool, CSVDE, works similarly to LDIFDE but uses Microsoft Excel-style comma-separated file formats.

More advanced directory synchronization programs take time to develop, or are available for purchase from third-party suppliers.

Many directory synchronization programs are much more sophisticated than the LDIFDE examples shown above. To avoid causing replication storms, customers should only have to import the full contents of a foreign directory once; after that, only incremental changes should be synchronized. Directory synchronization utilities must often map namespaces, which vary from environment to environment, during synchronization; for example, Active Directory services might break the *rapport.com* domain up into *rapport.com* and *consulting.rapport.com*, but Lotus Notes or NDS might represent all of *rapport* as *O=rapport*. Directory synchronization utilities must also be flexible and configurable to allow customers to filter or map attributes and objects from one environment to another.

Using LDIFDE for Import/Export

The following are examples of commands that will interchange information between LDIF-formatted files and Active Directory services using the LDIFDE tool:

- **IMPORT:** *ldifde -i -f INPUT.LDF* would import all the changes from the file INPUT.LDF into the current domain namespace, provided it was run from an administrator account with sufficient privileges.
- **EXPORT:** *ldifde -m -f OUTPUT.LDF -s caesar.rapport.com -d "dc=rapport,dc=com" -r "(objectClass=*)"* would access the server *caesar.rapport.com* to export all objects and attributes from the *rapport.com* domain into the file OUTPUT.LDF.

Active Directory technology provides considerable assistance to the developer, not only by offering LDIFDE and ADSI access from Visual Basic and VBScript, but also by implementing a proprietary change notification service as an LDAP extension. Through the change notification service, a program can register with Active Directory services to receive updates whenever a change is made to part of the namespace. This relieves the developer from having to code tedious merge, compare, and update logic. In a future release, Active Directory technology might implement LDAP standards for change notification or replication, as these standards emerge. Directory synchronization will become a much easier process for both customers and developers. In early 1999, Microsoft also published an LDAP-based control (called DirSync) and submitted an informational IETF draft describing the tool.

Developers can also make use of Active Directory services' change notification service for directory synchronization.

Meta-directory Services

Complex enterprise environments will contain a diverse mix of directories. Active Directory services will replace some of these directories, such as the Microsoft Exchange directory. Some directories might migrate to Active Directory services, but must coexist with it during the migration. Others will remain in coexistence with Active Directory services.

On top of this diverse enterprise directory topology, customers must build integrated directory management processes, or meta-directory services, if they wish to improve security, improve the accuracy of data, and reduce the cost of duplicate administration. Meta-directory services are tools and technologies enabling users to deploy a consolidated directory of directories designed expressly to work together with their existing e-mail, NOS, human resources, and other directories through sophisticated multi-master replication and object merging capabilities. Figure 8-8 shows a simplified example of the way a meta-directory can take full advantage of the technology of Active Directory services and other directories.

Figure 8-8 *Meta-directory scenario with Active Directory services.*

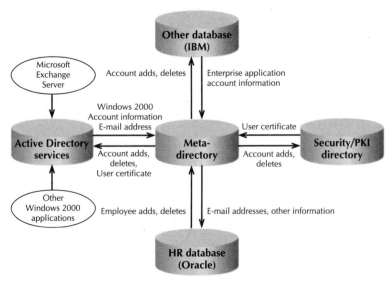

Because the meta-directory supports both multidirectional entry synchronization (join) and attribute-level synchronization between directories, it offers great flexibility. For example, in Figure 8-8, the authoritative source for the e-mail address could be Microsoft Exchange Server; Active Directory services could provide the network logon ID, employee adds and deletes by the human resources department, user certificates by the security system, and enterprise application account information by an IBM database. These attributes, arriving from various authoritative sources, could be automatically synchronized to the others in turn where needed, increasing the wealth of information in all directory repositories without requiring manual effort. The human resources department could also act as the authoritative source for entry existence, so that an employee leaving the company would automatically have his or her accounts deleted from all directory databases.

Meta-directories enable multiple authoritative sources for directory attribute management.

Meta-directories Defined

In 1996, The Burton Group formalized the meta-directory concept, describing a functional specification of join, centralized registration, attribute flow, and other directory services. They also provide a definitive meta-directory Frequently Asked Questions (FAQ) resource at *http:// www.tbg.com/tbghome/metafaq.htm.*

Essentially, meta-directory services consolidate subsets of the information in multiple directories, including data on people, groups, roles, organizational units, locations, and other resources. This consolidation creates a join, or a unified view, of the different directories in an organization. The meta-directory makes that unified view accessible via LDAP and Web-based access protocols. Meta-directory services also manage the relationships between existing directories, allowing data to flow between connected directories in a flexible, but controllable fashion.

Because meta-directories can feed information to Active Directory services, or propagate information from it, they represent a complementary technology.

Customers who want to maximize the role of Active Directory services in their enterprise environment can speed the process using meta-directory technology. Not only can the meta-directory feed heterogeneous directory information to Active Directory services, it can also help integrate Windows 2000 into the overall enterprise environment, enabling Active Directory services migration to occur more rapidly. Some customers will even choose to implement meta-directory services that use Active Directory services as their meta-directory repository. Note that in mid-1999, Microsoft acquired meta-directory vendor ZOOMIT Corporation and its VIA product. Initially, the product is available from Microsoft for limited distribution only. However, customers can also obtain meta-directory services from other vendors, such as Control Data Systems, IBM, ISOCOR, Novell, or Siemens. Microsoft does plan to build elements of the VIA product into a future release of Active Directory services.

Summary

Active Directory tech-nology replicates do-main information and forest configuration information in a site-sensitive manner.

Active Directory technology uses advanced multi-master replication technologies to copy information about users and resources across large domains efficiently, even when domain controllers are located in disparate sites with varying network bandwidth topologies. Active Directory technology replicates across domains to create the Global Catalog for domain trees or domain forests.

Customers must plan replication topologies carefully.

Using the information in this chapter, customers can do more than understand how Active Directory services works, they can also plan for it. After designing a domain namespace, the first step is to gather detailed information about the network topology and plot out the location of Active Directory sites by putting well-connected controllers into the same site or into low-cost site links, and grouping controllers separated by low-speed WANs into high-cost site links. Proper planning of domains, sites, site links, and site link bridges is necessary to optimize replication.

Good development practices can, in turn, ensure that products coexist well with Active Directory services and do not create replication issues for customers. Developers must internalize the notion that replication is pervasive in Active Directory services, and design their products accordingly. Active Directory–enabled programs should deal with latency or multi-master replication–induced states by storing all configuration in a single object where possible, avoiding interrelated properties, and linking complex directory-based data structures into object sets where necessary.

Developers should not create replication issues for customers.

Customers and developers should also plan for heterogeneous directory environments and evaluate directory synchronization tools capable of supporting migration to or coexistence with Active Directory technology. Use LDIF, VBScript, or the future Active Directory Synchronization Manager to deal with the simpler scenarios. Use meta-directory services to cope with complex directory data relationships.

Customers and developers should plan for heterogeneous directory environments.

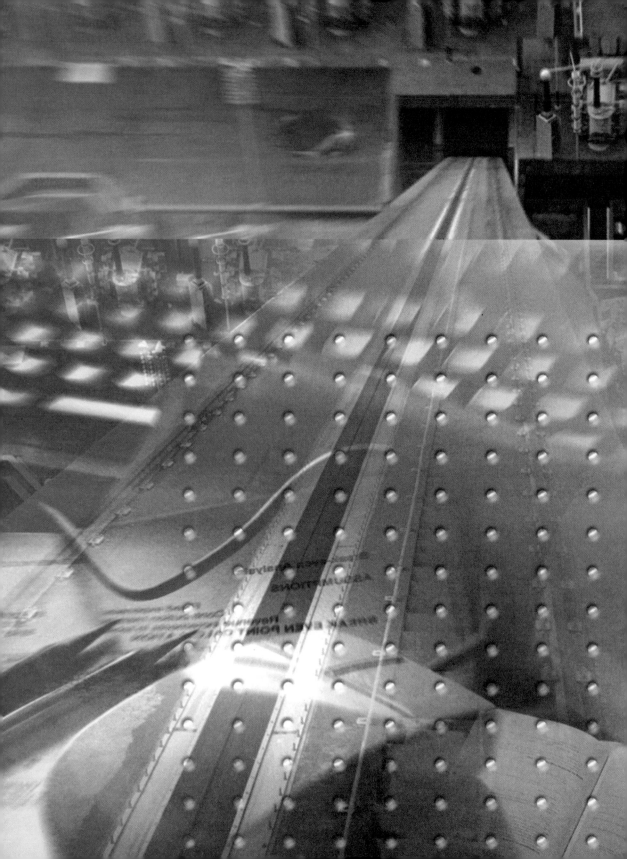

Security Overview: Kerberos, Certificates, and Access Control

Microsoft Active Directory directory services plays a key role in providing the distributed security of Microsoft Windows 2000. It acts as the repository for security account information, security groups, Kerberos credentials, X.509 public key certificates, and security policies. Windows 2000 services are designed to trust the secure operation of Active Directory services, relying on it to store encrypted password information and to exercise appropriate control over changes to security groups, restrictions, credentials, or policies. As Microsoft's White Paper, *Secure Networking Using Microsoft Windows NT 5.0 Distributed Security Services,* puts it: "This fundamental relationship of Security and the Active Directory is achieved only by complete integration of the directory with the Windows NT operating system, and is not otherwise available."

This chapter introduces Windows 2000 security architecture, Kerberos, single sign-on (SSO), public key infrastructure (PKI), access controls, and security administration capabilities. It explains how Windows 2000 and Active Directory services deliver manageability through tight integration of directory and security services, and

Active Directory services is the trusted repository for Windows 2000 distributed security.

how they add considerable flexibility through an array of administration tools and features. It also identifies a number of directory- and security-related administration, performance, and interoperability issues, and offers recommendations for customers and developers.

Overview of Windows 2000 Security Architecture

Customers require more flexible, scalable security infrastructures to deal with complex intranets and external information-sharing requirements.

Since the mid-1990s, sprawling intranets connect entire enterprises. Although the power of a network is equal to the square of the number of interconnected nodes, realizing a network's full potential can happen only with adequate security and manageability. Many intranets have developed in a chaotic manner, exposing and enabling myriad applications, with each application having its own embedded security, directory, and management interfaces. Burgeoning levels of business-to-business commerce add to the difficulty by making boundaries between internal and external information systems blur or disappear. For example, when a large retailer, such as Sears or Kmart, subcontracts catalog ordering to another company, secure workflow processes are necessary to integrate the customer service systems of both organizations. Large entertainment conglomerates, such as Disney or Time-Warner, deal with thousands of partners over the Internet. In each case, information must always be available on-line, must be current, and must have controlled access. Customers require more flexible, scalable security infrastructures to deal with these complex intranets and external information-sharing requirements.

Windows 2000 accommodates customer security management needs by integrating directory services with the operating system.

The Windows 2000 security architecture provides customers with a flexible and scalable security infrastructure through centralized administration of users and groups in the directory, replication of account information, delegation of administrative control, and support of directory and authentication standards. This architecture tightly integrates Windows 2000 with Microsoft desktop applications, development tools, and BackOffice applications, as well as with independent software vendor (ISV) partner applications written specifically for and integrated with Windows 2000.

There is tension within the technology industry concerning the relative importance of interchangeability and integration, such as that found within Windows 2000 and between Windows 2000 and the rest of the Microsoft and ISV product lines. Experts disagree, for example, on whether tight integration between directory and security services is desirable. Customers need to understand that, because of tight integration in Windows 2000, interchangeability of directory and security in Windows 2000 is limited; they cannot fully mix and match Microsoft's Kerberos protocol, Active Directory services, and other directory and security components with equivalent components from other vendors. Some experts believe that security is impossible unless customers lock down the directory through very tight integration. Other experts believe that vendors should dedicate themselves to providing component interchangeability through open standards and protocols, the so-called best-of-breed approach. It is important to acknowledge that these different schools of thought exist, that neither is absolutely right or wrong, and that each offers a set of tradeoffs to customers, who must work to understand their choices.

Experts disagree on how much integration of directory, security, and other services is appropriate.

Windows 2000 implements a distributed security model based on three tenets (Figure 9-1): the trusted domain controller, delegation of trust between services, and object-based access control in the operating system. First, each client in a domain establishes a direct trust path by securely authenticating to its domain controller. The trust path extends to other domain controllers with which interdomain trust relationships exist. Second, clients never get direct access to resources; instead, network services build a client's access token and impersonate the client by using its credentials to carry out requested operations. Third, the Windows operating system kernels use the security identifiers (SIDs) in the access token to verify whether the user (or any groups of which the user is a member) is granted the desired access rights defined by the access control list in the target object.

The Windows 2000 distributed security model is based on trusted domain controller authentication, delegation of trust between services, and object-based access control.

Figure 9-1 *Tenets of trust in Windows 2000.*

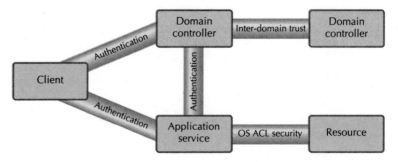

Built-in access control makes some administrators all-powerful, but other users have prescribed permissions.

Default Windows access controls prescribe different access permissions for administrators and users. In Windows 2000, administrators have full control over the operating system. Administrators can perform any and all functions that the operating system supports, and can grant to themselves any right that they do not already possess. Default security settings for users, however, prevent them from compromising the integrity of the operating system and installed applications, from installing applications that can be run by other users, or from viewing other users' private data.

Distributed systems security services and single sign-on (SSO) are primarily based on Kerberos and SSL standards.

Active Directory services provides the store for all domain security policy and account information, ensuring availability through replication to multiple domain controllers. Once a user logs on to a domain controller, he or she has single sign-on access to many Windows 2000 applications and services from Microsoft and independent software vendors. The logon process uses the Kerberos Version 5 authentication protocol, which is a mature Internet security standard for shared secret logon and trusted authentication servers that act as brokers between clients and network services. Each domain controller implements a Kerberos Key Distribution Center (KDC) and supplies clients with the Kerberos tickets they need to use Windows 2000 applications and any other cross-platform network application enabled to use Kerberos Version 5 authentication.

The Kerberos protocol will have an important role in securing intranets.

Through its Security Support Provider Interface (SSPI), Microsoft has made Kerberos support a mandatory certification requirement for vendors wishing to display the Microsoft Windows 2000 logo.

Kerberos has already made some inroads through the Open Software Foundation's Distributed Computing Environment and UNIX infrastructures. It seems likely that, as Windows 2000 deployment widens, applications using the Kerberos protocol will proliferate, and Kerberos will be widely deployed as a security protocol on intranets.

Although the Kerberos protocol is a good approach to security within an intranet, its reliance on a trusted authentication broker between clients and services is not the right model for loosely coupled, mutually suspicious parties in a global e-commerce environment. Microsoft recognizes that public key technology, as embodied in standards such as the Rivest, Shamir and Adelman (RSA) and X.509 Authentication Framework specifications, is more appropriate on the Internet. Windows 2000 bundles a number of public key infrastructure components, including the Microsoft Certificate Server, Secure Sockets Layer (SSL), Internet Key Exchange for Internet Protocol Security (IPSec), secure e-mail, and a Crypto API. These capabilities deliver strong authentication, data integrity, and privacy across public networks.

Public key infrastructure (PKI) support extends distributed systems security to support smart cards, extranets, and e-commerce.

As we saw in Chapter 7, "Planning Namespaces, Domains, and Schema," Active Directory technology supports user, group, and computer account information within a hierarchical namespace. For parts of an enterprise that share a common schema, domain forests or trees can be defined, where each domain is the security boundary of accounts and security policies. Because all domains in a forest trust one another automatically in a transitive way, and because universal groups in the forest's Global Catalog are available to all domains, managing trust relationships, permissions, and interdomain access is much easier than in Windows NT 4.0.

Active Directory services simplifies security administration and uses the hierarchical namespace to structure policy-based management.

Within each domain, customers can organize accounts into different organizational units (OUs). Customers can configure or delegate access controls and group policies defined in the directory through the Group Policy administration tool for each OU. In addition, the Active Directory Users and Computers snap-in provides graphical tools for interactive administration, and ADSI enables batch scripts to automate administration.

Windows 2000 provides supports many protocols, including Kerberos Version 5, NTLM authentication, and SSL/TLS, through SSPI.

The Kerberos protocol is just one of the security protocols that Windows 2000 supports. Others include the public key protocols mentioned previously, and Microsoft Windows NT LAN Manager (NTLM) security. Windows 2000 provides a backward compatible implementation of the NTLM protocols, but NTLM security is not required once a domain has fully upgraded to Windows 2000 and applications are no longer using NTLM.

Log On with Kerberos, Smart Card, and NTLM

Support for multiple authentication protocols lets clients log on and request access to resources in any trusted domain.

As long as they contact a Windows 2000 domain controller in a native mode or mixed mode domain, Windows 2000 or Windows NT Workstation clients using either Kerberos or NTLM authentication protocols can access resources across a domain forest via Windows 2000's transitive trusts. It is even possible for a user to log on with a smart card holding a digital certificate. If, however, the client requests access to resources through a Windows NT 4.0 domain controller in a mixed domain, the client will only have access to resources in domains that are available through existing Windows NT–style one-way explicit trusts. Windows NT 4.0's explicit trusts remain unchanged as a result of the upgrade from Windows NT 4.0 to Windows 2000.

Mastering Kerberos and Single Sign-on[1]

Kerberos enables single sign-on.

As we have seen, Windows 2000's transitive trusts in a domain forest greatly extend the scope of resources that either a Windows 2000 or a Windows NT Workstation client can access after logging on to a mixed- or native-mode Windows 2000 domain. It is the Kerberos protocols that provide this extended reach, referred to as single sign-on.

---

1. Parts of this chapter are derived from *Cryptographic Systems,* a report by Jamie Lewis and Phil Schacter, The Burton Group, February 9, 1999.

Kerberos is the central authentication protocol for Windows 2000. Originally developed by the Massachusetts Institute of Technology for the Project Athena network, Kerberos has undergone several major revisions. In Greek mythology, the three-headed dog, Kerberos, guards the entrance to Hades—the underworld. Like the dog with three heads, the Kerberos protocol involves three parties: a client on the network, at least one service being accessed, and at least one Key Distribution Center that acts as trusted broker arbitrating the client's authentication to services. RFC 1510 describes the current IETF Kerberos Version 5.

Kerberos is an IETF RFC and has become the central authentication and security protocol for Windows 2000.

Kerberos Basics

Using Kerberos, a requesting principal (the client) establishes secure communications with another principal (the service) by first identifying itself to the Kerberos server, as shown in Figure 9-2, steps 1 to 3.

The Key Distribution Center authenticates clients, establishing tickets for secure communication between network nodes.

Figure 9-2 *The Kerberos security protocol in action.*

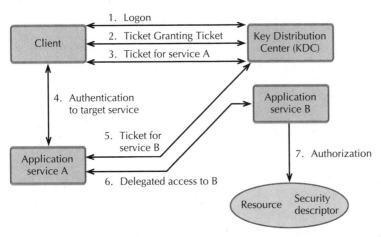

To do this, the client sends its identifier (in the clear) to the Kerberos server. The KDC then initiates authentication by sending the current time stamp encrypted with the master key for that account to prevent password-guessing attacks (step 1).

The KDC authenticates the client.

The KDC issues a Ticket-Granting Ticket, which the client can use to obtain tickets for authentication to other services on the network.

If the Kerberos server recognizes the requesting client, the server and the client also exchange a Ticket-Granting Ticket (TGT) (step 2) consisting of the session key, the requester's name, the expiration time, and other information—all encrypted with the server's private master key. From that point on, the requester must supply this Ticket-Granting Ticket to get a service ticket for any principal with which it wants to establish a secure session (steps 3 and 4). After a configurable time limit (sometimes 24 hours), a TGT expires and must be renewed.

The service trusts the client's service ticket issued by the KDC and communicates securely with the client using a KDC-provided session key.

Having established its identity to the Kerberos server, the client can present a valid Ticket-Granting Ticket and ask for a session with another network principal, which we will call the target. The Kerberos server then generates a new ticket, often called a service ticket, that will authenticate the requesting principal to the target service. The client authenticates to the target service, and client and service communicate securely using a KDC-provided session key. At this point it is up to the target service to decide what access privileges to grant to the client. Note that requests for service tickets for various applications can occur many times during the course of a user's session.

Kerberos Delegation

Sometimes clients ask a service to perform actions that require support from other services.

A Kerberos client sometimes asks a service to perform tasks on its behalf that require the service to set up secure sessions with other network entities. For example, a Kerberos client might access a travel reservation application through its Kerberos credentials. The application might access a travel service, which might in turn access a reservations database service; each service impersonates the client using its credentials to delegate access to the other service without requiring users to reenter passwords.

Delegation allows trusted services to perform tasks on behalf of the user that can involve multiple services as part of the same application.

Kerberos V5 allows clients to delegate ticket-requesting authority to target principals by asking for a separate Ticket-Granting Ticket on behalf of the target. The target service can allow still other network entities to obtain their own Ticket-Granting Tickets on behalf of the original requester, while using their own network layer addresses. Once again, it is up to the downstream target services to decide, as a matter of security policy, whether to grant access to the client using delegated access. Note, however, that delegation is not always enabled; in the Windows 2000 environment, administrators can turn it on or off for individual computer or service accounts, using the Trusted For Delegation account control option. In Figure 9-2, steps 5 and 6 illustrate the role of delegation in a Kerberos environment; access is delegated from service A to service B, a step distinct from earlier logon and authentication and later authorization (step 7).

Kerberos Realms

Attempting to support all users with a single KDC in very large networks can create performance and security problems. In addition, separate organizations might wish to interoperate securely using Kerberos, but separately control administration of accounts in Kerberos databases. To handle these situations, Kerberos allows managers to divide principals into different Kerberos realms, or domains as Windows 2000 refers to them. Assuming two domains have established trust at the KDC level, a principal in one of the domains can obtain tickets usable for accessing resources in the other domain. Administrators can organize domains hierarchically, with designated shortcuts between those that communicate frequently. Users then can use single sign-on capabilities to resources in the various domains.

Kerberos can interoperate securely across multiple administrative realms, or domains, using interdomain trust relationships.

Kerberos clients can access resources in remote domains by obtaining additional TGTs. In Windows 2000, for example, when a client must access a server in a remote domain, it asks the domain controller (DC) in its home domain for a referral ticket, a TGT that it can present to the ticket-granting service at the remote domain's controller. As long as it has a trust relationship with the remote domain, the local domain controller replies by sending the client a TGT encrypted with the remote DC's interdomain key. The client then uses the remote domain's TGT to request service tickets to resources in the remote domain from the remote DC.

Clients can access services in remote domains.

Windows 2000 Distributed Security Implementation

Domain controllers implement the NETLOGON service for domain trust, as well as KDC and Active Directory services.

To provide single sign-on throughout a domain forest, Windows 2000 implements a Kerberos Key Distribution Center, NETLOGON, and Active Directory services on every domain controller. Given sufficient domain controllers in a domain, the vital KDC service (without which no access to network resources can occur) remains available, and the multi-master replication of Active Directory services keeps account information synchronized. The KDC runs as a privileged process along with Active Directory services. Both services manage sensitive information, including passwords for user accounts. Otherwise, the KDC's responsibilities are limited to ticket issuing, whereas Active Directory services handles user, group, and policy management in the directory repository.

The Windows 2000 client implements Kerberos under the SSPI.

Microsoft implements Kerberos in a security provider under the SSPI in Windows 2000 clients and servers. The Kerberos security provider manages the Kerberos protocol exchanges transparently to applications. It caches TGTs and service tickets in its Local Security Authority for speed, going back to the KDC only when necessary.

Dfs, DCOM, RPC, and other services have been Kerberos-enabled in the Windows environment.

The server message block (SMB) client and server underlying the distributed file system (Dfs), Distributed COM (DCOM), LDAP authentication, and Microsoft's authenticated RPC, all use Kerberos automatically for authentication through SSPI. Through these and other methods, functions such as remote file access, file system management and referrals, Internet Information Server (IIS) access, remote computer management, DNS update, print spooling, IPSec, and bandwidth reservation requests are all secured. Through SSPI, it is possible to enable additional applications for Kerberos.

Windows 2000 Trusts

Windows 2000 domains in a forest are Kerberos realms with automatically configured two-way, transitive interdomain trusts.

All Windows 2000 domains in a domain forest have two-way, transitive trusts with all other domains. These trusts are based on interdomain trust accounts, and they enable users to access resources (subject to authorization) in multiple domains. In addition, customers can create explicit, non-transitive trust relationships between Windows 2000 domains, such as between the roots of two forests or a domain in one forest to a domain in a different forest. One-way, non-transitive trust relationships apply between Windows 2000 domains and Windows NT 4.0 domains. Trust relationships between domains do not determine the authentication protocol used between clients and servers. After establishing a trust relationship, application clients and servers can use either Kerberos or NTLM authentication.

Windows 2000 Access Control and Authorization

Once a client logs on and authenticates itself to network or application services, authorization and access control processes govern what it has permission to do. The Kerberos ticket contains the client's authorization data. The authorization data identifies the user's SID and group membership SIDs. The Kerberos Security Support Provider (SSP) protocol and the Local Security Authority (LSA) use authorization data to create the security access token that represents the client for impersonation by the service. Group memberships reflect roles the user has, for example, schema administrator, and these roles or groups determine whether a user may access a particular resource.

The authorization data in the client's service ticket contains its SID and group membership SIDs.

Figure 9-3 displays access control and authorization in the Windows 2000 environment. First the user requests access to a resource. The service calls the appropriate API to impersonate the client and then requests access to open a handle to a resource, such as a local file. The operating system uses the client impersonation token that was created during Kerberos authentication and obtains the resource's object security descriptor from a private store, such as the file system. The operating system then performs an access check to see whether one or more of the SIDs in the client's security token has the desired access rights in the resource's security descriptor, and returns a positive or negative response.

The operating system compares the SIDs in the user's access token with those in the target object's security descriptor to grant or deny access.

Figure 9-3 *The access control process at the operating system level.*

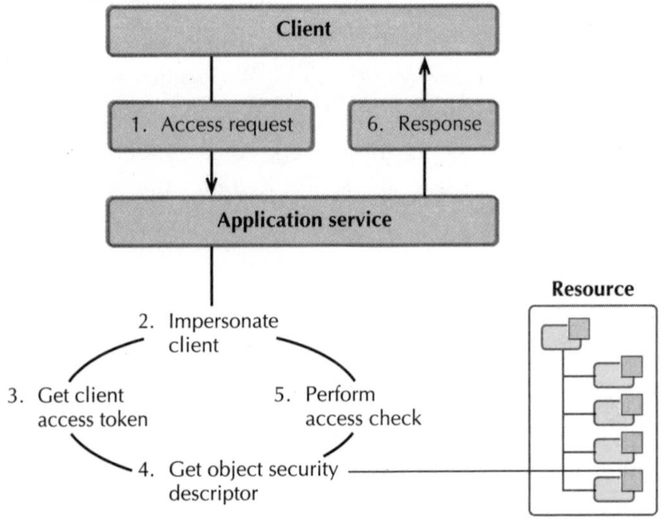

Cross-Platform Single Sign-on Support

Cross-domain trusts and third-party KDCs could enable single sign-on across Windows and UNIX.

One of the benefits of the Windows 2000 distributed security Kerberos implementation is a potential for cross-platform security interoperability with UNIX or other systems that provide Kerberos. Windows 2000 can interoperate with MIT Kerberos-based KDCs either by configuring the Windows client to log on to Windows using an account defined in the UNIX KDC or by using cross-domain trusts, enabling access to both environments.

Customers can set up clients to log on to both Windows and UNIX environments, as long as delegation is not required.

Any Windows or UNIX application that does not require impersonation can use a UNIX KDC as the Kerberos server. For example, a database application server with its own database authorization table could use name-based authentication to authenticate Windows clients and could provide session encryption using Kerberos tickets that a UNIX KDC has issued. However, lacking the Windows 2000 authorization data in the cross-platform mode of operation, the application server cannot impersonate the client and use the Windows 2000 access-control model.

Customers can also configure cross-domain trusts between a UNIX Kerberos domain and a Windows 2000 domain to enable a client or service in an originating domain to be authenticated to a server in another domain. However, authentication is only half the battle. The server in the destination domain must also authorize the client or service in the originating domain to access the requested resource in the destination domain. But complicating such interoperability is the fact that multivendor Kerberos environments have separate directory services and special means of expressing user authorization information. For example, in Windows 2000, the Kerberos service tickets carry user and group SIDs in the authorization data. But UNIX-based Kerberos implementations use other parameters. Mapping and propagating the directory entries, trusts, and permissions to make cross-platform Kerberos work currently requires specialized third-party products from vendors, such as Cybersafe.

Single sign-on to Windows and UNIX with delegation might be possible using cross-domain trust and third-party mapping software.

Marrying Kerberos and PKI Through the PKINIT Protocol

For customers who use public key security for authentication, the IETF is developing the PKINIT protocol, an emerging standard that integrates public key certificates with initial authentication with Kerberos. PKINIT allows clients to authenticate to a KDC using their X.509 certificate. The KDC verifies that the certificate is valid and that a trusted CA has issued it. The certificate contains a subject name that identifies the user in Active Directory services. The KDC locates the subject that the certificate identifies, and generates a TGT for the client. From that point onward, the client uses Kerberos authentication to get around on the network, with only the initial authentication process using public key security. This mapping of PKI to Kerberos makes possible the use of consistent authentication systems for both internal enterprise users and external partners. PKI would allow partners or contractors on a project, for example, to access a group account with limited privileges.

The PKINIT protocol allows public key users without an individual Kerberos account to use Kerberos services.

Certificate name mapping to Windows accounts is available in Active Directory services and in IIS.

Administrators can then define a one-to-one or many-to-one certificate-to-account mapping through the directory using the Name Mappings option in the Advanced Features Context menu on a container that appears in the Active Directory Users and Computers snap-in. Customers then can use these name mappings in IIS or other applications supporting public key authentication. It is also possible to set name mappings directly in IIS.

Security Support Provider Interface (SSPI)

SSPI hides complexity and ensures consistent security.

The Security Support Provider Interface (SSPI) is a Win32 API that applications and system services (such as Microsoft Internet Explorer and IIS) use to hide the complexity of security protocols that facilitate network authentication from applications, and to ensure consistent security in the Windows environment.

SSPI enables multiple security protocols.

SSPI also enables multiple security or authentication protocols, including Kerberos, NTLM, and SSL/TLS. Security providers use different credentials to authenticate the user, either public key certificates with TLS or PKINIT, or shared-secret credentials with Kerberos and NTLM. The security protocols interact with various authentication services and account information stores. Figure 9-4 displays the use of SSPI to enable multiple applications and multiple security protocols.

Figure 9-4 *SSPI links application protocols to security protocols.*

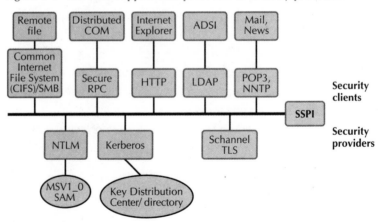

The NTLM security provider uses the MSV1_0 authentication service and the NETLOGON service on a domain controller for client authentication and authorization information. The Kerberos security provider uses a Key Distribution Center (KDC) for authentication service and Active Directory services as an account store. Secure channel services do not require an online authentication server because they use public key certificates issued by trusted certificate authorities. As we noted previously, SSPI is a mandatory component for product certification in the Windows 2000 logo program.

SSPI supports NTLM, Kerberos, and SSL/TLS protocols and authentication services.

Mastering Public Key Security

Public key encryption is the term for a symmetric style of encryption that issues two cryptographic keys to each user: a private key that is always kept secret, and a public key to be made freely available. With a user or application entity's public key, it becomes theoretically possible to provide security services—such as confidentiality, authentication, and integrity—to anyone, anywhere on the Internet, without the need for key management infrastructures or pre-existing accounts, through protocols such as Secure MIME (S/MIME) or TLS.

Public key cryptography could eventually provide security to anyone, anywhere on the Internet.

Public Key Basics

The public and private key pair are mathematically related. When an application encrypts data using one key, another application can decrypt the data only by using the other key. The mathematical complexity of the relationship between the public key and the private key ensures that it is virtually impossible to derive the value of the private key by looking at the public key, provided that the keys are long enough. The public key user generally retains a single copy of the private key in a software cryptographic module or on a smart card.

The public and private keys are mathematically related; one decrypts what the other encrypts.

If a sender uses the recipient's public key to encrypt data, only the recipient, who possesses the matching private key, can decrypt the message. Conversely, the sender can sign data using his or her private key, and anyone can verify the signature using the sender's public key. A successful signature verification authenticates the sender, because only a party in possession of the corresponding private key could have sent the message. This use of public key cryptography is known as the digital signature.

Encrypting with a recipient's public key enables delivery of confidential information, whereas encrypting with the private key authenticates the sender.

Using Public Keys for Encryption and Key Exchange

Public keys, generated by algorithms such as Rivest, Shamir, and Adelman (RSA) or Diffie-Hellman, come in sizes of 512, 1024, or 2048 bits. These keys are much longer than the 56, 128, or other bit lengths used for symmetric algorithms like the Data Encryption Standard (DES), or even Triple DES. Public key encryption therefore incurs a performance penalty. For this reason, cryptographic protocols like S/MIME and TLS typically combine public key and secret key technologies when encrypting large bulk data. This works in the following way. First, the cryptographic system renders a plaintext document confidential by generating a random secret key and encrypting it with a symmetric key algorithm (such as DES). It then in turn encrypts the randomly generated symmetric key with a recipient's public key, and conveys both the encrypted key and the encrypted document to the recipient, who uses its private key to decrypt the secret key and the secret key to decrypt the document. In this way, cryptographic systems take advantage of the asymmetric cryptography's inherent key management strengths, but retain symmetric cryptography's efficient performance.

Cryptographic protocols typically combine public key and secret key technologies when encrypting large amounts of data.

Digital Signatures

A *digital signature* is an encrypted digest[2] of a message or document created with the sender's private key. There is no confidentiality, since the message itself is not encrypted and everyone has access

Digital signatures use message digests encrypted with a private key to provide authentication and integrity services.

---

2. A message digest is a short, fixed-length digital string derived in a one-way fashion from a longer, variable-length message. The most common message digest standards are MD2, MD5, and Secure Hash Algorithm 1 (SHA-1). New systems should use SHA-1 for improved security.

to the sender's public key to decrypt the digest. Since only the sender's public key can decrypt the signature, the sender's private key must have encrypted it, and only the sender knows its private key. Thus, no one but that particular sender could have generated the digest representing the message in question. Also, the recipient can regenerate the digest against the message contents and compare it with the digest in the digital signature to prove the integrity of the message.

Public Key Management

Public key systems do not have the same key distribution problems that secret key systems have, because the users and services need only publish their public keys. There is no secret to convey to other parties. However, key management is still a serious problem with public key systems. Just because someone sees a published assertion that a certain public key is associated with a particular user does not necessarily make it so. An intruder could have published that key, pretending to be someone else. There must be a strong, verifiable link between the identity of a user or system and its public key. With public key technology, a trusted third party, the certification authority, provides this link by declaring which public keys belong to which users or services.

Public keys must have tight links to the identity of a user.

The certification authority (CA) creates a certificate (a plaintext data structure that lists the user's name, public key, and perhaps other identifying information), and then signs the certificate with its own private key and posts it in a publicly accessible place. To obtain a certified public key for a given party, users and services in general are free to use the certificate. Certificates are typically valid for a specified period of time, after which they expire unless the authenticated user renews them. In addition, a CA may revoke a certificate if it has been compromised. In either case, the CA is responsible for publishing certificate revocation lists (CRLs) on a timely basis, and anyone seeking to determine the authenticity of a published public key must check these lists. Managing expired keys and maintaining these lists are the most difficult tasks of public key cryptography. Figure 9-5 shows a certificate as it appears

Certification authorities create certificates to establish trust in users' public keys.

in the Windows user interface. Note that the Windows 2000 Encrypting File System (EFS) issued this certificate and restricted it for use with file recovery. It has a one-year validity period and a 512 bit public key.

Figure 9-5 *A certificate in Windows.*

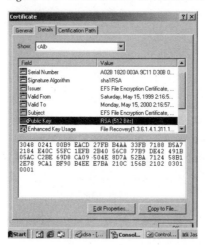

Hierarchical CA topologies, certificate trust lists, or cross certificates can establish trust in a CA's key.

Many organizations, such as banks, government agencies, ISPs, service bureaus, and private enterprises, operate or will operate CAs issuing certificates for internal or external use. The question remains whether a given CA's public key is actually valid, and whether the CA itself should be trusted. In general, organizations or communities of interest deploy a higher-level CA that publishes the public keys of lower-level CAs and protects them with its private key. This arrangement can extend throughout an indefinite number of levels in a hierarchy of authorities. Users subscribing to any CA in the hierarchy can trust certificates signed by any other CA in the hierarchy. A second approach, called *certificate trust lists* (CTLs), distributes the public keys of trusted CAs directly to network users and services. Yet another approach, called *cross certification*, involves two non-hierarchical CAs declaring mutual trust by signing each other's certificates to create cross certificates.

Public Key Infrastructure (PKI) Scenario

Now that we have covered the basics, we will briefly review the components of a PKI environment. The process begins, for example, with the user of a PKI-enabled product, such as Microsoft Outlook or Netscape Communicator, invoking PKI functionality for the first time by clicking a button in the user interface to digitally sign a document. As shown in Figure 9-6, this causes the client to enroll with a CA either directly or indirectly through an intermediate Registration Authority that validates the user's identity before authorizing a certificate. To enroll, the client software usually generates a public and private key pair and sends the public key along with the certification request to the CA via the IETF's Certificate Management Protocol (CMP), or via PKCS #10 formatted files conveyed through e-mail or Web-based upload and download. The enrollment software interacts with users, often asking them to sign a Certificate Practice Statement agreement.

New PKI users must enroll with a CA to obtain a certificate.

When a the client enrolls, the CA takes the following steps, as shown in Figure 9-6.

CAs publish the certificate in a directory for pickup by applications.

1. The client enrolls with the CA for a certificate.
2. The CA issues the certificate using the client's public key and provides the certificate to the client.
3. The CA publishes the certificate in a repository, such as an LDAP directory, from where a copy can be retrieved by applications or users to verify a digital signature or encrypt information; the CA also maintains revocation lists in the repository.
3a. The CA can, if directed by policy, push CRL information to clients.
4. Applications use the certificate and CRL information in the repository.

Figure 9-6 *A public key infrastructure scenario.*

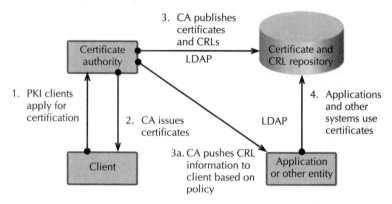

Microsoft PKI

Microsoft certificate services provide Microsoft's PKI.

Microsoft provides PKI capabilities with Windows 2000. A key element in the PKI is Microsoft certificate services, which enable customers to deploy enterprise CAs for issuing and revoking certificates. Certificate services are integrated with Active Directory services; the latter acts as the repository for CA location information, CA policy, certificates, and CRLs. Figure 9-7 diagrams the components of the Microsoft PKI, including PKI clients, certificate services, domain logon, Active Directory services, and domain administration. These logical components might physically reside on different machines, or they might be on one machine.

PKI enables a plethora of applications.

PKI applications Using certificate services and the Active Directory Domains And Trusts snap-in, customers can define their own CA, enabling PKI for a variety of applications, including:

- **Secure web access:** SSL/TLS, or secure channel, is available for server authentication, client authentication, and encryption. Customers can also map a user's certificate to an account. In the future, many new applications, such as databases and client/server systems, will also enable PKI-based single sign-on.

- **Secure MIME (S/MIME):** Products (such as Lotus Notes, Microsoft Exchange Server, and Microsoft Netscape Messenger) are beginning to provide secure e-mail interoperability based on S/MIME V2, migrating to S/MIME V3 for increased functionality. Exchange Server makes use of certificate services, but also requires its own key server to enable more advanced robust functionality than that currently available with certificate services. Such functions in Exchange Server include key histories (which allow the client to transparently decrypt a message encrypted with an expired but saved key) and key recovery (which allows a client to reclaim an encryption key after a disk failure).

- **Code Signing:** Code signing is important in enabling customers to verify both the publishers of the content and the content integrity at download time. Microsoft's Authenticode uses Crypto API and certificate services. Code signing is now required for many DLLs and drivers in the Windows environment.

- **Encrypting File System (EFS):** EFS supports transparent encryption and decryption of files stored in the Windows NT file system (NTFS). Each EFS user obtains a self-signed key pair and a certificate.

- **IP Security (IPSec) support:** The IETF has standardized IP security to provide a secure, interoperable standard for virtual private networks (VPNs). IPSec is gradually replacing proprietary VPN technologies like Microsoft's PPTP. For wide-scale deployment, IPSec uses a public key–based Internet Key Exchange (IKE) specification.

Figure 9-7 *Microsoft's public key infrastructure.*

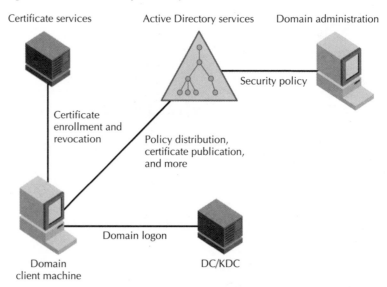

Certificate services   Active Directory services   Domain administration

Security policy

Certificate
enrollment and
revocation

Policy distribution,
certificate publication,
and more

Domain logon

Domain
client machine

DC/KDC

Microsoft supports hierarchical CA topologies and certificate trust lists.

Setting up certification authorities   Windows 2000 assumes a hierarchical CA topology to provide users or administrators with flexibility in determining which external certification authority roots (such as Verisign, Thawte, GTE Cybertrust) to trust. Because of X.509 certificate and CRL format support, a Windows CA can join a certificate hierarchy consisting of Microsoft CAs or CAs from other vendors. However, Windows does not support cross-certification; it uses certificate trust lists (CTLs) under the control of administrators or users.

Certificate services can be set up as a root or subordinate CA for internal or external use.

Administrators can set up the certificate services as an enterprise root CA, enterprise subordinate CA, stand-alone root CA, or stand-alone subordinate CA. Administrators should use enterprise CAs to issue certificates to users inside the enterprise, and should use stand-alone CAs to issue certificates to external (commercial) users. In either case, the administrator can join a hierarchy as a subordinate or become the root of a new hierarchy. Installation generates a self-signed CA certificate, using the CA's public/private key pair, or for a child CA, a certificate request to an intermediate or root CA. Windows supplies default policy modules

(Registration Authority software for user identity checking and other validation functions) for the four modes of CA configuration. Administrators can modify the policy or substitute different policy modules using the Certificates snap-in. Once set up, a CA cannot be renamed, although it is fairly easy to add or delete issuing CAs under a given root or to merge existing CA hierarchies by issuing a certificate from one of the root CAs certifying the other root as an intermediate CA.

Group Policy and Microsoft PKI   Certificate management is integrated with the Group Policy Object (GPO) that we discussed in Chapter 7, "Planning Namespaces, Domains, and Schema." Public key policies in the GPO can operate on a site, domain, OU, computer, or user basis to govern automated certificate enrollment of certificate types and templates for users and computers; CTLs for trusted enterprise CAs and Internet root CAs[3]; and a recovery agent holding backup copies of private keys used for encrypting file system data recovery.

> Certificate management integrates with the Group Policy Object and can operate at multiple levels.

Enrollment   Certificate services implements user certificate enrollment using a Web enrollment page on the same computer as the certificate service. This requires authentication for an enterprise CA and selection of a valid user template specifying certificate elements, such as naming, validity period, allowable cryptographic service providers (CSPs) for private key generation, algorithms, and certificate extensions. Windows PKI transfers keys and certificates between the client and service using PKCS #10 certificate request messages and PKCS #7 responses containing the resulting certificate or certificate chain. Users can also pick up CA root keys and CRLs through the enrollment Web page on the server. MCS also supports automatic enrollment of computer certificates for IPSec, which means that an administrator can configure this function through the Domain Policy object in Active Directory services.

> Certificate services provides automated policy-based enrollment for users and computers.

---

3. If a Windows client encounters a certificate that is not in its local CTL or in the GPO's CTL, it will generate an error message.

Crypto API

Cryptographic operations in Microsoft's PKI-based services, such as certificate services, Authenticode, IPSec, and Secure Channel, are enabled through Microsoft Cryptographic API (CAPI, or Crypto API), which runs on Microsoft Windows 95, Windows 98, and Windows 2000 workstations or servers. CAPI makes it possible for programs to obtain cryptographic and digital certificate services. Third-party applications can also use CAPI. Among CAPI's many sensitive functions is storage of private keys on a running computer; the U.S. National Institute of Standards and Technology (NIST) is currently evaluating Microsoft's CAI Cryptographic Service Provider (CSP) for certification as a Federal Information Processing Standard 140-1 compliant cryptographic engine.

As with ADSI and SSPI, Microsoft sandwiches CAPI in such a way that it contains both client and provider interfaces, allowing developers the flexibility to change underlying cryptographic logic while customers can add the applications without affecting one another. Microsoft ships a Base DSS and Diffie-Hellman Cryptographic Provider, but third-party vendors can also develop and market CSP plug-in modules with additional cryptographic services. CSPs might be software based or take advantage of cryptographic hardware devices, and can support a variety of algorithms and key strengths. Developers can use CSPs to customize selected pieces of the cryptographic puzzle; for example, a smart card CSP could use an existing CSP (such as the Microsoft Base Provider) to perform public and symmetric key operations, and would use the smart card itself to perform private key operations.

Mastering Access Control

Active Directory services is secured not only through Kerberos and PKI, but also through a comprehensive access control model that protects directory information and enables customers to delegate administration by organizational unit within a domain. This section discusses administrative delegation, access control models, administration tools, and programming practices.

Delegation of Administration

Delegation of administration enables customers to compartmentalize the security administration required within a domain. Customers can grant one set of administrators the right to manage a small set of users or groups within their area of responsibility but not in other parts of the organization. This provides support groups with local autonomy within the enterprise or allows external partners to administer accounts granting their users access to part of the enterprise network.

Customers can delegate administrative responsibility at the organizational unit or container level. To delegate, domain administrators select the Delegate Control option on the context menu of the container or organizational unit; this activates the Delegation of Control Wizard. From there, domain administrators delegate permissions to change properties on the container itself, to create and delete child objects within the container, or to update specific properties or child objects within a container. First, the domain administrator selects the delegate, then optionally the types of child objects (such as users, groups, or computers) that the delegate will administer, and finally assigns permissions on properties belonging to those objects. Figure 9-8 illustrates part of the Delegation of Control Wizard process.

Delegation allows customers to compartmentalize administrative functions.

Domain administrators can delegate administration at the OU or container level.

Figure 9-8 *The Delegation of Control Wizard.*

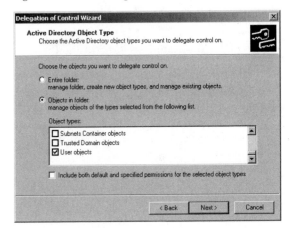

Access Control Models

The Active Directory
services access control
model derives from
Windows 2000 object-
based authorization.

Access control enables delegation and other features. The Active Directory access control model is similar to, and integrated with, the general Windows 2000 authorization model. In this model, Active Directory services checks the user's access token and required permissions to perform the requested operation against a security descriptor attached to the requested directory object. Based on the access check, Active Directory services grants or denies access.

A discretionary access
control list (DACL)
enables administrators to
set permissions at the
object and attribute level
for various users
and groups.

Each security descriptor contains a discretionary access control list (DACL) and a system access control list (SACL). The DACL is a set of access control entries (ACEs), each having a security identifier (SID) representing the *security principal* (user, group, or computer) to whom the ACE applies, and permissions that allow or deny users and groups rights to particular actions. An example of a permission attached to an object is the Read permission on the Telephone Number attribute. The DACL determines who can see the object and what actions they can perform on the object. The operating system never reveals the existence of an object to any user who is not represented in the ACL.

ACLs implement a secu-
rity policy governing
who can do what to
whom.

In effect, DACLs define a security policy for either a single protected entry or for an entire portion (or subtree) of the directory. For example, the security policy of the Rapport Communication company might be that by default no one can read or write to the Rapport directory. However, members of a group called Rapport administrators receive special dispensation to write to the directory, members of a Rapport employees group can read the directory, and members of the Rapport contractors group can also read the directory.

Authentication enables
access control by verify-
ing accessor identity.

To apply the ACLs, the directory needs some way to ascertain the identity of the accessor. Hence, almost all directory services provide a means to authenticate accessors through the submission of credentials. If the accessor submits no credentials, Active Directory services considers the accessor anonymous and affords him or her the lowest common denominator of privilege. Accessors can raise their privilege level by authenticating themselves with stronger credentials.

The system access control list (SACL) allows an administrator to audit users' access to objects and to view these security-related events through the security log in the Windows 2000 Event Viewer. The SACL specifies the group or user accounts to audit when accessing an object, the access events to audit, and a success or failure attribute for each access event. Active Directory SACLs can instruct the operating system to audit any read or write action against any attribute of an object, or any read or write action against individual attributes.

SACLs enable auditing of directory operations.

Types of Active Directory Services Permissions

- Create Child
- Delete Child
- Read Property
- Write Property
- List Contents
- Write Self
- Delete Tree
- List Object
- Control Access

Create Child or Delete Child can be specific to the type of object or general for any object under the container.

Read Property or Write Property can be specific to an individual property of the object or general for all attributes of the object.

Control Access can be specific to an individual control operation or general for all control operations on the object.

Extended rights provide
custom access controls.

As we discussed earlier, the access control in Active Directory services determines who can perform which operations on an object. The two major types of permissions are container operations and property-based operations. Active Directory services also provides an administrator with access control over custom operations that have no associations with container- or property-based operations. For example, a user class can be granted a Send As right, which an e-mail program can use to determine whether a particular user can send e-mail on behalf of another user. Access controls over these kinds of custom operations are called *extended rights*, and they are stored as access rights in the Extended Rights container within the Configuration container for a domain forest.

Inheritance of Access Rights

Access controls are
inherited from
containers.

Within an Active Directory domain, child objects inherit the ACEs from superior objects, such as Organizational Units, Containers, or the Domain object itself. Object inheritance propagates the ACEs assigned to an object or any of its properties to all children of this object within the domain. For example, a domain administrator can delegate departmental administration by enabling ACEs that grant Create Child and Delete Child rights at the OU level.

Inheritance is flexible
because it is object-
specific, and
administrators can turn it
off for a given child.

Although by default all Active Directory objects inherit from parent objects, domain administrators can choose to turn off inheritance for a given object. Inheritance is also object-specific because any given ACE applies only to a specific type of object or attribute. For example, an administrator can delegate control of users in an OU to a departmental administrator but leave other types of objects, such as groups or computers, under the control of the domain administrator. In sum, inherited access controls at the object, attribute, or extended rights levels provide enterprises with important tools for implementing top-down security policy.

Active Directory services
uses static access
controls.

Windows 2000 implements a static form of access rights inheritance referred to as *Create Time* inheritance. This means that, unless customers turn off access control inheritance, access control information defined for a container flows down to the child objects in the container, where it is copied or merges with access rights already stored in the new object. Any future changes to inherited access rights at higher levels in the tree propagate down to all affected child objects.

Operating systems are designed to optimize access control verification because it occurs frequently. Static access controls yield good performance because, at the time of an operation, all the information necessary for an access check is already there. However, changes to inherited ACLs of domains, containers, or OU entries with many children is CPU and IO intensive, because Active Directory services propagates static access controls. To avoid problems, customers should invest some planning time up-front so that access controls, once created, change infrequently.

Static access controls yield better lookup performance than dynamic access controls, but they have some disadvantages.

Access Control Administration

Administrators can manage access controls on an object and its children using the Active Directory Users And Computers snap-in. With advanced features enabled, an administrator with sufficient privileges will see a Security tab on the object's property sheet. After selecting the security tab, the administrator will see the security descriptor for the object, as shown in Figure 9-9.

Administrators manage access controls using the Active Directory Users And Computers snap-in.

The access control administration screen is divided into two windows (Figure 9-9). The upper window contains the list of ACEs, and the lower window contains the privileges for the selected ACE. The selected ACE displays the name of the user or group to which it applies. By default, when a new object is created, Active Directory services builds ACEs for the domain security groups (such as Administrators), for groups with delegated access (such as consulting admin), and for special categories of users such as Self, Authenticated Users, and Everyone (anonymous users).[4] An

Active Directory services sets up a number of ACEs by default when an object is created, but administrators can change the settings.

---

4. The default privileges for most ACEs derive from the object class definition and can be changed using the Active Directory Schema snap-in.

authorized administrator can add new ACEs, remove ACEs, or change permissions in an ACE of an individual entry. Finally, the security property sheet allows enabling/disabling access control inheritance for an entry, and an advanced view that displays granular permissions for every property of the object.

Figure 9-9   *Administration of access control.*

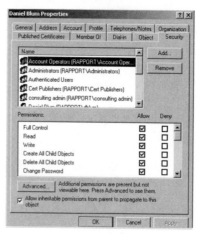

Access Control and the Developer

Developers need to provide users and administrators with control over security aspects of their applications.

Developers need to ensure that their applications take security into account. For example, if a service accesses the directory, it should impersonate each client in a separate Bind operation when binding on the client's behalf. If an application uses group-based access control, it should allow the administrator to reset the group members. If it becomes necessary to add new object classes to the directory, be sure to define sensible default security descriptors on the new classes. In other words, a program should equip its users and managers to deal with security; they will quickly get lost if they have to manipulate application security settings separately from the application's own interface.

Developers should code defensively to avoid install-time privilege problems and run-time access control errors.

Because Active Directory services uses the same access control model as other Windows resource managers, such as the file system and the registry, a directory application can use either the Win32 Security API or the ADSI access control objects to read, modify, and create security descriptors on directory objects. But access control can affect programs in subtle ways, and the programming is complex. For example, Active Directory services might return lookup errors even when the target object exists, if a service does not have access to read attributes on the object. Property modification, object creation, or object deletion fails if a program lacks privileges. Developers should run with the minimum privilege required (in the context of a service account, or using the logged-on user's credentials) and separate installation operations into phases, such as domain container changes and configuration container changes, to give the administrator a chance to change to the correct account. Also, programmers should be cautious about batching Write or Create operations.

It is usually a good idea to use security groups to define and delegate administrative roles associated with an application server or to identify the users and computers that are granted access to the service's objects in the directory. However, developers should minimize the number of groups required to avoid unnecessarily adding SIDs to users' access tokens (thereby slowing logon). Programs should refer to the group by its GUID to make it move- or rename-safe. In some cases, developers can program extended rights in lieu of group-based access control.

Minimize the number of security groups.

Best Practices

By following best practices in Active Directory directory services and Windows 2000 distributed security deployment, customers can build a flexible but secure enterprise NOS infrastructure. These best practices involve a combination of people, process, and technology recommendations.

Security best practices are a set of guidelines for people, process, and technology deployment and use.

The domain controller is the key to Windows 2000, but with Kerberos in a large network, a single domain controller can become a single point of failure and a performance bottleneck. If the domain controller goes down, no one can obtain tickets for secure sessions. If the network design funnels all ticket requests

It is vital to replicate and physically protect domain controllers.

into a single domain controller, response time could be unacceptably slow. In addition, users who must connect to the server through slow wide-area links experience inconvenient delays. To meet these difficulties, deploy multiple domain controllers, any of which can authenticate users and establish secure sessions. Each domain controller must also be physically protected, that is, kept in a locked room on secure premises.

Administrator privileges must be carefully guarded.

The administrator has great powers on a Windows 2000 system. Any user in possession of the password to the administrator account has or can configure full privileges on the domain controller. Customers should jealously protect access to the administrator account and the domain controller through network, computer, and personnel security measures.

Institute procedures for network security, computer security, and personnel security.

Network security means shutting down those services, or ports, on the domain controller that are not needed. When possible, deploy applications on member workstations or servers rather than on the domain controller; those applications that must run on the domain controller should run as service accounts.

Computer security means setting strong password policies (requiring lengthy, cryptic passwords that cannot be reused) and locking down accounts after invalid logon attempts. To simplify configuration and close any loopholes, use the Microsoft Security Configuration Editor to set an entire domain controller to run in a high secure mode.[5]

Delegate administration using the principle of least privilege and provide thorough training.

Enterprises must also enforce personnel security. The administrators group should be kept quite small by limiting membership and delegating routine administrative duties to less-privileged users. Follow the principle of least privilege when delegating, giving second-tier administrators only the privileges they need to perform well-defined functions. The domain administrators that remain

---

5. Setting high secure mode will break some applications. Customers must test this capability with their key applications, possibly reserving it for use in their most sensitive domains, such as a banking system. Developers should test their applications to make sure they work in high secure mode.

should be trusted personnel who have been through background checks and have thorough training in secure administration procedures, such as normally logging on with a less-privileged account and using the *run as* command to perform sensitive operations in the administrator context.

Like domain controllers with their KDC components, the machines that host CAs must be physically protected. One recommendation is that large enterprises create a Root CA, generate subordinate CAs, and take the Root CA offline to protect it completely. The CA private key that signs the enterprise's user, computer, or subordinate CA certificates should be protected, ideally by the use of cryptographic hardware. Back up each CA periodically to avoid serious administrative and security problems attending its potential loss. Thoroughly plan the PKI ahead of time; once a Root CA has been established and certificates have been issued, changing anything becomes increasingly difficult.

Thoroughly plan the enterprise's PKI ahead of time, and protect the machines hosting the public key certification authority function.

Vendors such as Entrust Software Technologies, Baltimore Technologies, Xcert, or GTE Cybertrust offer features such as the following: the ability to PKI-enable existing or legacy applications; provide dual key support for encryption and signing; support key histories for decryption or validation of old documents; recover an encryption key after the user loses a password or a hard drive; use multi-tiered Registration Authority support; and centrally generate public/private key pairs. Customers who require some or all of those features might want to consider best-of-breed PKI products. Also, an enterprise might become part of an e-commerce community of interest, which dictates or encourages use of a common outsourced certification authority such as Verisign or Thawte. However, the certificate services PKI from Microsoft is more tightly integrated with Windows 2000 than that of other vendors. Adding a third-party CA might bring additional functionality only at the expense of integration if an enterprise loses Microsoft certificate services strengths, such as automatic enrollment of computers in Microsoft's PKI. Although it is a good idea to consider third-party PKI products, investigate integration issues with the

There are various feature-rich PKI products on the market.

vendors. For example, at press time one startup vendor, called Elock, used a Cryptographic Service Provider (CSP) to add functionality to Microsoft certificate services, rather than trying to replace them.

Use high-strength encryption wherever possible.

Encryption in Kerberos or PKI is only as strong as the length of the keys customers choose, but large, international enterprises often have difficulty deploying strong encryption using products from United States vendors, such as Microsoft, due to United States export restrictions.[6] Another complicating consideration is that while longer key lengths are more secure, they can slow performance. If an enterprise has sensitive applications or networks, one possibility is to get the strong encryption release from Microsoft and augment the enterprise's computers with hardware accelerators, depending on performance requirements. Another choice is to use faster, export-level encryption and deploy stronger encryption just for a sensitive application. If strong encryption is necessary for a multinational corporation with headquarters in the United States, customers will need to use or obtain a government license to export strong cryptography to foreign offices and subsidiaries. An enterprise with headquarters outside the United States should consider using unrestricted PKI from international vendors, third-party PKI, and application products from international vendors, especially those that can layer strong encryption on top of the Windows 2000 infrastructure.

Security depends on mature implementations.

Real security is more than a matter of technical features or even key lengths. The most difficult issue is making sure that products using cryptographic systems do not contain implementation flaws that make the system ineffective, no matter what algorithm they use. Such product design flaws can undermine the best algo-

---

6. As of 1999, it appears that due to successful RSA Challenge attacks, 40-bit RC4 and 56-bit DES have reached the end of their usable life. For many applications, Triple DES is taking the place of DES or RC4, and is virtually unbreakable in the foreseeable future. In the longer term, the U.S. government will select a new generation Advanced Encryption Standard (AES) to replace DES by 2001. Also, for sensitive applications, RSA public key lengths of 768 bits or higher are now advised.

rithms using fully adequate keys, as many fault analysis attacks have shown in the past. For this reason, it is useful to wait out the inevitable 6- to 12-month cycle of real-world testing, bug fixes, and enhancements before deploying highly sensitive applications on a new platform.

Real security is a matter of developing appropriate security policies and then living by those policies. Customers should have an up-to-date security policy that incorporates the best practices described in this chapter, as well as other practices appropriate to their business environment. This security policy should define rules of the road for people, processes, and technologies. Customers should also have an integrated enterprise security architecture, as well as operational plans, training plans, and implementation plans that fully factor in the tenets of their security policy.

Bulletproof security policies must underpin people, processes, and technologies.

Summary

Active Directory services plays a key role in providing Windows 2000's distributed security by acting as the repository for security account information, security groups, Kerberos credentials, X.509 public key certificates, and security policies. To fulfill its trusted function, Active Directory services imposes security restrictions over access to and modification of the directory content. It supports an access control model whereby end users must have granular access rights to perform directory operations, such as adding, deleting, or modifying entries. Just like other Windows 2000 security services, the directory makes use of Kerberos, the Security Support Provider Interface API, Secure Channels, and the Microsoft Certificate Server to authenticate directory users and protect directory traffic over the network. In addition, Windows 2000 and Active Directory services retain core operating system support for Windows NT 4.0 security identifiers and security descriptors, as well as for the NTLM protocol when necessary for backward compatibility.

Chapter Ten

Migrating to Active Directory Services

We have discussed the features of Microsoft Active Directory technology, but not how customers will deploy Active Directory services. As this book goes to press, many questions remain unanswered about how quickly the product will be adopted and how well it will perform in large-scale production environments. This chapter begins by discussing networking and directory market perspectives, such as the expected adoption rate of Active Directory services and the product's impact on the overall competitive landscape. We then recommend best practices and methodologies that customers should use in preparing for, and then performing, migration. Finally, we will take out the crystal ball and look into the future to see where Microsoft, Active Directory services, and the directory industry will head over the next few years.

Migration, in this book, means much more than just the actual movement of accounts into a new database. Here we define *migration* as the entire process of getting from today's directory-less Microsoft Windows NT environment to a more stabilized Microsoft Windows 2000 environment where Active Directory technology can deliver its many benefits. Particularly in complex enterprise environments, moving accounts is just a small part of

This chapter examines the market impact of Active Directory services, present-day migration issues, and future trends.

Migration is the entire process of moving from today's directory-less Windows NT environment to a fully stabilized, manageable, directory-enabled Windows 2000 environment.

the process; considerable effort must also go into planning, optimization, ongoing management, and coexistence within a multivendor environment.

Market Perspectives

Microsoft Windows NT is deployed across the spectrum of small, mid-size, and large complex enterprises.

Today, Microsoft Windows NT Server provides basic NOS and general-purpose application hosting to a broad spectrum of users, ranging from the very small enterprise with fewer than a hundred users, to large enterprises with thousands of users. Generally speaking, the larger the enterprise, the more likely it is to have a complex environment with multiple network operating systems (such as NetWare and Solaris), Windows NT domains, sites, and administration support groups.

The larger and more complex the environment, the more difficult it has been to manage Microsoft Windows NT 4.0 Server.

Windows NT Server has performed well and been relatively easy to manage in simpler environments, but in complex environments, deployment, management, and operations have often been quite difficult—largely because Windows NT 4.0 lacks an enterprise-spanning directory that replicates across domains. Customers deploy too many domains and find administration cumbersome, often requiring third-party products, such as Novell's NDS for Windows NT, or products from independent software vendors (ISVs), such as Entevo Corporation, FastLane Technologies, or Mission Critical Software.

Active Directory Services:
Upsides, Downsides, and Unknowns

Once Active Directory services can be fully deployed and stabilized, it offers many advantages.

With many improvements in features and functions, Active Directory services represents a great leap forward beyond Windows NT 4.0 Server. Some of the major advantages of the product are its thorough integration with Windows security, graphical administration, and management; single logon and directory for network services and integrated applications; separation of user and machine identities to enable roaming; increased availability of domain controllers through multi-master replication; hierarchical delegation of administration; improved remote administration of Windows environments; backward compatibility with Microsoft Windows NT; flexibility of APIs and client providers; integration with Microsoft Exchange Server; and support for DNS, LDAP, Kerberos, and PKI standards. As I have said throughout the book, I am highly positive about Active Directory technology in general.

On the downside, however, Active Directory services is a large complex product, even when considered by itself—and it only comes bundled with the entire Windows 2000 Server package. Despite its complexity, the product lacks flexibility in certain areas: for example, the Global Catalog provides only one view of information, the directory forest provides only one schema, and there is no partial replication within domains. During deployment, DNS integration can become technically and politically difficult. In addition, achieving directory management, migration, and coexistence will be difficult in complex environments, at least during the early years of deploying Active Directory services.

Active Directory services and the migration process also have some disadvantages.

The good news is that Microsoft is working to integrate meta-directory functionality acquired from the ZOOMIT Corporation and domain migration technology acquired from Mission Critical Software. Coexistence and migration tools from third-party vendors are also maturing. These products will create a layer of integration that facilitates migration, change management, schema diversity, and interoperability. We will discuss this further in the *Future of Active Directory Services* section of this chapter.

In the long run, meta-directory and coexistence tools from Microsoft and other vendors will reduce the disadvantages of migrating to Active Directory services.

Many operational issues about Active Directory services are still being discovered. For example, Microsoft and solution partners have benchmarked Active Directory services with millions of objects in the lab, but do we know how big forests, domains, and OUs can get in the chaos of the real world? What kind of reliability and performance will customers of Active Directory services see in production? Where will the pressure points be as Microsoft migrates the huge Windows NT installed base, developer community, and solution delivery channels? How complex is group policy, and how much work is required to get real value out of it?

Much remains unknown about deploying Active Directory services.

How much real cross-platform LDAP, Kerberos, and PKI inter-operability will we actually see? To its credit, Microsoft has done a great deal to ready Active Directory services for mass deployment in 1999; it has supported large beta distributions, early adopter programs, early internal deployment of Active Directory services, aggressive new application certification programs, and training for channel partners and solution providers.

Adoption Timing

Many customers will not migrate to Active Directory services immediately.

Adoption and migration to Active Directory services will take several years, and Microsoft has said it will support Windows NT 4.0 Server for two years after the Windows 2000 release date. Many customers will wait for distribution of one or two Windows 2000 service packs before starting their migration in earnest; others might wait longer, seeking to realize a return on their Y2K-motivated investments in Windows NT 4.0 or recent versions of NetWare.

Deployment of Active Directory services will hit critical mass in 2002 or 2003.

In predicting the timing for adoption of Active Directory services, it is worth noting that, whereas large enterprises are keenly interested in the improved manageability and scalability that Windows 2000 brings, small enterprises will be motivated more by new application opportunities or de-motivated by compatibility issues. Answers to the questions posed in the list of unknowns will do much to determine the pattern and pace at which customers adopt Active Directory services. My own prediction is that adoption of Active Directory services will begin to hit critical mass (that is, it will capture a large percentage of the installed base) sometime in 2002 or 2003. Windows 2000 Professional (the workstation client product) will proliferate faster than the server.

The Competitive Landscape

There are many LDAP and meta-directory choices on the market.

Microsoft Active Directory services is hitting a market that is increasingly crowded with good LDAP server and meta-directory offerings. During the long march to Windows 2000's mass adoption, Microsoft still needs to justify to customers why they should rush to Windows 2000 rather than staying with Windows NT 4.0,

NetWare, and third-party directory products such as the Netscape Directory Server. After a long period of anticipation, customers can now benchmark and test server operating systems from vendors such as IBM, Novell, and Sun Microsystems, and directories from vendors such as IBM, ISOCOR, Netscape Communications, and Novell against a released product from Microsoft!

Customers' decision to deploy Active Directory vs. another general-purpose directory will be tightly coupled with the role customers determine for Windows 2000 in the enterprise overall. On the server operating system level, customers who have made a strategic commitment to another distributed server operating system for high-end applications (such as Sun Solaris) might find no reason to switch to Windows 2000 just yet. Other operating systems will continue to have advantages for high-performance, high-availability applications because they, unlike Windows, are optimized for a single hardware platform. Eventually, however, Windows 2000 Data Center will close the gap on scalability differences from UNIX vendors. Windows 2000 will also pose a challenge for Novell, which has remained competitive in part by providing enterprise directory services that now, through Active Directory services, will also be available from Microsoft.

> Active Directory services and Windows 2000 pose a serious long-term challenge to established server and directory offerings.

Despite its relatively late arrival, Active Directory services will eventually raise expectations in the enterprise directory market. Basic white-pages directory functionality will become a commodity, like TCP/IP. For customers, this is good news. As we saw in Chapter 1, "Introducing Active Directory Services," directories are just too important not to be provided in a flexible, ubiquitous, general-purpose manner. But even after the introduction of Active Directory services, Microsoft and its competitors will be able to find new directory niches in e-commerce and advanced administration or in system management and development arenas. Even when an infrastructure element is free (like TCP/IP), there is still scope for lucrative enhancement and innovation.

> The good news for customers is that Windows 2000 will eventually make vitally needed directory functionality into a commodity.

Preparing for the Migration

Enterprises should first fit Active Directory services and Windows 2000 into the context of an enterprise IT architecture plan, and then develop the Active Directory services architecture.

Migrating to Windows 2000 and Active Directory services is a significant effort. Ideally, before beginning migration planning, enterprises will have a high-level enterprise network architecture that sets the direction for their whole network computing environment. Within the strategic planning context described by that architecture, they should determine whether, or when, to migrate to Windows 2000 and, if appropriate, construct an economic justification for the move. Once the decision is made—or even while it is being made—the enterprise should develop an Active Directory services architecture document with blueprints for eventual namespace, administration, physical topology, and security design. This architecture, discussed in the *Envisioning* section of this chapter, should be designed early—even if just as a first pass—to prevent bottom-up (rather than centrally initiated) deployment of Windows 2000 from proceeding in a vacuum. Bottom-up deployment can lead to naming, schema, security, and administration conflicts that make later migration to Active Directory services more difficult.

Enterprise Network Planning Process

The enterprise IT architecture describes structural blueprints for an overall enterprise network computing and applications environment.

Particularly in complex enterprise environments, Active Directory services and Windows 2000 do not stand alone; they must be integrated with the rest of the enterprise infrastructure. Customers should have a documented overall enterprise IT architecture; if not, developing one should take a high priority, quite apart from Windows 2000 considerations. The enterprise IT architecture usually comprises blueprints for the structure of an enterprise network computing and applications environment and should describe enterprise standards for computing platforms, applications, network services,[1] management, security, and network infrastructure.

---

1. Different architecture models describe network services in different ways. The Burton Group's network services model enumerates file, print, directory, security, messaging, Web, object services, and network management services. See *The Network Services Model: New Infrastructure for New Business Models,* published at *http://www.tbg.com,* July 12, 1999.

The architecture determines what standard protocols or other interfaces the enterprise will require, as well as standards for specific products and services the enterprise will use. The driving considerations behind these architecture decisions include business needs, installed base, key vendor partnerships, and other factors. Today, an enterprise IT architecture should consider not only the organization's internal systems, but also its externally facing e-commerce systems. In both the internal and external cases, the architecture might call for the flexibility to deploy best-of-breed solutions, take advantage of integrated product suites such as Microsoft's, or combine both approaches. The enterprise might require, for example, that all desktops run a recent Windows desktop operating system, that all enterprise server applications run on IBM OS/390, Sun Solaris, or Windows NT 4.0 Server, and that all directories support LDAP.

> The architecture standardizes interfaces and products to be used in the enterprise environment.

It is important that the customer's enterprise IT architecture drive deployment of Active Directory services (or that of any other network computing component), and not the reverse. At one extreme, a customer might deploy Microsoft's off-the-shelf Active Directory product, DNS, DHCP, and MMC snap-in services with no third-party network operating system tools. At the other extreme, a customer might minimize use of Active Directory services to support shared Windows applications running at the workgroup level only, and look elsewhere for DNS, DHCP, and other components. Thus, enterprise architectures should prescribe either a large, medium, or small role for Active Directory services, and this should, in part, determine how to deploy it.

> The enterprise IT architecture should drive Active Directory services and Windows 2000 deployment.

Migration Decision Process

Because Microsoft has integrated its own applications, APIs, tools, and network services so tightly with Active Directory technology, the decision whether to deploy the product is simple. Customers and enterprises who use Microsoft Windows NT 4.0 today, or who plan to use it or Windows 2000 as a network or application

> Almost all customers will eventually deploy Active Directory services and Windows 2000 in some capacity.

The Business Case for Windows 2000 Migration

By early 2000, there will be significant potential business benefits to gain by migrating to Windows 2000 and Active Directory services. Customers must make sure these benefits apply to them. It is important not to deal with the Windows 2000 upgrade emotionally (based, for example, on whether or not decision-makers are favorably disposed toward Microsoft, are enthused by particular Windows 2000 features, or fear for their job security). Instead, build the business case by determining an annualized return on investment (ROI) based on estimates of migration cost, economic values of pre- and post-Windows 2000 infrastructure, and any long-run cost savings from improved administration.

A customer whose Windows NT deployment has scalability problems and is relatively unstable might derive a good ROI from migrating. But a customer with a diverse population of Macintosh, UNIX, and Windows 3.*x* desktops running on older hardware, many Intel servers running on older hardware, and slow but widely distributed wide area network (WAN) topologies will have difficulty deploying Windows 2000 and its value-added functions (such as IntelliMirror) and will see a relatively lower ROI.

Customers who can predict a significant ROI should begin early Windows 2000 migration and deployment. Customers who cannot derive an acceptable ROI can congratulate themselves on having a good infrastructure that does not need replacement yet or should ruefully consider long-term plans for migration in light of overall enterprise IT environment remediation efforts.

server, are going to deploy Active Directory services. By the same token, customers who are committed to Microsoft Exchange Server as a messaging system are going to deploy Active Directory services the next time they upgrade Exchange Server.

Simply put, Windows 2000 migration is a matter of *when,* not *if,* for many customers, but the question of timing is still important. Migrating to Windows 2000 in many cases requires significant physical upgrades to desktop workstations, server hardware, network bandwidth, and even site facilities. It requires changes in administrative models, and although these changes might be for the better, they require time and money to make. Customers must overcome numerous political and organizational issues, and all this activity will surely affect other projects that might be more critical to the enterprise line of business. Customers must carefully examine the business case for proceeding with Windows 2000 at any given time.

Customers must carefully examine Windows 2000 deployment timing.

For customers who are reading this in late 1999 or early 2000 and who, like the vast majority of enterprises, have at least some Windows NT servers in their environment, I recommend conducting a business case before beginning migration to Active Directory services. After midyear 2000, it remains to be seen how rapidly Windows 2000 service packs solidify the product, how quickly compelling Windows 2000–based applications emerge, and how long Microsoft plans to continue to sell Windows NT 4.0 and to support it. If all goes well for Microsoft, the migration decision will be simpler by 2001, and the business case will become less important.

Early adopters of Windows 2000 should conduct a business case to determine the economic rationale for proceeding with deployment today in their unique enterprise environment.

Performing the Migration

Once they have determined the right time for Windows 2000 migration, customers must identify the critical success factors on which the migration depends, then execute an effective migration methodology. This section walks readers through one methodology and examines some of the factors critical to success.

Customers must identify critical success factors and follow a migration methodology.

Critical Success Factors

The following are factors critical to the success of Windows 2000 migration:

- A good deployment plan proceeding against an architecture that has been validated through a pilot

- A deployment plan that accounts for dependence on hardware upgrades, application upgrades, pre-migration housecleaning of the Windows NT environment, testing, and site preparation

- An organized Windows 2000 migration team that supports development and execution of the architecture and deployment plans; the team must facilitate consensus in the organization on many aspects of deployment

- Accurate cost estimates, budgets, and funding in place before activating end-user migration steps

- Meta-directory services as an essential tool for customers who have a large, complex, existing directory environment to be integrated with Active Directory services

- Third-party migration tools to speed up migration, particularly by helping with pre-migration Windows NT 4.0 housecleaning or provisioning accounts during the period of coexistence with Windows NT 4.0, NetWare, and other environments

Methodology Overview

Microsoft's four-step migration methodology consists of envisioning, planning, developing, and deploying.

In working with early adopters during its Joint Development Program (JDP) for Windows 2000, Microsoft and JDP partners crafted a four-step methodology for migration. Because this methodology is similar to other migration recipes, it forms the basis of the following discussion. Microsoft's four-step method consists of envisioning, planning, developing, and deploying. These steps, and their relationship to an enterprise IT architecture, are shown in Figure 10-1. The upper part of the figure identifies a basic methodology suggested by The Burton Group for ongoing enterprise architecture planning; the lower part shows the steps in migrating to Active Directory services. Note that each enterprise must conduct planning for Active Directory services and Windows 2000 in the context of multiple enterprise architecture threads (or parallel activities), and that early envisioning and planning stages of migration can parallel the process of planning an iterative enterprise IT architecture.

Figure 10-1 *Enterprise IT and Windows 2000 architecture planning.*

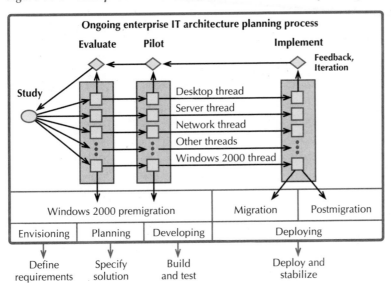

Envisioning

During the envisioning phase, customers should first conduct a detailed assessment of the enterprise network, desktop, directory, security, NOS, and other environments. What hardware and software need to be upgraded? What are the enterprise standards or conventions for user, group, and machine naming and administration in the existing NOS, network, and directory environments that Windows 2000 affects? What are the security and auditing policies and standards? Are these standards and conventions being enforced? What is the profile of a typical user in different parts of the organization?

Customers should assess their environments during the envisioning phase.

Next, customers must define the business and technical goals and requirements for Active Directory services and Windows 2000. These requirements are determined by the enterprise environment and the enterprise architecture. At a high level, enterprise goals for Windows 2000 might include: to deploy all features of value to the enterprise with minimal disruption to end users' production environments; to increase security; and to minimize administrative

Next, develop business and technical goals and requirements.

overhead during and after migration. Requirements derived from these goals can cover many areas, including availability, applications, interoperability, functionality, and rollout timeframe.

Once the requirements are known, it is then important to estimate budget and timelines for the upgrade. Note that at this point in the process, information is available to produce a business case (see the sidebar, *The Business Case for Windows 2000 Migration*). This business case might or might not contain a detailed estimate of ROI, but it should at least include a high-level vision statement, project plan, solution description, and risk assessment. Other important deliverables coming out of the envisioning stage are a functioning core team responsible for migration to Windows 2000, manager and senior technical training, and executive buy-in.

Budget estimates, timetables, high-level plans, team building, and executive buy-in are key deliverables at the envisioning stage.

Planning

During the planning phase, enterprises must develop an Active Directory services architecture, a master project plan, and a master project schedule, and deploy a laboratory testing environment for Windows 2000. Note that an initial first pass of the architecture should have been devised early in the process to establish the namespace guidelines, so that bottom-up deployment of Windows 2000 does not create undesired conventions. During the migration planning phase, however, it is important to produce an even more detailed architecture whose elements include a finalized namespace, organizational unit layout, domain and domain controller siting, administrative conventions, and basic security policies. During this phase, customers should also involve hardware, software, third-party tools, and services vendors; procure hardware; and investigate other resources that will become necessary during the migration process.

Planning includes the development of architecture, a master project plan, a master project schedule, and a testing environment.

The master project plan should also determine the migration methodology. With Microsoft's Domain Migration snap-in or third-party tools, customers can choose between migrating their existing Windows NT domain structure in place and unchanged to a Windows 2000 domain structure, or restructuring the Windows

Choose between the in-place or restructuring methodologies for domain migration.

NT domain structure while moving the information. They can choose to conduct the migration as a straight cutover from Windows NT or by cloning a copy of the Windows NT domains into Windows 2000. We will discuss and analyze these options in the section, *In-place Domain Migration vs. Restructured Domain Migration*.

We must emphasize again that because Windows 2000 and Active Directory services bring a host of changes in their wake, customers must link migration planning back to the enterprise IT architecture and strategic planning initiatives. For example, it might be important to coordinate a new Pentium III (or higher) desktop rollout with Windows 2000 installation, testing, and user training program elements. Another key coordination point is integration of Windows 2000 with the enterprise DNS. Still more issues arise when customers want to link Active Directory services with existing business processes and tools for centrally registering accounts or IP addresses.

Link the Windows 2000 architecture plan with related IT architectures, such as the enterprise DNS.

A final recommendation is to build a safety margin into the plan when sizing the resources the enterprise will need for deployment. Allocate more bandwidth, hardware, and staffing capacity than the actual estimated requirements. Refine the risk assessment to include monitoring processes and early warning thresholds for problems that might occur after deployment begins, such as network congestion at key chokepoints or slow response time on new domain controllers.

Build safety margins for bandwidth, hardware, and staffing into the plans.

Developing

During the developing phase, enterprises must test the planned Active Directory services and Windows 2000 architecture, applications, and migration processes to develop effective and highly repeatable rollout and post-rollout operations procedures and tools. To validate the architecture and any custom tools or processes, the migration team must fully define an operational environment—including applications—and conduct proofs of concepts and pilots involving real users. Key tasks include:

Developing includes testing, validation, tools, and processes.

- Define specific success criteria, if this was not done earlier.

- Extend the testing environment from the initial Windows 2000 laboratory to include multiple site and domain proofs of concept, and eventually a pilot user community.

- Measure, simulate, and test the impact that Active Directory services will have on the network.

- Test and automate the deployment processes (or actual movement of accounts) as much as possible. Test procedures for unattended desktop or server installation, and develop a mass production strategy to speed installation of domain controllers. For example, use Microsoft's SysPrep utility to duplicate an image of a properly configured domain controller install disk. SysPrep not only copies an image of the deployed domain controller, but it regenerates the image on a second machine with new SIDs and new hardware driver detection.

- Modify any in-house account registration, access administration, and address management tools to work with Active Directory services, or replace those tools.

- Install, configure, and test any third-party migration, directory synchronization, password synchronization, cross-platform single sign-on, access administration, or meta-directory tools planned for later production, unless the enterprise has deferred these to a later phase of deployment.

- Develop and test processes for disaster recovery. Ask questions like: What if the Active Directory database becomes corrupted and is replicated in that state to every domain controller in a large domain? How will the enterprise recover? Then determine the probability of the event and develop contingency plans and procedures.

- Test application compatibility with new and old versions of all major distributed workgroup applications or utilities, such as Lotus Notes, Novell GroupWise, or PeopleSoft.

The deliverables of the developing phase are lessons-learned documents, updates to the architecture, project plan, project schedule, risk assessment, and complete operational procedures for conducting mass migration and managing Windows 2000 domains once they are in place.

Developing must prepare the enterprise for the challenge of large-scale production rollout.

Deploying

At this point, all the budgets, blueprints, and install builds should be in place. But customers are dreaming if they think this means a smooth, automated migration that proceeds exactly on schedule and without a hitch! No plan survives contact with the real world, and no test results are repeatable in the face of thousands of enterprise users and hundreds of administrators and developers. Prepare sites, install new desktops and servers, train administrators and users, move accounts, and run test procedures—but expect the unexpected. During the planning and developing stages, risk assessment and remediation strategies for the deployment process should already have been established. Continuously measure against the expected thresholds for network and domain controller performance. When deployment is complete, focus on stabilizing the environment, measuring availability and performance, and adjusting domain controller topology and site topology as necessary.

While deploying, prepare for the unexpected, move accounts, then stabilize the resultant Windows 2000 environment.

Migration Concepts

When planning migration, customers must understand key concepts such as the difference between mixed and native mode Windows 2000 domains, in-place vs. domain restructuring migration methodologies, the logical order in which to migrate domains, DNS coexistence issues, and general coexistence issues.

Mixed and Native Mode Domains

Windows 2000 domains can exist in either mixed or native mode. These modes relate to the authentication infrastructure of a domain, that is, the domain controllers. Even when a domain has only Windows 2000 domain controllers and has been switched to

Windows 2000 mixed and native modes primarily affect the handling of authentication and authorization.

native mode, clients and servers running earlier versions of Windows NT and clients running Windows 9.x can exist within the domain. Figure 10-2 diagrams the evolution of Windows NT mode to mixed mode and then to native mode.

Figure 10-2 *Mixed and native modes, their features and compatibility.*

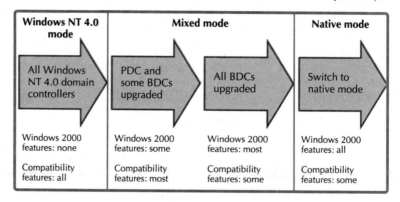

A domain is in mixed mode from the time of primary domain controller (PDC) upgrade until the administrator decides to switch the domain into Windows 2000 native mode. Mixed mode provides maximum backward compatibility with earlier versions of the operating system because applications that do not work well with Windows 2000 can continue accessing a Windows NT domain controller, and sites operating Windows NT domain controllers can continue with their pre-migration administration and operations policies, training, and procedures.

Mixed mode provides maximum backward compatibility to Windows NT.

Once all domain controllers are running Windows 2000, it is possible to switch the domain from mixed mode to native mode. The Active Directory Domains and Trusts snap-in is the tool that accomplishes this. At this point, the domain uses only Active Directory services multi-master replication between domain controllers, and no additional Windows NT domain controllers can participate in the domain through single-master replication. Native mode also enables the Windows 2000 universal groups and domain local groups, as well as group nesting functions. These advantages, plus the opportunity to make Windows 2000's

Native mode domains can use universal groups, domain local groups, and nested groups.

Why Remain in Mixed Mode?

There are reasons to remain in mixed mode for some time, particularly in a small to midsize domain and forest where Windows 2000's sophisticated group functionality is less critical than in larger, more complex environments. Customers should remain in mixed mode if they:

- Have Windows 2000 stability, training, or resources issues that make it inconvenient or risky to remove all Windows NT backup domain controllers (BDCs)
- Cannot upgrade some Windows NT BDCs because they still have applications that must run on or with a Windows NT 3.x or 4.0 domain controller and will not run on Windows 2000
- Recognize that the security environment around a particular domain controller is sufficient for it to act as a read-only BDC, but not sufficient for Windows 2000 multi-master write access to an entire domain and forest
- Require fallback capability to Windows NT (by promoting a BDC to PDC and forcing resynchronization of the account database)

promised improvements in security, scalability, availability, and manageability available throughout the domain, are the main reasons to upgrade to native mode.

In-place Domain Migration vs. Restructured Domain Migration

There are two types of domain migration methodologies. The first is in-place domain migration, by which customers upgrade an existing Windows NT PDC. The second is restructured domain migration, where the customer uses a specialized tool to consolidate multiple Windows NT domains into a single Windows 2000 domain, or to accomplish other restructuring schemes.

In-place domain migration upgrades Windows NT PDCs without changing the domain structure.

In-place domain upgrade   To accomplish an in-place domain migration, an administrator simply inserts the Windows 2000 distribution CD-ROM into the primary domain controller and upgrades the machine to a Windows 2000 domain controller. After the upgrade, all Windows NT accounts now exist in Active Directory services. In-place domain migration is appropriate when the customer's current domain structure maps directly to Active Directory services; the existing server hardware has sufficient CPU, disk, and memory resources; and the existing server siting is sufficiently secure.

Restructured domain migration moves or copies Windows NT domain information into a Windows 2000 domain.

Restructured domain upgrade   To accomplish a restructured domain upgrade, customers must set up an empty Active Directory domain with new hardware, move or copy users from one or more Windows NT domains, generate new SIDs in the Windows 2000 domain, and add the new SIDs to new or existing ACLs[2] so that users can continue accessing existing resources (a process

---

In-Place Domain Migration Pros

Depending on a customer's situation, in-place domain migration might or might not be appropriate.

Here are the advantages of in-place domain migration:

- It does not require special migration tools to accommodate restructuring scenarios, to re-stamp user and group security identifiers (SIDs) for different domains, or to update resource access control lists (ACLs) with new SIDs.
- After upgrade, the existing Windows NT domain structure remains intact in Windows 2000; this makes it possible to roll back from Windows 2000 fairly easily, if required.
- There is no need to move computers and re-connect to new hardware.

---

known as *re-ACLing*). Operations such as moving and copying, SID generation, and re-ACLing generally require an automated tool. The restructuring approach is appropriate when a customer wants to migrate directly to a newly designed and optimized Active Directory hierarchy.

Typically, restructuring involves consolidating multiple Windows NT domains into a smaller number of Active Directory domains. For example, as shown in Figure 10-3, a customer might consolidate four account domains into three Windows 2000 domains,

> Typically, restructuring means consolidating many Windows NT domains into a few Windows 2000 domains.

---

2. ACLs and SIDs were discussed in Chapter 9, "Security Overview: Kerberos, Certificates, and Access Control."

In-Place Domain Migration Cons

Following are the disadvantages of in-place domain migration:

- Customers must upgrade one domain at a time, which is a problem in larger organizations that have multiple account domains (containing user accounts) and hundreds of resource domains (typically containing applications or machines at a site level).

- In-place migration does not allow for reconfiguration or cleanup of existing domains during the migration process.

- Customers cannot generate an Active Directory services hierarchy on the fly during the domain upgrade or merge Microsoft Exchange Server mailbox and other configuration during the migration process.

- In-place migration lacks the rich tools found in domain restructuring products for collision handling, migration testing and simulation, auditing, or domain cloning (see the *Restructured domain upgrade* section of this chapter).

Restructured Domain Migration Pros and Cons

Depending on a customer's situation, restructured domain migration might or might not be appropriate.

First, here are the pros of restructured domain migration:

- Restructured domain migration, if done before account migration, encourages pre-migration cleanup in the Windows NT environment.
- The resultant Windows 2000 environment is on target, with no need for a second restructuring later.
- Restructured migration makes it possible to reduce risk or improve staging by migrating subsets of users.
- Restructured migration can optionally take place without impacting the Windows NT environment, thus reducing risk.

And here are the cons of restructured domain migration:

- It is more complex and requires more planning.
- More sophisticated tools are required to automate the process, especially if customers want to maintain access to the old Windows NT environment for a time after initial migration.
- It requires additional hardware to support dual environments if cloning techniques are used.

and many resource domains into organizational units within the Active Directory services structure. Note that restructuring can be accomplished, in principle, before or after moving domains into Windows 2000; but the sidebar, *Restructured Domain Migration Pros and Cons*, assumes restructuring during, not after, the move from Microsoft Windows NT 4.0.

Figure 10-3 *Restructuring during domain migration.*

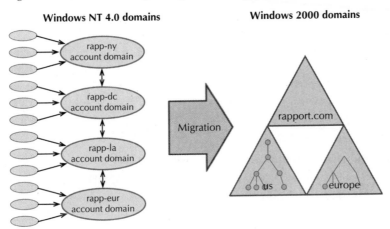

Other Migration Considerations

Customers should understand the implications of moving and copying, DNS integration, the proper order of domain migration, and other issues.

Issues associated with moving and copying users and groups   In-place migration is destructive of the original Windows NT environment. Domain restructuring tools from Microsoft and third parties, however, often provide a cloning option. With cloning, the tool copies the user accounts and groups from Windows NT to Windows 2000 and generates new SIDs for Windows 2000. But as we learned in Chapter 9, "Security Overview: Kerberos, Certificates, and Access Control," the operating system access control processes compare the user and group SIDs in the user's access token against the ACL in the resource's security descriptor. Because copied or moved user accounts or groups must have new SIDs, they will no longer match resource ACLs.

Moving or copying domain information changes SIDs.

One approach to the new SID problem is re-ACLing, or adding the new SID to the ACLs of all the resources where the old SID

Re-ACLing can be messy.

exists. Re-ACLing, however, can become messy if a customer maintains a dual environment for any length of time, or if user group memberships change during migration.

To avoid re-ACLing in some cases, Microsoft provides a SIDhistory attribute in Active Directory services for objects that represent security principals, such as users. Microsoft or third-party utilities built on new Win32 APIs update SIDhistory with new and old SIDs as part of the operation when moving a user or group. The logon process then adds all the SIDs from SIDhistory to a user's access token when he or she logs on. SIDhistory has its limits, however, and there are certain user or group migration situations in which it cannot be used.

The bottom line is that moving users and groups is complicated with Windows 2000. Any mistake causing users, groups, SIDs, and ACLs to become inconsistent can bring on trouble. Readers making the detailed migration methodology decisions should carefully study more detailed documentation available from Microsoft, as well as the manuals of the tools to be employed. Pilot carefully, back up religiously, and validate everything, especially early in the Active Directory services life cycle when all the tools are beta, just out of beta, or still new.

Order of migration   In general, Microsoft makes the case that Windows NT workstations and servers can be upgraded any time, but there are some general ordering recommendations for upgrading domain controllers. First—and most basic—Windows customers must upgrade the PDC first, then the BDC, during in-place migration of a single domain.

During migration of multiple domains, customers generally get the best value from migrating account domains, which have intensive user administration and can benefit from improved scalability and administrative delegation of Active Directory services. Start with the account domains over which the migration support team has the most control or where the risk of disruption to mission-critical business processes is minimal.

Other Migration Issues

Other miscellaneous issues can come up during migration.

- **Old gear:** Migration support goes back only so far. Customers with old hardware running Windows 3.*x* or earlier, Windows NT Server 3.1, or Windows NT Advanced Server 3.1 will need to upgrade to Windows 9.*x* or Windows NT 4.0 on the client, and Windows NT Server 3.5.1 or later on the server before commencing migration using Microsoft's software.

- **LAN Manager Replication (LMREPL):** LMREPL is often used in Windows NT environments to replicate logon scripts from an exporting DC to a number of importing domain controllers in the domain. The File Replication Service (FRS) replaces this service in Windows 2000 Server. However, Windows 2000 Server does not support LMREPL in mixed or native mode, so customer migration plans should include a strategy for migrating LMREPL to FRS.

- **WINS and NetBIOS:** NetBIOS is a 1980s-era Microsoft programming interface that identifies network resources using unique names in a flat namespace. WINS supports registration and name resolution of dynamic mappings from NetBIOS names to IP addresses. Both NetBIOS and WINS have known scalability issues in large enterprise networks. Windows 2000 does not require NetBIOS and WINS, but neither can be eliminated until the entire domain is running on Windows 2000 domain controllers, member servers, and clients, with no old versions in sight.

Migrate resource
domains where applica-
tions are compatible
with Windows 2000.

During migration of resource domains, customers should first migrate those containing applications that can immediately benefit
from, or be upgraded to use, Windows 2000 features. For example, moving from Exchange Server 5.5 to the next major Exchange Server Platinum release requires upgrading the Exchange
Server resource domain. Additionally, consider upgrading or consolidating domains with many workstations, because they can
make use of Windows 2000 infrastructure components, such as
Microsoft IntelliMirror. Avoid resource domains containing applications that do not work with Windows 2000, or have not been
tested, until it is time to upgrade or replace those applications.

DNS migration   As we noted in Chapter 7, "Planning
Namespaces, Domains, and Schema," Microsoft offers three
choices for integrating a new Active Directory services installation with an existing DNS that used to support the existing enterprise network, intranet, application, and other architectures.

Adding Active Directory
services to a new DNS
domain is the easiest
approach.

1. **Create a completely new DNS domain for each Active
   Directory services forest root.** This is the simplest and
   easiest approach because it creates no political or technical issues around replacing an existing DNS or testing
   existing intranet applications, but it means that Active
   Directory services does not get the enterprise's domain
   name. For example, the main enterprise DNS would keep
   rapport.com, and Active Directory services would get
   ad.rapport.com. This has less practical significance than
   one would expect, because the Active Directory services
   developers thoughtfully separated the naming of users
   from the naming of domains using the UPN suffix feature
   discussed in Chapter 5, "First Contact with Active Directory Services." However, including the extra *.ad* does
   make all domain names longer, which can mean extra
   typing when users need to log on remotely or perform
   other functions that explicitly reference a domain.

2. **Integrate Active Directory services into an existing
   domain.** Let Active Directory services' DNS replace the
   former DNS server occupant of *rapport.com*, for example.
   On the plus side, this approach reduces the number of

DNS servers to support. On the other hand, conflicts could result between rival camps of administrators (UNIX vs. Windows NT); existing DNS maintenance procedures might have to change in affected domains; and existing intranet applications might need retesting.

3. **Install Active Directory services in an existing domain.**
Configure Windows 2000 components to use an existing DNS that supports both Dynamic DNS functions and the SRV RR record[3] to work with Active Directory services. Again, this reduces the number of DNSs to maintain. However, existing DNS products do not have Microsoft's proprietary site optimizations that direct end-user logons to the nearest domain controller by matching subnet IDs (optionally using configured mappings). If users get logged on to distant domain controllers, then their logon, authentication, and directory access performance suffer.

Using an existing DNS in place of Microsoft's DNS can be risky in large, complex domains.

Coexistence challenges   During and after migration to Active Directory services there will be a number of coexistence issues. Other infrastructures, such as UNIX domains, Novell NetWare networks, enterprise applications, and secure intranet Web-based application environments, have very different directory and security infrastructures from Microsoft's, and customers will demand integration among these environments. There will be some convergence and consolidation of directory functionality into Active Directory services and Novell's NDS, but overall, customers require tools to synchronize directory entries, accounts, and passwords; move accounts; establish Kerberos, PKI, or other kinds of security trust relationships; share resources; and even (in some cases) foster consistency among groups, roles, and other access administration structures. In the sections to follow, we discuss migration tools, some of which allow customers to accommodate complex migration and coexistence scenarios involving Windows NT 4.0, Windows 2000, NDS, Exchange Server, and other infrastructures.

Customers also require tools for migration from and coexistence with NetWare, UNIX, and other networking environments.

---

3. Windows 2000 services uses the Service Resource Record (SRV RR) to locate domain controllers, as discussed in Chapter 2, "Active Directory Services and Industry Standards."

Meta-directory services are vital to provisioning coexistence, especially once migration is complete—or on pause.

Migration Tools

Migration tools are important assistants for moving to Windows 2000. There will be many such tools, including Microsoft's domain migration offerings, as well as products from other vendors.

Microsoft's Domain Migration Tool

Late in the release cycle of Windows 2000, Microsoft moved to provide a domain restructuring migration option.

During the Joint Development Program (JDP) in 1999, Microsoft customers requested support for domain restructuring, as well as in-place migration, noting that third-party tools tended to be expensive and that customers would like to see more migration functionality built into the base offering. Microsoft listened and purchased software from Mission Critical Software. During the last stages prior to the release of Windows 2000, Microsoft integrated the functionality from Mission Critical Software with its own code to create Microsoft's own Domain Migration tool. Due to release logistics and timing, however, this snap-in tool is not included in the initial Windows 2000 CD-ROM; it is only available via download.

Domain Migration offers wizards for common Windows 2000 migration scenarios, as well as other functionality.

The Domain Migration snap-in is a GUI tool that includes wizards for migration between Windows NT and Windows 2000 domains, and for restructuring Windows 2000 domains. It provides reporting on migrated users and computers, expired computer accounts, accounts referenced in ACLs, and name conflicts, and it creates audit records in the application event log. It also offers some Undo capabilities and re-ACLing agents for Windows NT 3.51, Windows NT 4.0, and Windows 2000 machines.

Domain Migration enables options for incremental user and group migration.

Domain Migration makes it possible for customers to move users and groups incrementally from Windows NT domains to Windows 2000 native mode domains, or to move resources from Windows NT domains into Windows 2000 native domain OU containers. It also addresses restructuring of Windows 2000 domains by allowing incremental user, group, or resource moves between domains, where the originating domain could be in mixed mode.

To maintain resource access and facilitate user migration, the Domain Migration snap-in supports the following features:

Domain Migration enables SIDhistory and re-ACLing options.

- Mirroring trusts if needed
- Moving users and groups in user-determined groupings
- Moving computer accounts in user-determined groupings
- Cloning users and groups while updating SIDhistory
- Cloning local groups in user-determined groupings while updating SIDhistory and maintaining memberships
- Re-ACLing servers and workstations if needed to remove or replace redundant SIDs or handle cases where SIDhistory cannot be used

Other Migration Tools

Customers should evaluate, plan for, or use their migration tools from third-party vendors if one or more of the following circumstances applies:

Some scenarios call for third-party tools.

- The Domain Migration snap-in does not support the desired migration scenario
- Extensive Windows NT domain housecleaning and continued maintenance is necessary before or during migration
- Migration scenarios require customization and scripting
- Corporate mergers and acquisitions are in the offing
- There are multivendor migration and coexistence requirements involving older versions of Windows NT, any versions of NetWare, or Exchange Server 5.5 or earlier

Another approach is to use a combination of Microsoft Domain Migration basic utilities, such as MoveTree or ClonePrincipal, with custom-developed scripts. But this requires considerable in-house expertise.

Lower-level migration utilities are also available.

The following vendors are easy to find on the Web and offer some of the industry's leading third-party Windows NT domain management and migration products:

- **Entevo:** Entevo's product suite includes DirectAdmin, DirectScript, DirectAdmin NDS Plus Pack, DirectMigrate 2000, and DirectMigrate for NDS. These products provide a virtual directory solution enabling a single point of administration for Windows NT, NDS, and Windows 2000, complete with role-based delegation, searching and reporting, and migration and consolidation facilities. DirectScript adds ADSI-compatible objects for developing custom management applications and remote Web-based administration tools.

- **FastLane Technologies:** FastLane's DM/Manager supports Windows NT and Windows 2000 domain restructuring. DM/Administrator overlays a hierarchical directory structure on Windows NT domains to improve manageability and security. FastLane suggests that customers use their product to introduce and model Windows 2000 management practices prior to migration. DM/Reporter reports on Windows NT domain and Microsoft Exchange Server environments, helping users tighten security, clean up bad or obsolete data, and enforce naming conventions and standards.

- **Mission Critical Software:** The original source of Microsoft's Domain Migration tool, Mission Critical provides the OnePoint Domain Administrator with automated domain consolidation and reconfiguration, modeling and optimization, migration from NetWare to Windows 2000, and automated population of Exchange Server directory from NDS data.

Future of Active Directory Services

The first release of Windows 2000 is only the beginning. Important changes await Active Directory services and directories in general.

Future Microsoft Developments

In future releases, Microsoft will continue enhancing Active Directory services and security integration, not only to support intranet security, but also to extend Microsoft's infrastructure further into extranets and e-commerce. Microsoft will strive to simplify Active Directory services administration through improved tools, and to improve coexistence by building in meta-directory services. Microsoft will also work to enhance Active Directory services' usability for end users, administrators, and programmers, and to heighten scalability.

Future releases of Active Directory services will continue to work on the basics: security, integration, coexistence, scalability, usability, and administration.

On the one hand, customers have complained that Microsoft's service pack releases often mix too many features with needed bug fixes. On the other hand, Microsoft has been criticized for long delays in rolling out major releases. Recently, Microsoft changed its policy; the company will no longer put features into service packs, but will instead limit service packs to bug fixes—something that enterprises require for stability's sake. At the same time, Microsoft will attempt to issue major operating system releases with new functionality more quickly, perhaps every 18 months rather than every three years. Given Microsoft's broad, complex product line and its aggressive development culture, stabilizing product release cycles will be a challenging effort for the company.

Microsoft also plans to stabilize its product release cycles.

Microsoft will continue tightly integrating Active Directory services with security and enabling applications to use the integrated features. Many of the enhancements will come on the public key infrastructure (PKI) side. For example, additional applications will be developed that automatically enroll themselves to obtain a certificate, and additional processes might be put in place to automatically reissue or revoke certificates when an employee's role changes or when a certificate's work is done. Microsoft currently recommends that users employ smart cards and avoid software that embeds encrypted private keys in software. Recognizing that not all users will employ smart cards, however, Microsoft might enhance Active Directory services to provide centralized, private key storage. This technique, which CyberSafe Corporation,

Improved directory and security integration is in the offing.

Entrust Technologies, Novell, and others have pioneered, allows users to roam around the network, obtaining a copy of their private key from the directory as needed, using a password.

Microsoft will improve Active Directory services' usability as a product and as a programming platform.

The Domain Migration snap-in (covered in the *Migration Tools* section) is only the beginning; Microsoft will add more administrative tools as Web downloads or in option packs. Currently, Microsoft has teams doing usability testing to optimize the product's human interfaces. Microsoft also wants to make Active Directory services a better platform for developers, in part through improved APIs and documentation, but also through improvement to the replication infrastructure that will allow the product to contain a wider range of information (including larger, more volatile data items) and remove some of the pitfalls now facing the programmer. Microsoft might create different replication contexts or scopes; for example, DHCP lease information might only need to be replicated to domain controllers on a subnet, whereas user accounts need to be replicated domain-wide. Also, replication could be enhanced with multiple queues or classes of service, allowing high-priority changes to flow around changes to large attributes, reducing delays and increasing security in some cases.

Continued work will go into improving performance, including 64-bit platform support.

Microsoft continues tweaking Active Directory services performance using an ever-expanding set of benchmarking scenarios. Enhanced replication technology would have a significant impact on scalability. Also, Windows 2000 support for 64-bit Merced processors will allow extremely large directories to use huge amounts of memory.

Increasing schema flexibility within forests or domains is a goal, if Microsoft can determine a good approach.

It is easy to say that supporting federated schemas (or multiple schemas) within a forest or domain would simplify application and directory administration and deployment, but Microsoft must be careful not to make them more complicated by changing the way Active Directory services defines the schema today. Currently, clients can bind transparently to an object using serverless binding (or by connecting to Active Directory services without specifying the target server) and still obtain the same query result, no matter which domain controller answers an LDAP request. With multiple schemas, domain controllers might hold different views of content, and developers would have to worry about which domain controller they should access. Microsoft is still researching requirements and design solutions for schema flexibility.

At the time of writing late in 1999, the ZOOMIT acquisition is still very recent, and little solid information is available about Microsoft's plans for integrating Active Directory services and ZOOMIT VIA. However, Microsoft is likely to develop real-time synchronization between the two products in the short term, and in the long term, ZOOMIT VIA will probably share a unified store with Active Directory services. ZOOMIT VIA has many interesting features, such as hashed search, centralized private key storage, and built-in support for the join and attribute flow meta-directory services. Eventually, VIA's identifiable functionality will be fully assimilated into Active Directory services; someday the only visible part of the former product might be new directory integration and coexistence snap-ins. Once integrated, Microsoft's meta-directory services will make it easier for large enterprises to support multiple forests with minimal duplication of effort. They can also be used to maintain extranet directories synchronized with partners.

Lastly, meta-directory services acquired from ZOOMIT VIA will enrich Microsoft's directory product line.

Industry Changes

Vendors continued working to extend the boundaries of directory interoperability in 1999. Work on LDAP access control and replication continued in the IETF. A Directory Interoperability Forum was launched to encourage common directory middleware APIs, among other things. A Directory Services Markup Language (DSML) effort began to create a mapping between LDAP content and the Extensible Markup Language (XML). In this regard, many in the industry see great synergy between directories and XML, highlighting potential XML roles for importing and exporting objects and attributes among directories; publishing directory namespaces and schemas; mapping among directory namespaces

Vendors' eagerness for directory interoperability led to various efforts in 1999.

and schemas; querying, locating, and filtering directory objects and attributes; and incrementally replicating and updating directories.

XML/directory integration can be used to dynamically generate personalized applications.

One vendor, Bowstreet, has taken XML/directory integration even further, developing an entire application framework that builds personalized extranet applications dynamically, based on traditional user and group directory information, as well as XML templates stored in the directory. Other vendors, such as Radiant Logic, also have creative approaches that could extend the value that directories can provide through integrating LDAP and XML.

Microsoft is participating in some of these efforts, but only monitoring others.

Microsoft is participating in the DSML effort but remains skeptical of the others, highlighting, for example, the difficulties of trying to define full equivalence of replication and access control in an innovation-driven area like directories. Microsoft has some legitimate technical concerns, and so far, standardized LDAP access control and replication remains elusive. But many bright technical people and their companies are continuing to push the envelope, and they could meet with some success.

Summary

Active Directory services offers enterprises significant value. It will ease administration, increase security, enhance functionality, and make it easier to deploy applications in the Windows environment. By directory-enabling new Windows clients and encouraging thousands of developers to write applications against existing general-purpose directories, Active Directory services is helping to usher in a seminal shift to directory-based network computing.

However, migration will be a major effort that must not be underestimated. Customers must work to understand how Windows 2000's considerable advantages over Windows NT in terms of cost of ownership and functionality can benefit their organizations. They must conduct extensive assessment, planning, and preparation efforts before making the great leap forward to Active Directory services.

I hope that this chapter and this book will not only facilitate readers' understanding of Active Directory services, but also will help in the migration process.

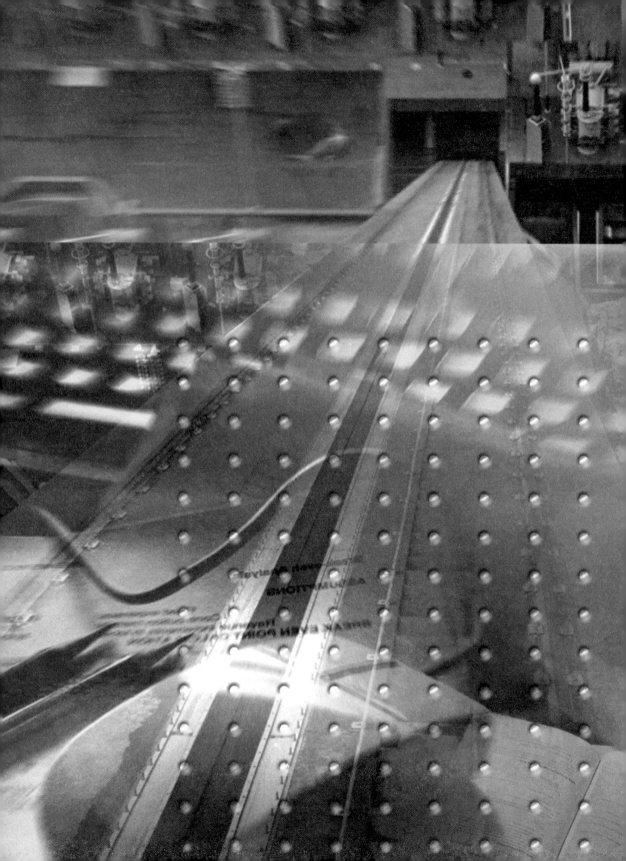

Glossary

access control entry (ACE) An elements in an access-control list (ACL). Each ACE controls or monitors access to an object by a specified trustee.

ACE *See* access control entry.

Active Directory Domains And Trusts snap-in The Windows 2000 utility that helps administrators migrate from mixed-mode to native-mode domain infrastructure.

Active Directory Service Interfaces (ADSI) A published API specification and a set of software libraries that developers can use to access various directory services. Much like an application can call the Windows printing APIs to print documents, an application can call ADSI to interact with directories.

ADSI *See* Active Directory Service Interfaces.

ADSI objects The representations of computers, users, files, servers, printers, and print queues that are defined as elements in ADSI.

ADsPath A COM display name, in either OLE or URL format, that uniquely identifies a directory entry regardless of directory service implementation. In LDAP, the ADsPath contains the X.500 distinguished name, such as *cn=danielblum,ou=consulting,dc=rapport,dc=com.*

API Application Programming Interface.

ARPANET A large wide area network created in the 1960s by the U.S. Department of Defense Advanced Research Projects Agency for the free exchange of information between universities and research organizations.

attribute A single property that describes an object; for example, the make, model, or color that describes a car. In the context of directories, the main components of entries in a directory, such as an e-mail address.

Authentication Framework Part of the 1988 ITU/ISO X.500 specifications defining the format of digital certificates used in multiple applications. Also referred to as X.509.

authentication tickets   Permissions to access resources indirectly, granted to clients and applications by a Kerberos Key Distribution Center (KDC).

auxiliary class   Contains a list of attributes, similar to an *include* file. Adding the auxiliary class to the definition of a structural or abstract class adds the auxiliary class's **mustContain** and **mayContain** (as well as **systemMustContain** and **systemMayContain**) attributes to the definition.

base object   The distinguished name of an entry used in an LDAP search request operation.

Bind request   Typically, the first operation in an LDAP interaction. The Bind operation exchanges authentication information between the client and server.

CA   *See* certification authority.

certificate revocation list (CRL)   A list of expired or invalid certificates published by a certification authority (CA).

certificate trust list (CTL)   An approach to validating certificates by which public keys of trusted CAs are distributed to network users and services.

certification authority (CA)   An organization that issues digital certificates for use in the security and verification operations of public key technology. With Windows 2000, any organization can act as its own CA using Microsoft Certificate Server or a third-party product.

chaining protocol   A protocol that allows two servers or Directory System Agents (DSAs) that implement the same standard or product specification to respond cooperatively to user queries.

CN   *See* common name.

COM   Component Object Model.

common name (CN)   A type of attribute description within the LDAP/X.500 information model that is a property of the object itself and is usually used in distinguished names.

container   An entry in the directory information tree (DIT) that contains other containers or leaf entries.

CORE Directory System Agent (DSA)   The process that manages all physical storage of Active Directory s<<<ervices through the ESE database.

country (C)   An attribute in the LDAP/X.500 information model.

Create Time inheritance   A static form of access rights inheritance supported by Windows 2000.

CRL *See* certificate revocation list.

cross certification An approach to validating public keys in which two non-hierarchical CAs declare mutual trust by signing one another's certificates.

CTL *See* certificate trust list.

DACL *See* discretionary access control list.

DAP *See* Directory Access Protocol.

DEN *See* Directory-Enabled Networks consortium initiative.

Dfs *See* distributed file system.

digital signature The use of public key cryptography to provide content integrity and originator authentification.

directory access protocol (DAP) The protocol that governs communications between X.500 clients and servers.

Directory-Enabled Networks (DEN) consortium initiative An industry-wide initiative of network infrastructure vendors and directory vendors to develop schematics for managing security, policy, and other confirguration needed by network devices. The goal is to improve allocation of network resources, services, and privileges.

directory information tree (DIT) The global tree structure of the LDAP/X.500 namespace.

Directory Services Markup Language (DSML) A language developed cooperatively by vendors with the aim of creating a mapping between LDAP content and the Extensible Markup Language (XML).

directory synchronization Unidirectional or bidirectional communication between a pair of established directories to maintain updates in both.

Directory System Agent (DSA) The directory server that answers requests from directory clients through supported access protocols. The DSA contains the directory database, access controls, and other content.

directory system protocol (DSP) Handles the interaction between X.500 DSAs.

discretionary access control list (DACL) A set of access control entries (ACEs) that lets administrators set permissions for users and groups at the object and attribute levels.

distinguished name (DN) A hierarchical name in the LDAP/X.500 information model, consisting of a relative distinguished name (RDN) plus the RDNs of all its container (or parent) entries.

distinguished value One or more of the values (such as *cn=Mark Dale*) that are part of a directory entry's relative distinguished name.

distributed file system (Dfs) A file system spanning multiple servers. Shares on multiple machines can be grouped into a single volume, the contents of which appear to clients to be in a single share.

Distributed interNet Applications Architecture (DNA) Microsoft's application architecture framework, which embraces and integrates the Internet, client/server, and PC models of computing for a new class of distributed computing solutions.

DIT *See* directory information tree.

DN *See* distinguished name.

DNA *See* Distributed interNet Applications Architecture.

DNS *See* Domain Name System.

domain forest One or more noncontiguous domains or domain trees that share a common schema, configuration, and Global Catalog.

Domain Migration snap-in A migration tool that includes wizards for migrating from Windows NT to Windows 2000 domains and for restructuring domains.

Domain Name System (DNS) The standard by which hosts on the Internet have both domain name addresses (for example, *rapport.com*) and numerical IP addresses (for example, 123.45.6.7).

domain tree A set of domains that form a contiguous namespace through a set of hierarchical relationships.

DSA *See* Directory System Agent.

DSML *See* Directory Services Markup Language.

DSP *See* directory system protocol.

EFS *See* encrypted file system.

Encrypted File System (EFS) The system, available through public key technology, which permits users to designate that certain files or folders should be encrypted transparently to applications.

enterprise directories The centralized repositories for maintaining all objects within an organization.

enterprise IT architecture A detailed description of an enterprise's network computing and applications environment, including standards for computing platforms, applications, network services, management, security, and network infrastructure.

entry A collection of attributes that contain values within a directory's hierarchical naming structure. In the LDAP/X.500 information model, each entry has a distinguished name (DN) and a relative distinguished name (RDN).

extranet   An extension of a corporate intranet using Internet-based technologies for secure communication with the enterprise's suppliers, customers, and trading partners.

Global Catalog   One or more domain controllers that contain subset attribute information for most entries in a Windows 2000 domain forest and that replicates domain schema, configuration, and partial user or other resource entries. The Global Catalog provides a way to centrally maintain information about users and universal groups for access control purposes.

GPE   *See* Group Policy Editor.

GPO   *See* Group Policy Object.

Group Policy Editor (GPE)   A Windows 2000 snap-in that allows customers to create custom profiles for groups of users and computers.

Group Policy Object (GPO)   An object created by the Group Policy Editor snap-in to hold information about a specific group's association with selected directory objects, such as sites, domains, or organizational units (OUs).

in-place domain migration   A migration method by which an existing Windows NT primary domain controller is upgraded to a Windows 2000 domain controller.

integrated zone storage   Storage of zone information in an Active Directory database rather than in a text file.

Internet Key Exchange (IKE) for IPSec   One of the public key infrastructure components bundled with Windows 2000 for delivering strong authentication, data integrity, and privacy across public networks.

IPSec   Internet Protocol Security. *See* Internet Key Exchange.

KCC   *See* Knowledge Consistency Checker.

KDC   *See* Key Distribution Center.

Kerberos   A distributed authentication and privacy protocol that protects information on a network between devices and enables single sign-on. Used in the Windows 2000 security model.

Kerberos Ticket-Granting Ticket (TGT)   The ticket granted to a client after the authentication process, which the client uses to request service tickets as needed for access to services.

Key Distribution Center (KDC)   An online trusted broker used in Kerberos distributed security operations.

Knowledge Consistency Checker (KCC)   A service on each domain controller that calculates and configures intersite and intrasite domain replication topologies every 15 minutes.

LDAP *See* Lightweight Directory Access Protocol.

LDAP Data Interchange Format (LDIF) An information format typically used for bulk import and export of directory information between LDAP-based directory servers, or to describe a set of changes that are to be applied to a directory.

LDAP V3 The third version of the LDAP protocol; adds extensibility, strong authentication, international character set support, schema publishing, and other features. The standard for data distribution across the network.

LDAPMessages The protocol data units by which an LDAP client communicates with an LDAP server.

LDIF *See* LDAP Data Interchange Format.

leaf An object at the lowest level of a directory tree or domain, such as user, group, or computer.

Lightweight Directory Access Protocol (LDAP) A specification for client-to-directory access protocol that provides rich directory services in a simpler form than the X.500 standard.

Lightweight Internet Person Schema (LIPS) An industry specification defining attribute types for use with LDAP. Established in late 1996 at the Network Applications Consortium.

LIPS *See* Lightweight Internet Person Schema.

meta-directory services Tools that meet critical multivendor integration requirements that go beyond the limits of directory synchronization; for example, the ability to join information about people who are scattered throughout multiple directory systems, synchronize passwords, or automatically create accounts in multiple applications or systems when administrators add a person to the directory.

meta-interfaces The COM interfaces through which developers gain access to information about a defined object and what the object represents.

Microsoft Management Console (MMS) A set of Windows 2000 Professional utilities that allow authorized administrators to manage the directory remotely.

Microsoft Windows 2000 platform software development kit (SDK) Documentation that provides information about the latest technologies supported by Windows 2000 and previously released platforms. The Windows 2000 Platform SDK includes corresponding header files, import libraries, and code sample for creating applications on the various Microsoft operating systems.

migration   The process of moving an enterprise's computing resources from one environment (such as Windows NT) to another environment (such as Windows 2000).

mixed-mode domain   A migration concept that provides maximum backward compatibility with earlier versions of Windows NT. In mixed-mode domain, domain controllers that have been upgraded to Active Directory services allow servers running Windows NT versions 4.0 and earlier to exist within the domain.

multi-master replication   A replication scheme supported by Active Directory services and other products that ensures that directories remain updated and writable even if one or more servers fail; any server within a domain can process and replicate updates.

namespace   The method or conventions by which objects in a group of cooperating directories or databases are hierarchically structured and named.

naming context   In LDAP/X.500 standards, a namespace partition extending down from a root container to a lower boundary of leaf entries, or containers controlled by another administrative authority. Each naming context is controlled by a DSA, or in the case of Active Directory services, by a group of domain controllers.

native-mode domain   A migration concept in which all domain controllers are running Windows 2000, the domain uses only Active Directory services multi-master replication between domain controllers, and no Windows NT domain controllers can participate in the domain through single-master replication.

Netscape Mission Control Desktop   A directory-enabled tool used to manage Netscape Web browser profile and configuration items with the help of an LDAP directory server, usually Netscape's.

network directory   A file or database where users or applications can get reference information about objects on the network.

Novell's Z.E.N.works   A directory-enabled tool that manages desktop profile and application configuration items using Novell's Novell Directory Services (NDS).

object class   Defines the schema for entries and establishes which attributes a directory entry contains; specifies which attributes in an entry are mandatory, which are optional, and which are used for naming.

object identifier (OID)   An internationally registered number used for uniquely identifying network information types, such as directory object classes and attributes.

object set   A contiguous subtree with child counts on the container entries and GUIDs stamped on each object in the set; recommended for complex applications that must store multiple objects and attributes in the directory. Object sets can allow developers to detect both partial update and version skew.

OID   *See* object identifier.

Open Systems Interconnection (OSI) model   A layered architecture developed by the ISO that standardizes levels of service and types of interaction for computers exchanging information through a communications network. The OSI model separates computer-to-computer communications into seven layers or levels, each building upon the standards contained in the levels below it.

operational attributes   Attributes used by servers to configure the directory system itself. Retrievable from the root of a DSA's naming context (called

RootDSE), they provide information about the server's supported naming contexts, supported schema, alternate (backup) server, supported protocol extensions, supported controls, and supported authentication features.

organization (O)   A type of attribute description within the LDAP/X.500 information model.

organizational unit (OU)   A type of container object used within the LDAP/X.500 information model to group other objects and classes together for easier administration.

OSI   *See* Open Systems Interconnection model

OU   *See* organizational unit.

partition   The information area beginning at a branch of a directory tree and continuing to the bottom of that tree and/or to the edges of new partitions controlled by subordinate DSAs.

PKINIT protocol   An emerging standard that integrates public key certificates with initial authentication through Kerberos.

protocol data unit (PDU)   A variable-length protocol element that contains data and control information.

public key cryptography   An asymmetric encryption scheme that uses a pair of keys to code data. The public key encrypts data, and a corresponding secret key decrypts it. For digital signatures, the sender uses the private key to create a unique electronic number that can be read by anyone who has the corresponding public key, thus verifying that the message is truly from the sender.

RDN *See* relative distinguished name.

referral An LDAP operation that advises the client to contact another server (specified as a URL) when the server initially contacted does not hold the requested information.

relative distinguished name (RDN) The name of an object within its current level in the directory hierarchy. For example, from its own mailbox, v-rossl is the RDN of the v-rossl mailbox object, while its distinguished name (DN) might be *O=Trager,cn=Boston,cn=recipients,cn=v-rossl.*

relative identifier (RID) The portion of a security identifier (SID) that identifies a user or group in relation to the authority that issued the SID.

replication protocol A protocol that allows two or more DSAs implementing the same standard or product specification to synchronize all or part of their information content so that when content changes are made to one DSA, these changes are automatically sent to the other DSA.

Request for Comment (RFC) Any protocol, operational recommendation, requirements document, or other informational document published by the IETF.

restructured domain migration A migration method by which many Windows NT domains are consolidated into a few Windows 2000 domains; accounts, users, and other enterprise computing resources must be copied or moved, not just upgraded.

RFC *See* Request for Comment.

Rivest, Shamir and Adelman standards (RSA) Standard algorithms that generate public keys for encryption and key exchange.

SACL *See* system access control list.

SAM Security Account Manager.

SASL *See* Simple Authentication and Security Layer.

schema Defines the logical structure of a directory database.

SDK Software development kit.

Secure Sockets Layer/Transport Layer Security (SSL/TLS) Two of the security authentication protocols enabled by the Security Support Provider Interface (SSPI) in Windows.

Security Support Provider Interface (SSPI) A Win32 API used by systems services and applications to hide the complexity of multiple security and authentication protocols; also used for authenticating via SSL, Kerberos, NTLM, and other protocols.

Simple Authentication and Security Layer (SASL) Part of the Bind request, where the client specifies its version, the user name it is binding as, and its simple or (for LDAP V3 only) strong credentials. SASL supports Secure Sockets Layer (SSL), Kerberos, HTTP Digest, and other security methods.

simple credentials The password specified by clients as part of LDAP V3 Bind request operations.

single-master replication A replication scheme supported by Windows NT 3.*x* and 4.0 and by as other products, in which a single domain controller or other kind of directory server owns a group of entries. Updates can be made only at that server, which replicates information to other servers. Only one replica of a database in a given partition is writable, while all other copies are read only.

site link A group of sites that can communicate at uniform cost via some intersite transport. A typical site link would connect just two sites through IP and corresponds to an actual WAN link. Administrators can create a site link for an intersite transport (IP or SMTP) by specifying two or more sites, a numeric cost, a replication frequency, and a schedule of time periods when the sites might be unavailable, such as during business hours or other times of high rates for a dial-up line.

site link bridge A grouping of site links defined by an administrator for the purpose of further controlling replication topology by disabling automatic (or transitive) routing between site links.

SSL/TLS *See* Secure Sockets Layer/Transport Layer Security.

SSPI *See* Security Support Provider Interface.

standard zone storage Storage of zone information in a text file rather than in an Active Directory database.

strong credentials In LDAP Bind request operations, the use of digital certificates or other methods to provide robust authentication.

structural class A type of object class that defines naming rules for its entries and determines both an entry's content and its position in the namespace.

syntax The structural rules of an attribute, such as whether it can be an integer or string, and whether the attribute can be multi-valued. Syntax is specified by an attribute-definition object in Active Directory services.

system access control list (SACL)   A list that allows administrators to audit users' access to objects and to view these security-related events through the security log in the Windows 2000 Event Viewer.

TGT   *See* Kerberos Ticket-Granting Ticket.

tickets   A feature of the Kerberos security model, by which clients are granted access to objects and resources only indirectly, through services. Application servers use the service ticket to impersonate the client and look up its user or group security identifiers

TLS   See Transport Layer Security.

Transport Layer Security (TLS)   The IETF's version of Secure Sockets Layer (SSL), which provides a secure communications channel between Internet clients and servers.

unique ID (UID)   A type of attribute description within the LDAP/X.500 information model.

update sequence number (USN)   A counter maintained by each domain controller and incremented with every initiated Active Directory update transaction. Every Active Directory entry stores the USN existing at the time of its creation and the USN of its most recent modification; every Active Directory attribute value stores the latest USN.

urgent replication   A push mechanism used by the Security Account Manager (SAM) and the Local Security Authority (LSA) to immediately update domain controllers (disregarding the pause interval) about any newly locked-out accounts, relative ID (RID) pool changes, or changes to domain controller machine account information.

USN   *See* update sequence number.

values   The content of attributes, such as an individual phone number. For a car, *blue* might be the value for the color attribute.

virtual private network (VPN)   A set of nodes on a public network such as the Internet that communicate among themselves using encryption technology so that their messages are as safe from being intercepted and understood by unauthorized users as if the nodes were connected by private lines; functionally enhanced by centralized directory services.

VPN   *See* virtual private network.

X.500   A set of recommendations adopted by the ITU and ISO for standardizing directory protocols used in both public-access and private computer networks.

X.500 documents protocols for client/server systems that maintain and access directories of users and resources.

X.509 *See* Authenticated Framework.

ZAW *See* Zero Administration initiative for Windows.

Zero Administration initiative for Windows (ZAW) A Microsoft-led initiative designed to reduce PC costs of ownership via centralized administration of user logon, applications, security, and other resources through Active Directory services.

zone In DNS standards, the namespace partition formed by each domain within the global namespace or within an enterprise namespace. Each zone is controlled by an authoritative DNS server, or in the case of Active Directory services, by a group of domain controllers.

Index

authorization, Windows 2000, 239–40
auxiliary object classes, 187

B

backup domain controllers (BDCs), 102–3
Base DN parameter, in ADSI searches, 150
base object, 51
BDCs (backup domain controllers), 102–3
Berkeley Internet Name Daemon (BIND), 42–43
best practices, security, 259–63
BIND (Berkeley Internet Name Daemon), 42–43
BIND boot file, 43
binding
    with ADSI
        to multiple namespaces, 148
        to objects in the directory, 146–47
    guidelines on, 148
Bind operation, LDAP, 50–51, 109
Bowstreet, 296
browsing, 119
builtin containers, 180
Burton Group, The, 274

C

caching servers, 39
Cairo, 60
canonical name, 182
CAPI (Crypto API), 252
Certificate Management Protocol (CMP), 247
Certificate Practice Statement agreement, 247
certificate revocation lists (CRLs), 71, 245, 247,
    248, 250, 251
certificates, public key (certificate services), 71,
    72, 91, 241–43, 245–52, 261, 262, 293
    Microsoft certificate services, 248
Certificate Server, Microsoft, 69–71, 233
certification authorities (CAs), 245
    enrollment of new PKI users, 247
    Microsoft PKI and, 248
    setting up, 250–51
chaining protocol, 37

change notification, 41
class store objects, 186
clients, 36
    Active Directory, 117–22
        administration, 122
        browsing, 119–22
        components of, 91, 92–93
    thin and rich, 63–64
CMP (Certificate Management Protocol), 247
code signing, 249
Collection objects, ADSI, 156–57
COM automation interfaces, 143
common name, 182
Compare operation, LDAP, 53
Component Object Model (COM/COM+), 17,
    60. See also DCOM (Distributed
    Component Object Model)
    ADSI as based on, 138, 143
    as integrated framework, 76
    overview of, 74
computer objects, 185–86
computers, containers for, 180
configuration containers, 179–80
configuration-naming context, 178
Configure Your Server program, 126
container objects, 185
containers (container entries), 44, 54, 159, 170
    configuration, 179–80
    defined, 171
    domain, 180
    organizational unit (OU), 181–83
context menus, for new schema items, 195
cost of directories, 7–8
Create New Attribute screen, 190
Create Time inheritance, 256–57
credentials, 9–10
    in ADSI, 158
    simple, 51
    strong, 51
CRLs (certificate revocation lists), 71, 245, 247,
    248, 250, 251
cross-domain access, enabling, 61, 89, 104,
    170, 240, 241
Crypto API (CAPI), 252
cryptographic service providers (CSPs), 251

ODSI (Open Directory Services Interfaces), 137
OIDs (object identifiers), 46
   defining, for new object classes and
     attributes, 191
OLE (object linking and embedding), as
   ancestor of COM, 74
OLE DB, 64
Open Directory Services Interfaces (ODSI), 137
OpenDSObject method, 158
operational attributes, 48
opportunity costs of directories, 8
organizational units (OUs), 77, 95, 181, 183, 185
   access controls, 181, 183
   Windows 2000 security architecture and, 233
Outlook, directory-enabling, 80–84
Outlook 2000, 122

P

paging, server-side, LDAP searches and, 52
partitions, 172, 204
   replication and, 202
passwords, Compare operation for verification
   of, 53
PDCs (primary domain controllers), 102–3, 106
permissions, types of, 255–56
PKI. *See* public key infrastructure (PKI)
   standards
PKINIT protocol, 241–42
planning phase, of migration to Active
   Directory services, 276–77
policies, 181
policy-based administration, Windows 2000,
   77, 183
primary domain controllers (PDCs), 102–3, 106
primary name servers, 39
printers, searching for, 121–22
private keys, 243
property pages, for new schema items, 195
protocol data units (PDUs), 48
public key encryption, 243–52
   cryptographic protocols and, 244
   digital signatures and, 244–45
   overview of, 243
   performance considerations, 244
public key infrastructure (PKI) standards, 16,
   28, 233

Active Directory services' support for, 91
applications enabled by, 248–49
best practices guidelines, 261, 262
certification authorities (CAs), 245
   enrollment of new PKI users, 247
   Microsoft PKI and, 248
   setting up, 250–51
Crypto API and, 252
enrollment and, 247–48, 251
Microsoft, 248, 261
PKINIT protocol and, 241–42
scenario using, 247–48
third-party products, 261
public keys, 243
   cryptographic protocols and, 244
   management of, 245

Q

queries
   inverse, 40
   iterative, 39, 40
   recursive, 39, 40
QueryInterface method, 144

R

RDNs (relative distinguished names), 44
   defined, 172
recursive queries, 39, 40
referrals, LDAP, 50
Registration Authority, 247, 251, 261
relative distinguished names (RDNs), 44
   defined, 172
relative identifier (RID), 106
replication (replicas), 199–226
   Active Directory services and, 90, 102–3
   capabilities of Active Directory replication,
     204–5
   Dfs (distributed file system), 73
   directory performance improved by, 201
   domain controllers and, 208, 210–14
   in the enterprise, 213–14
   Exchange Server information store's support
     for, 81–82
   interdomain and intradomain, 206–7

security, *continued*
  best practices for, 259–63
  public key (*See* public key encryption)
Security Access Manager (SAM), urgent
    replication and, 209
Security Account Manager (SAM), 88, 94
Security Configuration Editor, 260
security identifier (SID), 69, 98, 182
security identifiers (SIDs), 69, 98, 231
security services, 37
  Windows 2000, 68–72
security standards. *See also* Kerberos; PKI
    (public key infrastructure) standards
Security Support Provider Interface (SSPI), 69,
    232, 242–43
  APIs, 93
  Kerberos implemented under, 238
Security Support Provider (SSP) protocol,
    Kerberos, 239
server message block (SMB), 60, 238
server objects, 186
service connection points (SCPs), 161–63
Service Resource Record (SRV RR), 42, 100,
    108, 109, 289
setting up Active Directory services, 123, 126
  configuring the server and, 126
  DHCP and, 129
  DNS and, 128
  domain controllers and, 126–27
signatures, digital, 244–45
Simple Authentication and Security Layer
    (SASL) protocol, Bind request and, 51
simple credentials, 51
Simple Mail Transfer Protocol (SMTP), 80
  Exchange Server's support for, 82
single-master replication, 201
single sign-on, 232
  cross-platform, 240–41
  Kerberos protocols and, 234, 237, 238, 240, 241
single sign-ons, 70
site links, replication and, 214–16
sites
  Exchange Server vs. Active Directory, 217
  replication and, 210–13
Sites And Services snap-in, 130, 215

smartcard, 234
smart cards, 293–94
SMB (server message block), 60, 238
S/MIME, 81
SMTP (Simple Mail Transfer Protocol), 80
  Exchange Server's support for, 82
sorting, server-side, LDAP searches and, 52
special-purpose directories, 3, 4, 7
SRV RR (Service Resource Record), 42, 100,
    108, 109, 289
SSL. *See* Secure Sockets Layer (SSL)
SSPI. *See* Security Support Provider Interface
    (SSPI)
StreetTalk, 60
strong credentials, 51
structural object classes, 187
structured storage, 64
Structure Query Language (SQL), 149
  ADSI searches and, 154
subclasses, 47
subdomains, 38
subschema entries, 48
synchronization (directory synchronization),
    200, 203, 220–23
  bidirectional, 221
  migration tools and, 220–21
system access control list (SACL), 159, 254
  auditing of directory operations and, 255
system containers, 180

T

TGT. *See* Ticket-Granting Ticket (TGT)
thin clients, DNA (Distributed interNet
    Applications) and, 63–64
Ticket-Granting Ticket (TGT), 69, 99, 109
  KDC and, 236
TLS (Transport Layer Security), 71, 98, 248
Transaction Server, Microsoft (MTS), 77–80
Transport Layer Security (TLS), 71, 98, 248
trees. *See* directory trees; domain trees
trust relationships, cross-domain, 89
two-phase commit transaction processing, 78
type element, 46–47

U

Unbind operation, LDAP, 50
Uniform Resource Locators (URLs), LDAP, 53
UNIX systems, single sign-on across Windows and, 240
unstructured storage, 64
Update operations, LDAP, 54
update sequence number (USN), 208–9
upgrading
    to Active Directory services, 125–26
    to Windows 2000 Server, 123–24
UPN (user principal name) suffixes, 131, 288
up-to-dateness table, 208–9
urgent replication, 209–10
User Datagram Protocol (UDP), 48
User Manager for Domains, 88
user objects, 185
user principal name (UPN) suffixes, 131, 288
users, containers for, 180
Users And Computers snap-in, 130, 132–34
Users and Computers snap-in, 233–34
USN (update sequence number), 208–9

V

VIA, ZOOMIT, 295
virtual list views, 53
virtual private networks (VPNs), 10, 29
volume objects, 186
VPNs (virtual private networks), 10, 29

W

wide area networks (WANs), 176
    replication and, 215
Windows NT LAN Manager (NTLM), 60, 92, 94, 109
    logon with, 234
    SSPI and, 243
Windows NT 3.x, 61
    organization of networks, 88–89
Windows NT 4.0, 17, 61
    administration of, 89–90

coexistence of Active Directory services with, 267
domain controllers, 102–3
enterprise-spanning directory lacking in, 266
organization of networks, 88–89
resource domains, 177
servers, 61–62
Windows 2000, 11, 15, 17
    migration to Active Directory services and, 265, 267–69 (*See also* migration to Active Directory services)
        business case for, 272
        timing of, 273
    mixed and native mode domains, 279–81
    policy-based administration in, 77, 183
    search functionality, 120–22
    servers organized into sites, 210
Windows 2000 distributed systems, 67–73
    Dfs (distributed file system), 72–73
    public key support in, 71–72
    security services, 68–72, 229 (*See also* Kerberos protocol; PKI (public key infrastructure) standards)
        access control and authorization, 239–40
        access controls, 232
        best practices, 259–63
        cross-platform single sign-on support, 240–41
        delegation of trust, 231
        implementation of, 238
        interdomain trusts, 238–39
        Kerberos realms, 237, 238–39
        overview of, 230–34
        PKINIT protocol, 241–42
        SSPI (Security Support Provider Interface), 242–43
        trusted domain controller, 231
    single sign-on capabilities, 70–71
Windows 2000 Server, 65, 66–67, 90
    configuring, 126
    installing, 124–25
    setting up Active Directory services and, 123
    upgrading to, 123–24
WINS (Windows Internet Naming Service), 287
    Windows NT 4.0 and, 89–90

X

X.400 standards, 29, 80
  Exchange Server's support for, 82
X.500 standards, 6, 11, 60
  hybrid domain component naming and, 46
  overview of, 31–32
  replication and, 203
X.501 recommendation, 44
X.509 Authentication Framework
    specifications, 31, 233, 241, 250
XML (Extensible Markup Language), 296

Z

Zero Administration Initiative for Windows
    (ZAW), 9
Zero Administration initiative for Windows
    (ZAW), 65, 77
zones, DNS, 38–40
ZOOMIT Corporation, 14–15, 226
ZOOMIT VIA, 295

Daniel Blum

Daniel Blum is a Senior Vice President and Principal Consultant at The Burton Group where he specializes in directory services, public key infrastructure (PKI), and e-business security consulting. He has consulted for some of the world's largest companies, and worked with trade associations and standards committees such as the Electronic Messaging Association (EMA), Network Applications Consortium (NAC), National Institute of Standards (NIST) and the Corporation for Open Systems (COS). He has written books, industry reports, and articles. He has delivered seminars throughout North America and Europe, appeared as an analyst on public television, chaired industry conference tracks, and been quoted in numerous articles. His column currently runs periodically with Network World, and more information is available on his consulting practice with The Burton Group at *http://www.tbg.com.*

The manuscript for this book was prepared and submitted to Microsoft Press in electronic form. Text files were prepared using Microsoft Word 97. Pages were composed by Helios Productions using Adobe PageMaker 6.52 for Windows, with text in Optima and display type in Optima Bold. Composed pages were delivered to the printer as electronic prepress files.

Cover Graphic Designer
Patrick Lanfear

Interior Graphic Artist
Jim Kramer

Project Editor
Lynn Finnel

Principal Compositor
Sybil Ihrig, Helios Productions

Technical Editor
Greg L. Guntle

Principal Proofreader/Copy Editor
Fran Aitkens

Proofreader
Deborah O. Stockton

Indexer
Maro Riofrancos